A Mixed Race

A Mixed Race

Ethnicity in Early America

EDITED BY

Frank Shuffelton

New York   Oxford
OXFORD UNIVERSITY PRESS
1993

Oxford University Press

Oxford   New York   Toronto
Delhi   Bombay   Calcutta   Madras   Karachi
Kuala Lumpur   Singapore   Hong Kong   Tokyo
Nairobi   Das es Salaam   Cape Town
Melbourne   Auckland   Madrid

and associated companies in
Berlin   Ibadan

Published by Oxford University Press, Inc.,
200 Madison Avenue, New York, New York 10016

Oxford is a registered trademark of Oxford University Press

Library of Congress Cataloging-in-Publication Data
A Mixed race : ethnicity in early America / edited by Frank Shuffelton.
p. cm.   Includes index.
ISBN 0–19–507522–6
ISBN 0–19–507523–4 (pbk.)
1. American literature—Colonial period, ca. 1600–1775—History and criticism.
2. American literature—Minority authors—History and criticism.
3. Ethnicity—United States—History—17th century.
4. Ethnicity—United States—History—18th century.
5. United States—Ethnic relations.
6. Ethnic relations in literature.
7. Ethnic groups in literature.
8. Ethnology in literature.
9. Ethnicity in literature.
I. Shuffelton, Frank, 1940–
PS186.M58   1993   810.9'920693—dc20
92–43927

9 8 7 6 5 4 3 2 1

Printed in the United States of America
on acid-free paper

Contents

Contributors

ROSALIE MURPHY BAUM teaches at the University of South Florida and is the author of numerous essays about American literature.

BETSY ERKKILA, Professor of English at the University of Pennsylvania, has written widely and perceptively about American poets and poetry. Her *Walt Whitman among the French* (1980) and *Whitman the Political Poet* (1988) are well known.

BENILDE MONTGOMERY pursues his scholarship on early African-American writers at Dowling College.

DANA D. NELSON is the author of *The Word in Black and White: Constructing Race in American Literature, 1628–1867* (1991), which contains a version of her contribution here. She currently teaches at Louisiana State University.

WILLIAM T. PARSONS was Emeritus Professor of American History and Pennsylvania German Studies at Ursinus College and the author of *The Pennsylvania Germans: A Persistent Minority* (1985) and numerous other books and articles on Pennsylvania German culture. He had also been an editor of *Pennsylvania Folklife*. He was pleased that among his many Pennsylvania German ancestors were Palatines, Swiss, Alsatians, and Swabians.

DOREEN ALVAREZ SAAR has done extensive work on Crèvecoeur's *Letters*, with essays in *Early American Literature, MELUS,* and *Studies in Eighteenth-Century Culture.* She teaches at Drexel University.

ROBERT SECOR, Professor of English at Pennsylvania State University, includes among his many books and essays on British and American literature the informative account "Seventeenth-Century Almanac Verse" in *Puritan Poets and Poetics,* ed. White and Meserole (1985).

JOHN SEKORA, Professor of English at North Carolina Central University, is the author with Darwin Turner of *The Art of the Slave Narrative* (1982) and has also written numerous other important essays on antebellum African-American writers.

DAVID R. SEWELL is the author of *Mark Twain's Languages: Discourse, Dialogue, and Variety* (1987) and teaches American literature at the University of Rochester.

DAVID S. SHIELDS's study, *Oracles of Empire: Poetry, Politics, and Commerce in British America, 1690–1750* (1990), has transformed our understanding of literary culture in eighteenth-century America.

FRANK SHUFFELTON has most recently published *Thomas Jefferson, 1981–1990: An Annotated Bibliography* (1992).

LUISE VAN KEUREN teaches in the Language and Literature Department at Green Mountain College.

DANIEL WILLIAMS, Associate Professor of English at the University of Mississippi, has published widely and authoritatively about early American criminal narratives.

A Mixed Race

Introduction

Frank Shuffelton

Reviewing the position of American literature in 1846, Margaret Fuller began with a consideration of what it meant to be American and to have a distinctively national literature, but she chose to come at her topic obliquely through a series of cultural oppositions and affinities. To be American was to be different from "those who think and write among us in the methods and of the thoughts of Europe," but it was also to "have no sympathy with national vanity." She pleaded guilty to "an undue attachment to foreign continental literature" because of its ability, in the example of "the great Latins," to offer "more sweetness and a richer flavor" than the English character. Yet an expansionist young America still could "prize the peculiar greatness . . . which has enabled English genius to go forth from its insular position and conquer such vast dominion in the realms both of matter and of mind." Nevertheless, if England stands to us as parent to child, what suits Britain with her "insular position and consequent need to concentrate and intensify her life, . . . does not suit a mixed race continually enriched with new blood from other stocks the most unlike that of our first descent."[1]

Central to her argument is this notion that Americans were already in 1846 "a mixed race," a fact perhaps more apparent to Fuller than to many of her New England friends, whom she would later shock by marrying an Italian nobleman and naming their child Angelo. Where many of her contemporaries thought of racial and ethnic mixture as contamination or "mongrelization," she saw this transformation of an original English ethnicity as a dynamic enrichment, bringing movement and newness to an otherwise static, inbred group, bringing in effect originality to "our" ancestral origins.[2] A visionary moment of Whit-

3

manian scope suggests the benefits that will flow from the invigorating ethnic mixture of Americans: "with ample field and verge enough to range in and leaver every impulse free, and abundant opportunity to develop a genius wide and full as our rivers, flowery, luxuriant, and impassioned as our vast prairies, rooted in strength as the rocks on which the Puritan fathers landed."[3] English descent may have been suitable to cultivate the genius of rocky New England, but the enormous variety of the American continent will demand "a wide and full" array of spiritual and cultural possibilities to match its "abundant opportunity."

Fuller's generous enthusiasm about the possibilities of the representative American self in 1846—her "we" is not merely editorial—is thickly inscribed with historical concerns of her time and ours. Her vision of the American character encapsulates important issues concerning ethnic experience in America, posed as it is historically between an earlier America that laid the foundations of our ethnically "mixed race" and the great immigration of the later nineteenth century that reaffirmed the pluralism inherent in that character. We should notice, first, her confidence that ethnic variety was a positive fact, an enrichment, of American experience, a confidence largely shared by the authors of the essays in the present volume. The peculiar quality of American life, for better or worse, is a function of the ethnic diversity and range of consequent cultural choices that come from being a people of "a mixed race." If the American continent held out abundant possibilities to the men and women who came to live on it—whether they came in the last four centuries or in the last two hundred and fifty—that abundance existed in significant part because they brought richly differentiated human possibilities to it.

We should also notice the unresolved and romantically evaded difficulties of Fuller's vision. If her welcome to the continual enrichment of the ethnic other differentiated her from the narrower Anglophilia of some of her contemporaries, her vision remained practically Eurocentric, and it centered on western Europe at that. In addition, her openness toward those who presented cultural alternatives to the norms of the hegemonic group was not always shared by her contemporaries in the age of the Know-Nothings, and it has not been true since, as waves of antagonism have risen against one immigrant group after another. If her definition of Americans as "a mixed race" was in some sense an attempt to distance herself from the crude nativism of antebellum America, it was also a maneuver to wrap an Anglo-American frame around the large variety of ethnic possibilities represented in the America preceding her (and perhaps to exclude some, such as the Africans and Native Americans, even if only by silence toward their possible contributions to our "mixed race"). Thus, if we feel ourselves superior to the Know-Nothings, we should remember the concern of some of our contemporaries about the changing ethnic character of the entering classes in our most prestigious universities and the introduction of new materials into the curriculum, the threat others feel at the rise of bilingualism in schools and workplaces, to say nothing of the continuing episodes of racism that still plague us nearly four centuries after the first European settlements in North America.

In welcoming the ethnic mixture that already constituted America, she thus invoked further complexities of American ethnic experience when she claimed that "a genius . . . to rise and work in this hemisphere" would only appear after "the fusion of races among us is more complete."[4] This is a "soft" version of the cultural imperialism implicit in the melting pot theory of American cultural development that foresees imported culture disappearing into but nevertheless transforming the culture it confronts on American shores. If more benign than the "hard" version that insists on the total submission of the cultural Other to the norms of a hegemonic culture, to total assimilation, it nonetheless similarly fails to deal with the enormously inventive ways people have of preserving, reinventing, and renegotiating their cultural differences in the face of alien values and practices. Envisioning an America already well on the way to an organic "fusion of faces," it also evades consideration of the interplay of culture and power in the ethnic experience, both of Fuller's own time and of an earlier, foundational America.

If we were already in 1846 a "mixed race," at least culturally if not genetically (but that, too), our mixture resulted from years of confrontation, conflict, negotiation, and cooperation between culturally varied groups of European immigrants, Native Americans, and kidnapped Africans. The winds from all quarters of the globe had been blowing for centuries, and the resulting American harvest was far richer and more complex than the mere infusion of "Latin" flavor into "English genius" implied by Fuller. The "mixed race" that America had already become in 1846 had differentiated itself from its putatively English origins through an almost dizzying array of confrontations and compromises with an array of other cultural possibilities. Her romantic, pastoral metaphors of national growth masked the suffering, the violence, and the excitement that went into making the American mixture, even as it masked the continuing presence of ethnic Others who threatened and were threatened by a myth of a European blossoming in the New World atmosphere.[5]

The scholarship on America's ethnic founding has been disproportionate in at least two ways: it has until recent years been stronger and broader in some disciplines, such as history, than in others, such as literary studies; second, it has, even in those areas in which it has thrived, been overshadowed by work directed toward later periods. There is a strong tradition, for example, of historical scholarship on the immigration and accommodation of individual ethnic groups in early America, ethnic local history so to speak, and there have been distinguished historians of the immigration process in general, from Marcus Hansen and Maldwyn Jones to Thomas Archdeacon, who have begun with considerations of early American immigration, even though their interests were more focused on events of a later period. However, because these historians have tended to consider ethnic interaction within the context of the immigration of already distinct groups, they have remained apart on the deepest conceptual level from historians of race and culture in America such as David Brion Davis, Winthrop Jordan, Francis Jennings, Richard Drinnon, and Bernard Sheehan. These scholars in their differing ways have focused on ethnic conflicts as struggles for power and domination drawn out over race and culture in terms not always compassed by immigration history conceived of as the history of the Americanization of different cultural groups.

The richness of historical scholarship on more than four centuries of ethnic experience in America, even if not always successfully integrated, has not been duplicated to the same degree in other disciplines. Sociologists, perhaps because of their overriding concern for contemporary issues and perhaps because of their understanding of what constitutes usable evidence, have had a great deal to say about questions of assimilation in this century but very little about early America. In addition, scholars of early American literature have until fairly recently largely failed to draw on the work of the historians of immigration and ethnic interaction or to respond to the elements of ethnicity in the work they studied, partly because of methodological positions that drew their attention in the direction of other aesthetic issues. Thus when interest in the Indian captivity narratives as literature blossomed in the 1960s, the discussion initially tended to focus on questions of genre, form, and theme; for those who were interested at that time in ethnicity and literature, the action was somewhere else.

Because the great migration in the years after 1890 and the more recent immigration from the Third World have both involved much larger numbers of immigrants than in earlier eras and have dramatically reinforced the contradictory values of assimilation and pluralism inherent in America's ethnic founding, scholarly attention, including that of literary scholars, has tended to focus on the last century rather than on the foundational period. When readers understood ethnicity in terms of an overemphasized or exoticized ethnic particularity, they most readily found texts amenable to such treatment by looking at materials from the last century or so, when a greatly enlarged population of cultural minorities, broad extensions of literacy, and access to a popular press enormously expanded the production of texts readily identified as "ethnic." Given this understanding of ethnicity, such readers would find the texts of early American ethnic confrontation and conflict insufficiently ethnic. One result of this has been to underestimate the significance of ethnicity for the so-called American experience. America in effect began with a confrontation on a beach somewhere in the western Atlantic between two culturally differing groups of people, and its subsequent development was fundamentally shaped by cultural interactions between Native Americans, Europeans, and Africans within the limits of a not always voluntarily or equally shared political community.[6] America was ethnic from the beginning, and to fail to understand this is to risk always the misconception that later immigration is a dilution or contamination of some supposed founding ethnic purity.

Recent scholarship on at least two fronts has changed our understanding of ethnicity in useful ways. The work of ethnographers and ethnographic critics such as Renato Rosaldo, Mary Louise Pratt, and James Clifford has shown that, in Clifford's words, "ethnographic texts are orchestrations of multivocal exchanges occurring in politically charged situations" and that cultural identity "can never be located solely in the continuity of a culture or tradition. Identity is conjunctural, not essential."[7] Ethnicity is performance rather than substance. In a parallel vein literary scholars such as Werner Sollors, William Boelhower, and Mary V. Dearborn have tapped sources as various as sociological theories of kinship and ethnicity, semiotics, and Marxist cultural studies to suggest that literary texts should be understood as "codes for a socialization into ethnic groups and into America" rather than as mimetic representations

of an essential ethnic differentness.[8] By seeing at the center of ethnicity
"not an entity or a content or a definable subject, but a dynamic relation,
a qualifying energy, in short an ethnic *kinesis*,"[9] such scholars have
introduced several clarifying and enabling notions for those who would
understand America's ethnic foundations.

First, if ethnicity is a dynamic relation between different cultural
groups, it manifests itself differently in what might seem to be the same
cultural group in different historical periods. "Germanness" in the eighteenth century will hardly be the same as German ethnicity in the years
after Bismarck; ethnicity is not a constant but an index of a cultural
group's continually changing self-understanding in the face of shifting
relations to the larger world. Ethnicity in early America might not present itself in the same terms as in early twentieth-century America.
Second, the "qualifying energy" of ethnicity implicates it always in
struggles for control over narratives, over values, over the self, and thus
ethnicity is not to be ascribed only to someone who is culturally other
than a hegemonic group but is operative within the narratives, the
values, and the selves of the dominant group as well. The English
immigrants to New England were not merely trying to impose their
culture violently or otherwise on the Native Americans; they were being
ethnically transformed themselves in the process of confronting and
being confronted by the people they found already on the ground (and by
the other Europeans in neighboring settlements). Finally, the business of
ethnicity is carried on by means of signs and markers that are generated
on both sides of a boundary of cultural confrontation. If we are to
understand more fully the ethnic foundation of America, we must attend
to the representation of ethnicity, which is not the description of an
essential, unchanging ethnicity, although that is often the pretense of
those we might look at, but the generation of signs with which groups
negotiate relationships variously hostile or accommodating with their
neighbors.[10] Ethnic semiosis certainly does not occur only in texts, but
textual understanding has nevertheless been the central procedure for the
recognition (and perhaps regulation) of ethnicity in that transplanted
version of Atlantic civilization that calls itself American culture.

The contributors to this collection, then, seek to extend a more self-
conscious consideration of ethnicity to early America, the years before
1800 that constitute the period of our ethnic founding. The essays presented here consider in various terms the conditions of ethnic representation that determined the "mixed race" that we had already become in

the first half of the nineteenth century, and those in the first section particularly focus upon relations that fall under the heavily charged signs of race. For European immigrants on their way to being ethnically transformed as Americans, the seemingly most obvious cultural others in early America, both in terms of difference and numbers, were the Native Americans and the African slaves, and it is impossible to understand later phenomena of American ethnicity without considering always the power of ethnic representations of and by these groups of people. Because neither the Native Americans nor the people of African origin shared the European immigrants' common ties to a Christian and classical past, they posed real alternatives to the European cultural understanding, and each of these groups had a large enough population that their very numbers seemed to challenge the possible continuance of European power or culture. (As the Native Americans' numbers diminished, at least in eastern North America, and they thus became less of a threatening ethnic other, the population of African Americans increased and seemed to become more worrisome.) Europeans became Americans, Americans became different from Europeans, because they had to confront significantly different ethnic groups that they would eventually include, sometimes reluctantly, sometimes violently, as part of the meaning of America.

In other words, Americans are both colonizers, and thus understandable in terms of the growing body of critiques of all European colonizers, but also the colonized, and thus perhaps unlike anyone besides other Americans, North and South. Dana D. Nelson thus examines the complicated, heteroglossic American colonial discourse on race by untangling the strategies and contradictions of two "colonizers who refused." Cotton Mather and William Byrd each were dissenting voices when they spoke in favor of the rights of blacks and Indians in, respectively, *The Negro Christianized* and the histories of the dividing line between Virginia and North Carolina, but for Nelson the key question is, "Given that the colonial author can never write outside the power motives of colonial discourse, what are the results of the interplay between resistance and consent?" She goes on to uncover the inevitably political and economic motivations that undermine both Mather's and Byrd's attempts to subvert racial tropes of difference, while reminding us that we should not deny their generous impulses as individuals even if thus undermined by institutional forces.

The heteroglossic complexities of ethnic discourse concern the next two essayists as well, particularly as they function in the Indian captivity narratives. David Sewell points out that to date the best-known analyses of the captivity narratives have been mythographic, emphasizing the survival of captive spirits, but that comparatively little attention has been paid to the way the narratives ultimately mediate experience through language. Sewell describes three strategies that the captivity narratives employ to deal with Indian discourse, the threatening language of the ethnic Other, as they engage themselves in an act of "cultural translation," rendering Indian discourse into a narrative form intelligible to European readers. For Sewell the captivity narrative is ultimately a means to insist on the inadequacy and distance of the ethnic Other, but Rosalie Murphy Baum's meditation upon the complex interplay between an imputed ethnic norm and a constructed ethnic Other explores the possibilities and limits of narrators who understand the world as "a whole, as totality, a system, instead of as a sum of self-contained societies and cultures." She finally suggests that different potentials for understanding or sympathizing with an ethnic Other are possessed by voices from the margins as opposed to those, like John Williams, who speak from somewhere near the center of their culture's assumed ethnic norm.

Baum's point is reinforced by her consideration of the ethnic discourse of Pierre Millet, a Jesuit missionary, and by her analysis of Williams's construction of French ethnicity in tandem with that of Indian ethnicity. Luise van Keuren's discussion of the representations of the Indian as humorist offers a different perspective on transcultural negotiations between the Native Americans and the white settlers. In an imperial world where the Native Americans are being brought under a colonial discourse, they speak with resisting, carnivalesque voices that can be represented by colonial writers as part of their own resistance to European, transatlantic domination. Van Keuren points out that the figure of the Indian humorist disappears from the literature after the American Revolution, thus implicitly reminding us of the historical dimensions of ethnic constructions. When white American writers felt after 1800 that they had become masters in their own house, they limited the spectrum of native voices to surliness and pathos, thus losing in their own imaginations of the Native American humorist.

The essays by John Sekora and Benilde Montgomery examine inaugural voices in what Henry Louis Gates, Jr., calls "the black tradition in English literature." Sekora examines the circumstances surrounding the

1760 publication of *Narrative of the Uncommon Suffering & Surprizing Deliverance of Briton Hammon,* the earliest slave narrative, in order to come nearer to an understanding of how black writing began in America. By attending to the historical context of the Seven Years' War, the publishing history of several Boston printers, and the generic models of the Indian captivity narratives, Sekora is able to demonstrate how "one kind of mythmaking likewise teaches another" in order to create in the narratives of the slave writers "the only moral history of American slavery that we have." Montgomery's ironically titled essay examines another pioneering black text with a similar awareness of the relevance of the Indian captivity experience for the representation of African-American ethnicity. Where Sekora's essay reveals the conditions under which a black voice can be produced, Montgomery shows Marrant as a voice discovering itself as it comes to understand a particular relationship between freedom and language. Marrant's resistance to any single set of ethnic categories, as Montgomery describes it, is fundamental both to his blackness and to his epitomization of a kind of "transethnic" culture that holds out as-yet-unrealized possibilities to all Americans.

The second group of essays hopes to indicate in some degree the diverse possibilities of ethnicity and its representation in early America. The essays by William T. Parsons and David S. Shields consider various cultural transactions among, respectively, the Pennsylvania Germans and the Jewish merchant families of New York and Philadelphia. Parsons discusses the complex situation of the German-speaking immigrants to Pennsylvania who eventually became the "Pennsylvania Dutch" and preserved their distinctiveness (under changing signs) up to the present moment. He looks at the distinctive language and the diverse cultural practices of the Germans that set them off from settlers from the British Isles, and he also points to the perceived diversity within the German-speaking community that tended to focus their ethnic gaze in upon themselves and upon their own differences and concerns. In his attempt to give a sense of the cultural project of the Pennsylvania Germans as a whole, Parsons emulates Christopher Sauer as a *Hoch-Deutsch Pennsylvanische Geschicht-Schreiber* for our own time, but Shields looks more closely at a small part of a much smaller community. The Jewish community in eighteenth-century America was small, and the Levy-Franks family was only a part of that, but in the years before the Revolution it was marked with a particular degree of economic success and cultural distinction. Shields examines the power of a full-blown cosmopolitanism to create a cultural arena in which Jewish and Christian intellectuals together participated in the neoclassical conversation of their age. But if the Pennsylvania Germans held in common with their English-speaking neighbors a compatible Protestant understanding, the religious difference of the Levys and the Franks finally provoked a crisis of identity when the possibility of intermarriage arose. That this would happen hardly seems surprising to a twentieth-century reader, but the situation looks rather different from within the context of literary play that Shields has uncovered.

The final two essays in this section look at the representation of ethnicity within the context of two major genres of popular literature in early America, jest books and the so-called gallows narratives. In his wide-ranging survey of ethnic confrontation in the jest books widely published at the end of the eighteenth and the beginning of the nineteenth centuries, Robert Secor examines how ethnic humor serves a range of functions from the hegemonic to the carnivalesque. He assigns the rise of specifically ethnic humor to this period that simultaneously embraces the dawn of the Industrial Revolution in England and the uneasy confrontation of a new national identity (or the lack of one) in the young American republic. If ethnic humor could be used as an aggressive maneuver to protect the social order by continuing the marginalization of some outsiders such as the Irish or the Africans, it would also be used, perhaps coercively, to stigmatize those such as the Germans who chose to remain outside the ethnic norm, as Parsons has suggested above. Marked everywhere by racism, ethnic humor could, however, treat Native Americans differently than Africans, but as Secor points out, with changing historical circumstances the representation of Native Americans changed from positive to pejorative, from the noble savage as *eiron* to the pathetic drunk. Complementing Secor's exploration of ethnic stereotypes, Williams considers how those gallows narratives dealing with executions for rape demonstrate the entanglement of ethnic prejudices with marginalizing narratives of self-gratification, hypersexuality, and social opposition. Williams is also sensitive to changing historical sensibilities, charting the changing legal and public attitudes toward rape as a crime against an almost unconsciously held ethnic map of passion and control.

The final section of this volume contains three essays focusing on ethnicity in the discourse of three major writers during the era of the Revolution and early republic. Phillis Wheatley's status as a major

writer was disputed by Thomas Jefferson, and later critics have sometimes described her as a merely imitative poet, mutilated by slavery and
internalizing the racist attitudes of the white world around her. Betsy
Erkkila, however, argues that she "transformed the discourse of liberty, natural rights, and human nature into a subtle critique of the color
code and the oppressive racial structures of revolutionary America."
Wheatley's *Poems on Various Subjects,* contends Erkkila, is "loaded
with the irony of a cause and a country at odds with itself," sounding the
revolutionary possibility of a society defined in terms not of white masculine authority but of the creativity of all its participants, female and
male, white and black. Erkkila's essay is a welcome addition to this
collection because it brings together the question of gender difference
and ethnic difference, two positions of social marginalization from
which arise similar and often collaborative strategies of resistance.

Crèvecoeur's *Letters from an American Farmer* first articulates the
melting pot principle in which "that strange mixture of blood, which
you will find in no other country," results from immigrants leaving
behind all their "ancient prejudices and manners" and receiving new
ones "in the broad lap of our great Alma Mater."[11] Doreen Alvarez
Saar meditates on the mechanism Crèvecoeur postulates as effecting this
transformation, and she finds that, even more than his image of the
melting pot, his defense of the work ethic becomes a continuing definition of the immigrant experience. Acceptance of the work ethic, she
argues, is the central drama of what Werner Sollors describes as the
consent tradition of American culture, and the exclusion of some groups
from the rites of labor is part of the larger pattern of racist exclusion.
Recognizing Crèvecoeur's text as the product both of a significant
American ethnic diversity already present and of the desire to assert a
homogeneous American character, Saar's essay also looks forward to a
later literature of American ethnicity whose foundations are already
here.

Thomas Jefferson's writings, even more than Phillis Wheatley's, are,
to use Erkkila's words, "loaded with the irony of a cause and a country
at odds with itself." Rejecting Wheatley's poetry as "below the dignity
of criticism," Jefferson in *Notes on the State of Virginia* advanced the
suspicion that blacks were "inferior to the whites in the endowments
both of body and mind." Given his particular intellectual and moral
authority, he thus took upon himself a share of responsibility for subsequent American racism and the system of slavery it seemed to justify. In

the long run his opening sentences to the Declaration of Independence articulated those principles of equality and natural rights that in American life have always most forcefully opposed racism, but in antebellum America he was ironically also an influential supporter of racism. In the last essay of this collection Frank Shuffelton attempts to confront one paradox concerning Jefferson's description of racially different groups, his contrasting attitudes toward American Indians and the people of African descent. While part of the answer certainly resides in Jefferson's rebuttal of Buffon's diminution of American biological possibilities, Shuffelton suggests that Jefferson was also unwittingly trapped by competing Enlightenment discourses of anthropology. In a society where, as Saar observes, blacks labor under the code of slavery, Jefferson was blinded to their genuine creativity and thus was blinded to the limits of his own anthropological categories.

From the moments when John Smith met Powhatan or Hobomok and Squanto stepped out of the forest, the ethnic others who were both saviors and threats to the English immigrants, American culture has come out of a continuing series of confrontations and collaborations between men and women from every place on the surface of this globe. Fuller's "mixed race" is not, as her language suggested, merely a matter of shared blood but a product of cultural transformations that began the moment Native Americans and Europeans and Africans first laid eyes on each other. (And if supermarket tabloids are to be believed, we should not limit the immigrants among us only to the natives of our planet.) Despite various attempts to create a myth of ethnic homogeneity before the Revolution, the multiethnic character of America was solidly founded well before that, and that ethnic founding was accompanied by both the promises and the problems associated with ethnic difference. The essays in this collection do not aim at an encyclopedic account of all the ethnic groups who participated in this founding, but they do hope to open up the possibilities of understanding to be gained from looking at early American culture from the viewpoint of the new scholarship of ethnicity. The Founding Fathers who gave us the Declaration, the Constitution, and the Bill of Rights were not types of the new Adam, but they were the sons of immigrants.

I would like to thank all the contributors to this volume for their outstanding cooperation and patience, and I am also grateful for advice and encouragement received at various times from Ronald Bosco, Cathy N.

Davidson, Leo LeMay, Carla Mulford, and Werner Sollors among others. Rosemarie Hattman, Lucy Peck, and Cynthia Warner helped prepare the final typescript, a service I deeply appreciate.

Notes

1. Margaret Fuller, "American Literature: Its Position in the Present Time, and Prospects for the Future," in *Papers on Literature and Art* (New York: Wiley and Putnam, 1846), Part II, 122–23.

2. Cf. William J. Scheick, *The Half-Blood: A Cultural Symbol in Nineteenth-Century American Fiction* (Lexington: University Press of Kentucky, 1979), for attitudes toward racial mixture.

3. Fuller, 123–24.

4. Fuller, 124.

5. One might also consider whether the scholarly interest in the thematics of "wilderness," even though it does take into consideration violence, suffering, and excitement, is not also somewhat of an evasion of the issues of ethnic formation. To ground American character on the "myth" of the frontier contextualizes it as an expression of individual psychology, even if supposedly "archetypal," rather than as a result of social experience; cf. Richard Slotkin, *Regeneration through Violence: The Mythology of the American Frontier, 1600–1860* (Middletown, Ct.: Wesleyan University Press, 1973), 6–14. Slotkin admittedly criticizes and exposes the myth of wilderness, but to resort to myth as a vehicle of interpretation always runs the risk of apology, of condoning rather than morally controlling power.

6. Stow Persons affirms the fundamental importance of ethnicity when he contends that "the early reactions of the Europeans to Indians were based on ethnic differences" and divides American ethnic history into two phases, before and after the closing of unrestricted immigration after World War I, thus portraying the great migration as a phenomenon continuous with the earlier settlement. "American Ethnicity in the Revolutionary Era," in Jaroslaw Pelenski, ed., *The American and European Revolutions, 1776–1848: Sociopolitical and Ideological Aspects* (Iowa City: University of Iowa Press, 1980), 38–53.

7. James Clifford, *The Predicament of Culture: Twentieth-Century Ethnography, Literature, and Art* (Cambridge: Harvard University Press, 1988), 10–11. See also Clifford and George E. Marcus, eds., *Writing Culture: The Poetics and Politics of Ethnography* (Berkeley: University of California Press, 1986), and Renato Rosaldo, *Culture and Truth: The Remaking of Social Analysis* (Boston: Beacon Press, 1988).

8. Werner Sollors, *Beyond Ethnicity: Consent and Descent in American Culture* (New York: Oxford University Press, 1986), 11. See also William Boelhower, *Through A Glass Darkly: Ethnic Semiosis in American Literature* (New York: Oxford University Press, 1987), and Mary V. Dearborn, *Pocahontas's Daughters: Gender and Ethnicity in American Culture* (New York: Oxford University Press, 1986), and the essays in Sollors, ed., *The Invention of Ethnicity* (New York: Oxford University Press, 1989).

9. Boelhower, 23.

10. As a caution, however, to interpreting ethnic codes as merely a system of signs abstracted from questions of power and survival, we ought to note Stephen Steinberg's protest against the "mystification of ethnicity . . . involving the reification of culture . . . whenever culture is treated as though it is a thing unto itself, independent of other spheres of life." *The Ethnic Myth: Race, Ethnicity, and Class in America* (New York: Atheneum, 1981), ix–x.

11. J. Hector St. John de Crèvecoeur, *Letters from an American Farmer,* ed. Albert F. Stone (New York: Penguin, 1981), 69–70.

I

Questions of Race
and Ethnicity

1

Economies of Morality and Power: Reading "Race" in Two Colonial Texts

Dana D. Nelson

Colonial Discourse and the Colonizer Who Refuses

The historical record documents, if nothing more certain, a continual and dynamic dialogue over issues of "race" among the Anglo-Europeans in colonial America. Current historical and social theory continue to reflect the disagreement of the historical record. Winthrop Jordan's comments of 1968 regarding the inception of slavery still hold:

> Unfortunately, the details of this process can never be completely reconstructed; there is simply not enough evidence (and very little chance of more to come) to show precisely when and how and why Negroes came to be treated so differently from white men, though there is just enough to make historians differ as to its meaning.[1]

But differences of opinion, then and now, are not necessarily a bad thing. Culture, as postmodern theorists seek to show, is made up precisely out of both consensus and dissent, formed out of—in Bakhtinian terms—heteroglossia.

For the purpose of remembering the heteroglossia of early American attitudes on race, scholars like Roger Bruns have amply documented a segment—however small at times—of the Anglo-European community who dissented from the various and more prominent racist theorizing of other American colonists.[2] These "colonizers who refused" complicated American colonial discourse on race by resisting the growing power of the dominative and justificatory social fictions that would arbitrarily subjugate one "kind" of people in order to maintain the privilege of another. Retrieving the voices of those colonizers who refused works at the most immediate level to refute simplistic assumptions that the Anglo-Europeans entered into racial oppression against Africans and Native Americans "unthinkingly" or because they somehow didn't know better. These voices highlight that the American colonialists did not slip into a practice already provided for by preexisting social, political, and economic institutions as much as they structured an ideological formation that would allow it to seem so—for themselves and others. (As various scholars have noted, it was not until Anglo-Europeans were firmly committed to economic and geographic expansion overseas that they became interested in developing theories of race.[3]

Just as important, these voices of dissent can be valuable for our contemporary dialogue on race for their intrinsic, as well as extrinsic, voiced powerful objections to oppressive social practices based on distinctions of race; Albert Memmi's portrait of the colonizer who refuses reminds us that these people were yet on the receiving end of a system predicated on racial privilege. Observing that the central experience of the colonizer is dominative privilege that is at once economic and psychological, Memmi depicts how the colonizer "realizes that this easy profit is so great only because it is wrested from others. In short, he [*sic*] finds two things in one: he discovers the existence of the colonizer as he discovers his own privilege."[4]

For the dissenting colonial, then, the structure of his or her experience becomes contradiction:

> It is not easy to escape mentally from a concrete situation, to refuse its ideology while continuing to live with its actual relationships. . . . [The colonizer who refuses] lives his [*sic*] life under the sign of contradiction which looms at every step, depriving him of all coherence and all tranquility.[5]

We can see, then, how the structure of colonialist praxis infiltrates and co-opts the colonialist's sense of self. Accordingly, we might assume that the colonialist discursive system will obliquely shape (and work to compromise) any attempt of a colonialist to differ from its arbitrary dispensation of privilege and oppression.

Recently, JanMohamed has argued along lines similar to those of Memmi that we must take into account the actual workings and effects of colonial legal and social institutions in order to fully understand colonialist discourse: "The dominant pattern of relations that controls the text within the colonialist context is determined by economic and political imperatives and changes, such as the development of slavery, that are external to the discursive field itself."[6] To put this another way, we must read in colonial discourse the patterns of power that sustain and justify it. This carefully constructed situation of power of the colonizer in relation to the colonized—what Said calls "flexible positional authority"—structures any utterance within the colonial context. And it creates an iron-clad dilemma for those who would speak against the system from their place *within*. Colonial privilege compromises the colonizer who resists at the same time it authorizes him or her to speak.

This places the colonial dissenter in an odd spot, where contradiction becomes a structural ambivalence. Ambivalence for the colonizer who refuses can be, as both Memmi and JanMohamed observe, a privileged stasis, a position that replaces real confrontation with moral outrage. As Memmi puts it, "indignation is not always accompanied by a desire for a policy of action. It is rather a position of principle"—principle that does not clearly challenge the actual balance of power between colonizer and colonized (for instance, in the case of Thomas Jefferson, whose clearly agonized reflections on slavery in *Notes on the State of Virginia* did not lead him to free his slaves during his lifetime).[7] Yet this recognition should not lead us to indict these writers out of hand. Just as these dissenting voices could offer a generative challenge to their larger culture, so too can the difference inscribed *within* any particular text be productive, opening new discursive valences for alternative social models. Edward Said puts the point this way: "we can better understand the persistence and the durability of saturating hegemonic systems . . . when we realize that their internal constraints upon writers and thinkers were productive, not unilaterally inhibiting."[8]

All of this indicates the need to carefully reassess colonial writings that dissent from colonialist discrimination and oppression. The key question becomes this: given that the colonial author can never write outside the power motives of colonial discourse, what are the results of the interplay between resistance and consent? Two colonial texts, Cotton Mather's *The Negro Christianized* (1706) and William Byrd's *Histories of the Dividing Line betwixt Virginia and North Carolina* (written between 1728 and 1730), provide a useful site for such an analysis. Typically, both writers are cited as progressive and open-minded in the racial issues they address. This is certainly so in the case of both, yet it seems important to press the questioning further. Accordingly, the discussion that follows examines the underlying motivations of each text and focuses particularly upon the economy of racial representation in each.

An Essay to Do Good

In 1706, Cotton Mather published a small pamphlet entitled *The Negro Christianized.*[9] The theme of the essay, "as we have opportunity let us Do Good unto all men" (6), anticipates in many ways a lengthier pamphlet Mather would publish four years later, *Bonifacius: An Essay to do Good.* Both tracts function as an essay at two levels: as a written text exhorting its audience to "Do Good," the text prescribes social action; as a performance, it becomes a good deed in itself that provides models for those seeking to "Do Good." In this capacity, the essays are social action.

The concept, "Do Good," that links both texts was one that had long before impressed the Puritan minister. As he explains in his preface to *Bonifacius,* "[There was a] passage, in a Speech from an Envoy from His Britanick Majesty, to the Duke of Brandenburgh Twenty years ago; *A Capacity to Do Good, not only gives a Title to it, but also makes the doing of it a Duty.* . . . To be brief, Reader, the Book now in thy Hands, is nothing but an Illustration, and a Prosecution of that Memorable Sentence."[10] It would seem, from the subtitle of *The Negro Christianized,* that this earlier work was similarly motivated: *An Essay to excite and assist that Good Work; the Information of the Negroes in Christianity.* Mather's good intentions extended beyond the mere writing of his text, as he recounts in his diary (May 31, 1706): "My Design is; not only to lodge one of the Books, in every Family in *New England,* which has a *Negro* in it, but also to send Numbers of them into the *Indies;* and write such Letters to the principal Inhabitants of the Islands, as may be proper to accompany them."[11]

The argument of *The Negro Christianized* is fairly straightforward. "It is a Golden Sentence," Mather begins, "that has been sometimes quoted from Chrisodem, That for a man to know the Art of Alms, is more than for a man to be Crowned with the Diadem of Kings. But to Convert one Soul unto God, is more than to pour Ten Thousand Talents into the Baskets of the Poor" (1). In this tract Mather proposes, against popular sentiment, that it is every Christian slaveholder's duty to Christianize his slave. Mather appeals to his audience's reasonableness: *"Show yourselves Men, and let Rational Arguments have their Force upon you, to make you treat, not as Bruits but as Men, those Rational Creatures whom God has made your Servants"* (4). Mather enumerates his reasons for such a proposal. First, God requires that any man's servants also be His. Second, a man does not deserve the title "Christian" unless he does everything in his power to ensure that all his household are Christian too. Third, Christian compassion requires that the owner do something for the improvement of his suffering and sinful slaves. Fourth, the compassionate owner will see the "incomparable benefit" of Christian consolation for his efforts. "A Good Man," observes Mather, "is One who does all the Good that he can. The greatest Good that we can do for any, is to bring them unto the fullest Acquaintance with *Christianity*" (9).

Mather overtly works to break down racial tropes, which he astutely perceives as a barrier to slaveholders' willingness to Christianize their slaves. After presenting his arguments for Christianizing the Negro as each slave owner's duty, Mather asks, "And now, what Objection can any Man Living Have?" Anticipating and answering to the "idle and silly cavils" of his audience, Mather tackles two major arguments of the day: that blacks do not have rational capacity and that dark skin color is an external manifestation of moral degradation.[12] He answers to both charges simply by asserting their irrelevance:

> It has been cavilled, by some, that it is questionable *Whether the Negroes have Rational Souls, or no.* But let that *Brutish* insinuation be never Whispered any more. Certainly, their Discourse, will abundantly prove, that they have *Reason. Reason* showes it self in the *Design* which they daily act upon. The vast improvement that *Education* has made upon *some* of them, argues that there is a *Reasonable Soul* in all of them. (23)

As for their color, which is also made an objection, Mather scoffs: "A Gay sort of Argument! As if the great God went by the Complexion of Men, in His Favours to them!" (24). In contrast with the dominative hierarchy that frames their social relationship, Mather argues for a horizontal rather than vertical space for Christian relations between slaveholders and slaves.

Despite Mather's good intentions and perhaps revolutionary assertions contradicting determinist racial theories, the text is more complicated and in the end more conservative than it seems at first glance. While establishing what seems to be a common ground between black and white men, Mather places their capacity for reason in opposition. Mather's address privileges white sensibility, basing itself from its outset on the reasonable persuasion of his white reader. Yet he markedly does not expect the same from the black slaves. Of them, Mather says— shortly after affirming their rational soul—"Indeed, their stupidity is a discouragement," and continues:

> But the greater their stupidity, the greater must be our Application. If we can't learn them as much as we would, let us learn them as much as we can. . . . And the more Difficult it is, to fetch such forlorn things up out of the perdition whereinto they are fallen, the more Laudable is the undertaking: There will be more of a Triumph, if we Prosper in the undertaking. (25)

The Negro may have a rational soul, but it is certainly not qualitatively the same soul as that of the white. In fact, it is fixed firmly in a relation inferior to the white soul. This position, coming later in his essay, begins to undermine his initial assertion. Winthrop Jordan is able to conclude that "Mather was completely decided [i.e., favorably] on the Negro's essential nature . . . despite his dreadful punning on the Negro's color."[13] Yet if, as JanMohamed urges, "any evident 'ambivalence' is in fact a product of deliberate, if at times subconscious, imperialist duplicity," we should analyze these apparent contradictions, rather than discarding them as irrelevant, since colonialist racial discourse often operates by such contradictory means.[14]

The color imagery—what Jordan characterizes as "dreadful punning"—subverts Mather's explicit intentions to discard categorization of Christians by color. The rhetorical device rife through this text—in fact the only trope seemingly available to Mather in distinguishing good from bad, saved from damned—is dark and light imagery. He may affirm the issue of the African's color a "trifle," but the figure of speech he uses immediately after this discussion in considering the difficulties of educating the black is loaded: "It may seem, unto as little purpose to Teach, as to wash an Aetheopian" (25).[15] Like Barthes's analysis of the cover of the *Paris Match,* with its seemingly benign signification of patriotism masking a more insidious apology for imperialism, Mather's text explicitly sponsors a liberal, humane reading of blackness while implicitly proposing a very conservative, commodified figuration.[16]

In fact, Mather's figurative language develops a covert text that works against his overt text throughout. He introduces slaves as ''the Blackest Instances of Blindness and Baseness,'' associating these qualities by alliteration. And while he reminds his readers parenthetically that it is not yet proven that the slaves are not descendants of Ham, he leaves room for doubt, which reinforces rather than undermines a persistent conceptual link in the text between skin color and moral degradation. He continues, ''Let us make a Trial, Whether they that have been Scorched and Blacken'd by the sun of Africa, may not come to have their Minds Healed by the more Benign Beams of the Sun of Righteousness,'' figuratively linking physical to moral condition (1–3). Later in the text, Mather further blurs distinctions between physical and moral condition, indeed, suggesting a conflation:

> We read of, *People* destroy'd for lack of knowledge. If you withhold *Knowledge* from our Black People, they *Destroy'd*. But their *Destruction* must very much ly at *your* door; *You* must answer for it. It was a *Black charge* of old brought in against the *Jewish Nation;* Jer. 2.34. . . . Surely, Things look very *Black* upon us. (16)

We see here the full range of passion that the color imagery is intended to evoke, and its confusing, even counterproductive effects for Mather's argument. It is at this point especially that Mather seems entirely trapped in what JanMohamed describes as Manichean allegory, as his color imagery of light and dark acquires a momentum of its own that begins to displace Mather's initial argument.[17]

This covert text of *The Negro Christianized* further works against the overt one by displacing the ostensible subject of the piece—the black— with his or her white owner as the recipient of benefit. In other words, it is the white Christian who clearly becomes the subject *and* object of the text, the black heathen only a means by which the Christian can advance himself or herself on a cosmic scale. The act of Christianizing the black is ''the noblest Work, that was undertaken among the Children of men'' (2)—''children of men'' clearly excluding the African slave. The black is an ''opportunity,'' a ''trial,'' a ''creature.'' ''Who can tell,'' queries Mather, ''but that God may have sent this Poor Creature into my hands, so that One of the Elect may by my means be Called; and by my Instruction be made Wife unto Salvation! The glorious God will put unspeakable Glory upon me, if it may be so!'' (3). The white Christian accrues eternal benefits, through acting upon black slaves—by making them "objects for the Nobles of Heaven to take Notice of!" (20). Important in this process, this material "object"—the Christianized Negro—will in fact serve to reflect the white master, says Mather: "It cannot but be a vast accession unto your Joy in Heaven, to meet your Servants there and hear them forever blessing the gracious God, for the Day when He first made them your Servants" (20). Like the saluting Negro on the cover of the *Paris Match,* Mather's slaves have no meaning of themselves but are rather an eternal index to white superiority; they will both literally (in this life) and figuratively (in heaven) stand for their Christianizing master.

Mather's interest in the benefits of "doing" highlights the economic dynamic that structures colonial discourse. Virginia Bernhard, in her essay "Cotton Mather and the Doing of Good: A Puritan Gospel of Wealth," observes that Mather's *Bonifacius,* unlike more somber English tracts that focus on the thanklessness of Doing Good, "abounds with optimism and constantly stresses both spiritual and temporal benefits which accrue to the individual who does good."[18] A similar optimism frames the argument of *The Negro Christianized.* "Benefits," "revenues," "accounts," "inheritances," "share," and "recompense" are all metaphors for the heavenly profits available to the Christianizing white. Even more emphatically, Mather underscores the temporal, specifically monetary rewards the plan will garner the reluctant slave owner: "Yea, the pious Masters, that have instituted their Servants in Christian Piety, will even in this life have Recompense" (20). The slaves will be more tractable, more dutiful and faithful, hence, more profitable. He observes that slaves "are to enjoy no Earthly Goods, but the small Allowance that your Justice and Bounty shall see proper for them" (19), clearly indicating that by contrast, the white man's privilege is the accumulation of worldly goods.

It is curious, then, when Mather departs from this theme in order to chastise those who would object to his plan on economic grounds. Mather introduces at this point the prevalent argument that baptism will entitle slaves to freedom, which can only mean pecuniary *loss* for the owner. His response is frankly scornful of such "base" concerns: "Man, if this were true; that a Slave bought with thy Money, were by thy means brought unto the Things that accompany Salvation, and though shouldest from this tie have no more service from him, yet thy Money were not thrown away" (26). He continues to reprimand the selfish owner/reader severely for several more lines. Then comes a remarkable shift in tone and argumentation: "But it is all a Mistake. There is no such thing. What Law is it, that Sets the Baptized Slave at Liberty? Not the law of Christianity, that allows of Slavery; Only it wonderfully Dulcifies and Mollifies and Moderates the Circumstances of it" (26). Mather herein considers the possible laws that might interfere and concludes, "The Baptised then are not thereby entitled to their Liberty" (27). Since the charm of Mather's proposal is the financial reward that owners will gain by their benevolent action, Mather's reassurance that such action will result in loss of neither money nor property is powerful and only barely disguised by the admonitory lecture.

Mather's plan for the actual process of Christianizing the Negro slaves also revolves around economic considerations. He proposes that busy white owners, who may not have time to devote to schooling their slaves in creeds and catechism, should "employ and reward" (29) white children and servants to perform the task for them.[19] Further, as incentive for the Negroes to learn, Mather proposes that owners offer *them* some small, "agreeable recompenses" as well. Throughout *The Negro Christianized,* Christianity and the condition of whiteness are linked to financial gain—not only will the owner recognize a metaphysical acquisition, he or she will see a physical, tangible benefit as well. Mather's plan is, in short, a scheme of cosmic capitalism. Money becomes the metaphor *and* the message. The black slave becomes a figurative as well as literal commodity, becomes commodified in the act of purchase as well as Christianization.

As we have seen, Mather's linguistic choices—racial tropes, loaded figures of speech, and a cost-effective logic—undergird the racialist economy of *The Negro Christianized.* But larger, extratextual economies are not irrelevant to the racist subtext of his pamphlet. In fact, Mather's motivation for writing *The Negro Christianized* was neither self-effacing nor self-sacrificing. On March 1, 1706, Mather records in his diary:

> I am exercised, in my Family, with the want of good Servants. . . . I plead, that my Glorious CHRIST appeared in the *Form of a Servant;* and therefore the Lord would grant good *Servants* unto those that were always at work for Him, and wanted the Assistences of such living Instruments. I resolve, that if God bless me with Good *Servants,* I will serve him with more Fidelity and Activity; and I will do something that not only my own

> Servants, but other Servants in this Land, and abroad in the world, May come to glorify him. I have Thoughts, to write an Essay, about the Christianity of our *Negro* and other *Slaves*.[20]

In one of the bitter ironies of life, God apparently did fulfill His end of the bargain; on December 13 of the same year, Mather records:

> This Day, a surprising Thing befel me. Some Gentlemen of our Church, understanding (without any Application of mine to them for such a Thing.) that I wanted a *good Servant* at the expence of between forty and fifty Pounds, purchased for me, a very likely *Slave;* a young Man, who is a *Negro* of promising Aspect and Temper and this Day they presented him unto me. It seems to be a mighty Smile of Heaven upon my family; and it arrives at an observable Time unto me.[21]

Mather names his slave Onesimus; in subsequent entries, he dutifully notes his children's successful completion of their catechizing the slave.

I do not mean by this to discredit either Mather or his good intentions for the slaves of New England. I do mean this as an example that points up the inevitably political and economic motivation of any racial characterization in colonial America (in fact, in *any* colonial situation). Mather sets out to undermine racial tropes; that his own text is overwhelmed by the language available to him in color imagery, and by his own pecuniary interest, should clue us to the ways in which discourse and institutions—as Michel Foucault points out—shape the author as much as vice versa. The compelling tension in *The Negro Christianized* results from Mather's attempt to resist colonialist discourse and his perhaps unconscious acquiescence to its financial motivations. His resulting complicity should not obfuscate the difficulty of his gesture: *The Negro Christianized* should be recognized for the social good it proposes and enacts, *along with* its fundamental prejudice and self-interest.

Dividing Lines

While Cotton Mather's text illustrates the imaginative bondage of the Manichean allegory, William Byrd's public and secret *Histories of the Dividing Line betwixt Virginia and North Carolina* exemplify the covert economy of power implicit in colonial discourse.[22] Together, the two *Histories* provide an interesting insight into Byrd's attitudes toward racial issues, one intended for a selected circulation and one composed for a more general, public audience. And, as Donald T. Siebert, Jr., cautions, "it is well to note . . . that neither account is purely public or private, that there is no net contrast in tone or intention between [the two *Histories*], as is often assumed."[23] Both texts provide an account of Byrd's struggle for self-definition among his fellows and among the continent's natives; both serve as well to define new territory for the colonies and new possibilities for action in those lands. Thus, both the secret and public *Histories* function in a proverbial capacity. They model strategies for social relations in the colonies, and they offer seasoned advice to men setting out to conquer the wilderness. And despite Byrd's apparently liberal attitudes and jocular narrative style, both texts urge a rigid social hierarchy, which seeks not to modify but to codify racial and social distinctions.

At the most immediate level, the *Histories* operate as a scouting guide. Especially in the public version, Byrd provides a detailed account of how to prepare for such an undertaking in the wilderness, how to negotiate the terrain, how to deal with dietary problems inherent to a backwoods diet, and how to cope with soggy campgrounds. Byrd actually goes to great lengths in the public *History* to equip his reader, offering recipes for such "Portable Provisions" that will best outfit the aspiring woodsman/explorer. He gives trapping advice and hunting tips, and, to improve the vigor of the backwoodsman, he urges eating plenty of bear meat. The importance of promoting and preparing such hardy adventurers is almost inestimable in terms of economic advantage they can provide the burgeoning settlement, as Byrd observes: "Such [continued] discovery would certainly prove an unspeakable Advantage to this Colony, by facilitating a Trade with so considerable a nation of Indians [i.e., the Cherokees]" (246). And the bear diet, Byrd underlines, will not only facilitate the physical vigor of those establishing dominion, it will also invigorate the project in another way: "I am able to say, besides, for the Reputation of the Bear Dyet, that all the Marryed men of our Company were joyful Fathers within forty weeks after they got Home, and most of the Single men had children sworn to them within the same time" (252).

Perhaps more importantly, although less explicitly, both *Histories* are guides to the maintenance of social order in the wilderness. As David Smith has noted, the *Histories* carefully delineate a social and political hierarchy. Previous scholars, presumably drawing on Byrd's request to the legislature, have estimated the travel party at about twenty men.

Smith, however, has more carefully established a figure of around fifty. The basis for such a large complement was social rather than technical or physical: "The hierarchy, in all its division, was not to deteriorate in the Great Woods. Gentlemen were still gentlemen, and needed to be served, and others below that rank needed to see them being served."[24] As the "Dividing Line" physically opened up new land for settlement, it textually delineated and maintained social order.

Not surprisingly, the text also addresses the issue of colonialist relations with the indigenous populations. Though his contemporaries accounted for the natives' failure at assimilation as being due to their own deficiencies, Byrd asserts that it is the English settlers who are at fault for their absurd aesthetic scruples and their immoral lack of Christian honor. Byrd proposes that the early settlers might have found a better way to establish harmonious relations with the Indians than by offering gifts of beads and cloth, and a more honorable means of gaining native lands: "The poor Indians would have had less reason to Complain that the English took away their Land, if they had received it by way of Portion with their Daughters" (4). It would, he indicates, have greatly dignified the legacy of the original settlers or have shared their enlightening influence, socially and racially. While this alternative seems to have repelled those settlers, Byrd insists that the natives are not as repugnant as generally depicted and makes an audacious comparison between the morality of the natives and that of the first settlers who exploited Indian hospitality: "Morals and all considered, I can't think the Indians were much greater Heathens than the first Adventurers, who, had they been good Christians, would have had the charity to take this only method of converting the Natives to Christianity" (3). Byrd dismantles opposition between white Virginians and native inhabitants at two levels: physical and moral. His comments explicitly contest the popular view of the day, that miscegenation would lead inevitably to the deterioration of the superior race. Racial characteristics, Byrd asserts, are not fixed. Rather, such differences are a factor of material and cultural circumstance: "The principal Difference between one People and another proceeds only from the Different Opportunities of Improvement" (120).

Byrd's initial arguments emphasize similarity over difference between Anglo-Europeans and Native Americans. This is a significant argumentative framework, for the descriptive choice of identity or difference will determine very different possibilities and a different relationship (horizontal or vertical) of power. Yet like *The Negro Christianized,* the subtext of Byrd's *Histories* finally serves to reinforce and essentialize cultural distinctions, reasserting the vertical power structure that Byrd's arguments initially challenge.

Both versions of the *Histories* pay close attention to the Indians encountered on the survey, and invariably these "portraits of manners" observations reflect conservative, not liberal, attitudes. For instance, one Sabbath day on the excursion, Byrd and his fellows question "our Indian"—a Saponi who used the hunting name of "Bearskin"—about his religion. Byrd relates Bearskin's comments to his public reader with a mind open enough to see certain affinities to Western religions, observing that Bearskin's account "contain'd . . . the three Great Articles of Natural Religion: The Belief of a God; The Moral Distinction betwixt Good and Evil; and the Expectation of Rewards and Punishment in Another World." Still, he more insistently finds in the religion a bent that is yet "a little Gross and Sensual," as much as "cou'd be expected from a meer State of Nature, without one Glimpse of Revelation or Philosophy" (202). At other points in the *Histories,* Byrd is willing to consider transatlantic cultural parallels which would dismantle racial opposition. Even when Byrd discusses as sensational a topic as the native scalping practices, he draws a comparison to a similar practice of the ancient Scythians, suggesting a European (albeit distant) origin for the natives (308). But her, and later, in recounting a native legend that bears striking parallels to Christ's earthly mission, he markedly refrains from drawing any significant connections between Bearskin's story and Christian belief. Rather than using Bearskin's testimony as an opportunity to further his initial tactics of undermining racial distinctions by emphasizing commonalities, his account of Saponi cosmology underscores a moral deficiency in the natives. In an account of an enterprise that is often noted for its *own* sensual bent, Byrd's pronouncement on Bearskin's heaven ("a little Gross and Sensual") contains its own irony.

In the public *History,* Byrd expands his portrait of Indian manners in a way that portrays an essential, rather than circumstantial, opposition between the two groups. For example, he notes, "It must b [*sic*] observ'd, by the way, that Indian Towns, like Religious Houses, are remarkable for a fruitful Situation; for being by Nature not very Industrious, they choose such a Situation as will Subsist them with the least Labour" (208). Later, he explains at length:

> I never could learn that the Indians set apart any day of the Week or the
> Year for the Service of God. They pray, as Philosophers eat, only when
> they have a stomach, without having any set time for it. Indeed these Idle
> People have very little occasion for a sabbath to refresh themselves after
> hard labour, because very few of them ever Labour at all. Like the wild
> Irish, they would rather want than Work, and are all men of Pleasure to
> whom every day is a day of rest. (262)

Unlike the industrious crew of men on the survey, who hazard swamp
and storm to stake an imaginary line, "the little Work that is done
among the Indians is done by the poor Women, while the men are quite
idle" (116).

We see the tendency of Byrd's account to essentialize the Indian no
more clearly than in the *Histories'* contradictory portrayal of Bearskin.
Hired as much to provide fresh game as to navigate the woods, Bearskin's actions serve to repeat and reinforce Byrd's observations of Indians in general. For instance, when Byrd acknowledges in the public
History the Saponi's hunting prowess, he indicates that Bearskin's success is due to a savage nature: "Our unmerciful Indian kill'd no less than
two Braces of Deer and a large Bear" (260). But when Bearskin fails to
round up enough food for the crew, it is attributed to what Byrd has also
explained as "Indian nature"—their inborn tendency to avoid work,
even if it means going hungry. The *Histories'* mythologized version of
Indian essence thus contains and naturalizes contradictions so that Indians can be at once "essentially" lazy when they fail to provide food
and "essentially" savage when they successfully furnish food—and
both ways morally inferior to the Anglo-Americans.

There is a tactical as well as descriptive objective for Byrd's commentary on Indian presence. Throughout his survey of the colonies' boundary, Byrd is attentive to the economic potential of the areas under survey. Mary Louise Pratt has pointed out the economic motives that
inevitably underlie colonial travel narratives like Byrd's *Histories*. Nowhere can this be more prominent than in the notion of the "survey"—
the fixing of an imaginary political and economic boundary between two
Anglo-European colonies. Like a real estate brochure, the public *History* in particular highlights the economic potential of the areas under
survey, tacitly encouraging further Anglo settlement and expansion.
Even through the awful Dismal Swamp, the vigilant commissioner speculates at the feasibility of draining the land in order to render it usable.

And while he plans for colonial appropriation, Byrd remains also aware of the "Indian Menace."[25]

Because of the colonists' aversion to intermarriage, they will have to face Indian resistance. Byrd points to the Carolinians' violent policy toward Indians and openly sympathizes with the native's revolt against "Tyranny and Injustice," almost applauding their war on "those little Tyrants" (304). But his analysis does not extend to Virginia's relations with the local natives (which highlights his attitudes toward both North Carolina and Native Americans). Interestingly, Byrd does not seem to regard continued violence from the Indians against Virginians as a serious threat; but given that he repeatedly depicts Indians as a dying breed, there is perhaps little wonder in his nonchalance.

The public *History*'s portrayal of the steadily decreasing Indian number is worth note. In much the same way that the two texts "fix" Indian nature, depoliticizing and dehistoricizing, the public version also explains the decreasing native population as the inevitable result of Indian savagery and intertribal warring (helped along by white disease and liquor). And, like John Underhill's pamphlet, *Newes from America* (1638), which promises bounteous land while narrating coincidentally the demise of the Pequots, Byrd keeps an eye on the attractive lands that become available through native depopulation. For instance, Byrd notes that the Usherees were formerly

> a very Numerous and Powerful People. But the frequent Slaughters made upon them by the Northern Indians, and, what has been still more destructive by far, the Intemperance and Foul Distempers introduc'd amongst them by the Carolina Traders, have now reduc'd their number to little more than 400 Fighting Men, besides Women and Children. It is a charming Place where they live, the Air very Wholesome, the Soil fertile, and the Winters ever mild and Serene. (300)

Innocent and apparently objective observations like this, JanMohamed would argue, reveal the extent of colonial duplicity. Byrd's description minimizes ("little more") while underscoring the degree of the "Indian Menace" ("Fighting Men"), at the same time it indicates the real source of concern that motivates the colonists' conceptual need for an "Indian Menace": the availability of fertile lands. The more the native population is "reduc'd" the more "charming Place[s]" are made available.

At points, the public *History* seems a virtual catalog of the demise of the various tribes. It notes the fate of Meherin Indians (decimated by the Catawbas) and assures the reader that the whole number of Indians in Nottoway is reduced to about two hundred, including women and children; these are, Byrd asserts, "the only Indians of any consequence now remaining within the Limits of Virginia" (116). As for the Carolinian Tuscaroras, although "heretofore very numerous and powerful, making within time of Memory, at least a Thousand Fighting Men . . . [now] there remain so few, that they are in danger of being quite exterminated by the Catawbas, their mortal Enemies" (290).[26]

Byrd's observations on the inevitability of Indian extinction are backed in the public *History* by Indian legend. Although skeptical of Indian religion, Byrd in effect confirms his own observations with this "odd legend" that the race will inevitably be killed off by "their God." Byrd passes by the opportunity to draw obvious Christian parallels from this native story of a perfect man sent to model behavior and encourage harmony among a dishonest and impious population. Like Christ, the messenger is scorned, harassed, and finally impaled on a tree. The test details how the native god becomes enraged at his people's failure to reform and their execution of his messenger. As a result, this god will never "leave off punishing, and wasting their People, till he shall be blotted every living Soul of them out of the World" (292). The "odd legend" sidetracks from the Indians' political, physical, and economic interaction with the whites and offers instead a mythic explanation for their extinction. As Barthes reminds us, myth is always a "value, never separable from the system that creates it . . . a perpetual alibi."[27] Interestingly enough, Byrd casually offers it as the summation of his story of Indian demise.

If the natives are not a physical threat to the Virginians, their dangerous influence manifests itself in other ways. Despite his unreserved and even mischievous banter on intermarriage, his own discussion of the "slovenly" and "tallow-faced" backwoodsmen who have intermarried among the Indians and have adopted their customs and habits counters his earlier assertions that such practice will "blanche" and socially improve the Indians, not vice versa. Rather, his account suggests that backwoods miscegenation has lead to traits of slothful sensuality he finds characteristic to the Indians, and he implies that the whites who live in the "lubberland" must assert their racial heritage of "Industry and Frugality" as the "two Cardinal Virtues" that will banish such undesirable traits (36).[28] Those who acquire what Byrd regards as affinities to the Indian way of life seem to Byrd degenerate and diseased, and he carefully marks the scabs and facial deformities that some exhibit due their lack of initiative in growing vegetables and relying instead in their diet on pork (54).

Richard Slotkin tries to reconcile these comments with Byrd's former, more liberal assertions on racial intermarriage by suggesting that he had an agenda for "proper" sort of intermarriage, as opposed to that which had taken place in the backwoods, among the frontiersmen.[29] It seems to me, however, that Byrd's arguments for the moral integrity that the whites would gain by intermarriage are subtly but completely countered by the cumulative message of the public *History* in particular. We might rehearse here the profoundly conservative undertone of Byrd's initial comments on racial union. The scheme for intermarriage includes no recognition of Indian culture or racial characteristics but instead a desire to "bleach" them—wash them of color—while at the same time civilizing them so that they disappear into European appearance and manner. Hand in hand with this suggestion is the real motivation: assimilation is a means to peaceful and relatively cost-free procurement of land title. Byrd's stake in colonial acquisition thus subverts his interest in racial fraternity. Like Cotton Mather's admonition against placing pecuniary concerns over Christian duty, Byrd's advice on racial integration remains philosophical at best.

In fact, we can push Byrd's stance on racial union one step further. Byrd notes that the white man never could bring himself to intermarry with the native women. Nor do the members of Byrd's company find any marriageable Indian women in their venture. Yet, as the company men take frequent and even violent advantage of local "tawnies," it becomes clear that *sexual* union is not repugnant at all. Rather, what are portrayed as the laughable antics of Byrd's cohorts reaffirm the right of might: Why gain honorably what can be taken by force?

In the end, both writers make bold attempts to subvert racial tropes of difference, yet both are compromised by economies of moral and economic privilege that structure colonial discourse. In fact, we might argue that the most generous impulses of *The Negro Christianized* and the *Histories of the Dividing Line* are subsumed by the power of colonial discourse and its economic interests. Kenneth Burke's formulation of the "bureaucratization of the imaginative" may speak to the dynamic we have seen in these two very different texts:

All imaginative possibility (usually at the start Utopian) is bureaucratized when it is embodied in the realities of a social texture, in all the complexities of language and habits, in the property relationships, the methods of government, production and distribution, and in the development of rituals that re-enforce the same emphasis.[30]

Acknowledging this dynamic between individual and institution, text and discourse, not only leads us to temper our idealism about the real-world efficacy of literary "resistance" (and concomitantly it should help us be more realistic in our expectations of those who attempt to work resistance from within dominant culture), but it also clues us always to question the institutional forces that shape any utterance—the contesting dialogue over the uses of power that we see inscribed in texts like Mather's and Byrd's.

Notes

1. Winthrop Jordan, *White over Black: American Attitudes Toward the Negro, 1550–1812* (Chapel Hill: University of North Carolina Press, 1968), 44.

2. See Bruns's important anthology of antislavery protest, *Am I Not a Man and a Brother: The Antislavery Crusade of Revolutionary America, 1688–1788* (New York: Chelsea House, 1983).

3. Both Jordan and Gossett comment on the development of Anglo racism toward Africans; see Jordan, 18, and Thomas F. Gossett, *Race: The History of an Idea in America* (Dallas: Southern Methodist University Press, 1963), 12. Alden T. Vaughan discusses how the growing emphasis on Native American racial difference paved the way for more aggressive Anglo-American territorial policies in "From White Man to Redskin: Changing Anglo-American Perceptions of the American Indians," *American History Review* 87 (1982), 917–53. Dorothy Hammond and Alt Jablow note a similar dynamic toward Africans in their study of British colonialism. See their study, *The Africa That Never Was: Four Centuries of British Writing about Africa* (New York: Twayne, 1970).

4. Albert Memmi, *The Colonizer and the Colonized* (New York: Orion Press, 1965), 7.

5. Memmi, 20.

6. Abdul JanMohamed, "The Economy of Manichean Allegory: The Function of Racial Difference in Colonialist Literature," *Critical Inquiry* 12 (Autumn 1985), 63.

7. Memmi, 20. Currently, Abdul JanMohamed and Homi Bhabha are debating the status of "ambivalence." See Homi K. Bhabha, "The Other Question—The Stereotype and Colonial Discourse," *Screen* 24 (Nov–Dec 1983), 18–36; and JanMohamed's "Economy of Manichean Allegory," especially 49–61 for a sample of this debate.

8. Edward Said, *Orientalism* (New York: Vintage Books, 1978), 14.

9. Cotton Mather, *The Negro Christianized. An Essay to excite and assist that Good*

Work; the Information of the Negroes in Christianity (Boston, 1706). All further references to this work will appear parenthetically in the text.

10. Cotton Mather, *Bonifacius: An Essay to do Good,* 1710 (Gainesville, Fla: *Scholars'* Facsimiles and Reprints, 1967), v.

11. See *The Diary of Cotton Mather,* Vol. I, 1681–1709 (New York: Frederick Ungar Publishing Co., 1911), 565.

12. For an excellent survey of early theories on the color of Africans, see Jordan's *White over Black,* especially Chap. VI, "The Bodies of Men," 216–65.

13. Jordan, 201.

14. JanMohamed, 61.

15. This phrase has a history that further complicates Mather's use as a less-than-naive contradiction of his earlier argument. It alludes specifically to Jer. 13:23, "Can the Ethiop change his skin / or the leopard his spots? / No more can you do good / you who are schooled in evil"—a passage that suggestively links skin color to moral condition. Furthermore, according to Winthrop Jordan, "Elizabethan dramatists used the stock expression 'to wash an Ethiop white' as indicating sheer impossibility" (15).

16. See "Myth Today," in Roland Barthes, *Mythologies* (New York: Hill and Wang, 1972), 109–59, especially 116–31.

17. JanMohamed explains that:

> the dominant model of power- and interest-relations in all colonial societies is the manichean opposition between the putative superiority of the European and the supposed inferiority of the native. This axis in turn provides the central feature of the colonialist cognitive framework and colonialist literary representation: the manichean allegory—a field of diverse yet interchangeable oppositions between white and black, good and evil, superiority and inferiority. (63)

18. Virginia Bernhard, "Cotton Mather and the Doing of Good: A Puritan Gospel of Wealth," *New England Quarterly* 49 (1971), 232.

19. We might here also question the striking superficiality of Mather's plan. In a culture where religious profession was considered a deeply *intellectual* matter, and where children were catechized only as a preamble to more extensive study in their adulthood, Mather's method—outlined at the end of the tract—is clearly either assuming that Negroes can't learn much after all, or is lacking in real commitment to the enterprise.

20. Mather, *Diary,* 554.

21. Mather, *Diary,* 579.

22. William Byrd, *Histories of the Dividing Line betwixt Virginia and North Carolina* (New York: Cover Publications, 1967). All subsequent references to this work will be included parenthetically in the text.

23. Donald T. Siebert, Jr., "William Byrd's *Histories of the Line:* The Fashioning of a Hero," *American Literature* 47 (1975), 537.

24. David Smith, "William Byrd Surveys America," *Early American Literature* 11 (1977), 303.

25. See Francis Jennings, who argues that the so-called Indian Menace was in fact "a boomerang effect of the European Menace to the Indians." *The Invasion of America: Indians, Colonialism and the Cant of Conquest* (New York: Norton, 1975), 37.

26. For those natives who remain, the public *History* outlines an interesting course of

action: subjugate them through trade—particularly of firearms. Thomas Morton may have been persecuted by the Puritans for selling rifles to the Indians, but Byrd insists it is a good idea, "because it makes them depend entirely upon the English, not only for their Trade, but even for their subsistence" (116). And practically speaking, arrows are silent, and therefore more dangerous—unlike the noisy rifle shot, which alerts the unsuspecting white immediately.

27. Barthes, 123.

28. Parrington discusses the social leveling associated with the lubberland in frontier literature in *Main Currents in American Thought: The Colonial Mind* (New York: Harcourt Brace Jovanovich, 1927), i: 139–42. Richard Slotkin, in his study *Regeneration through Violence: The Mythology of the American Frontier, 1600–1860* (Middletown, Ct.: Wesleyan University Press, 1971) provides a reading of Byrd's account of lubberland that, while similar in focus, diverges somewhat from my own (cf. pp. 218–20).

29. Slotkin, 222.

30. Kenneth Burke, *Attitudes toward History,* 3d ed. (Berkeley: University of California Press, 1984), 225.

2

"So Unstable and Like Mad Men They Were": Language and Interpretation in Early American Captivity Narratives

David R. Sewell

In *Regeneration through Violence,* Richard Slotkin prefaces a chapter on captivity mythology with William Carlos Williams's comment on the Puritans' ideological cohesion: "The jargon of God, which they used, was their dialect by which they kept themselves surrounded with a palisade."[1] But for early Americans language was a flimsy bulwark in anything more than an abstract sense; the palisade of language could always be breached by those physical incursions and confrontations that subjected hundreds of explorers, missionaries, and settlers to Indian captivity during the first three centuries of North American colonization. Perhaps in a fiction like Cooper's *Mohicans* a David Gamut might set up a wall of hymns and prayers formidable enough to dismay Mingo and Huron attackers; in reality, neither prayer, threat, nor discourse of reason was of much avail in altering the purposes of Indians who sought to take captives.

Captives were carried off to territory that was as unfamiliar linguistically as geographically. Often enough the linguistic code of their captors was strange; the Indians spoke no English, or only a version of American Indian Pidgin English of the sort that Europeans invariably called "broken English."[2] But even when one or more of the Indian captors were fluent in English, or when—less often—the captive spoke an Indian language, the captive found himself or herself in an unprecedented role as interlocutor: no longer the teacher, preacher, or tradesman empowered to proselytize or bargain with the Indians, but now the submissive object of pointed questions, violent imperatives, cruel jests. The models of conversation found in what we might call the colonial Berlitz guides, the various published vocabularies of and dialogues in the Indian languages, were accordingly rendered useless. Roger Williams, for instance, had begun his *Key into the Language of America* on an assumption of linguistic equality and harmony. "What cheare *Nétop?* is the generall salutation of all English toward [the Indians.] *Nétop* is friend." In his *Vocabulary of the Massachusetts . . . Indian Language* Josiah Cotton had taught his reader to question the validity of the very Indian speech acts that he was learning how to perform; in one dialogue an opening "how do you do" is followed immediately by the Algonquian phrase that translates a condemnation of Indian linguistic habit: "What is the matter that Indians very often no speak true?" But in the earliest captivity narrative published in British North America, Mary Rowlandson's of 1682, the first instance of Indian speech is a naked imperative that shows how the power relations have been reversed: "Come go along with us."[3] In a sense, the whole history of the American captivity is a response to that imperative, an attempt to deflect its force, deny its authority, correct it as ungrammatical in a syntax of Indian-white conversation in which the imperative mood is supposed to operate in only one direction.

Being a captive meant learning a new kind of dialogue, one in which the normal colonial power relations were inverted. And there is in fact a kind of language of captivity, one with rules that the Indians composed but that quickly became common knowledge among Europeans as well. For instance, in Charles Johnston's 1790 narrative of his seizure by the Shawnee we learn such "rules" of the captivity language game as this: Don't complain about the heaviness of your pack, or you'll be given one twice as large; don't complain about how tight your bonds are, or they'll be pulled so taut as to make sleep impossible. All microrules of this sort are instances of a more general principle, one that William Fleming in his 1756 narrative calls "a Policy to counterfeit a chearful Behaviour."[4] The most overarching discursive requirement for captives is that they not give vent to their natural feelings. This is a rule that can be both learned and taught; Fleming is sorry when he is unable to impart it to a young man taken prisoner shortly after himself:

> The unhappy Youth not being accustomed to such Treatment as he now met with; and not being apprized of the bad Consequences that might attend the least Resistance, discovered great Uneasiness, and could not be prevailed upon to keep silent: Had not the *Indians* been acquainted with the English tongue, I should have thought it my Duty to admonish him to a Compliance with their capricious Humours . . . but as I could advance nothing to mitigate his Grief but what might tend to betray my Intentions . . . I was obliged to be entirely silent.[5]

Even torture, the most terrifying and by any measure the most inhuman and illogical act to which the prisoners were subjected, was among the Indians a social and therefore a communicative performance. Its game-like nature becomes obvious when one reflects upon its structural similarities to what we might call its degenerate forms in the play of modern civilized society: blindman's buff, for example, or the classic carnival game of throwing balls to hit a spring that will dunk the victim in a water tub; in both, teasing and mocking the victim is de rigueur for the participants. The primary semantic rule of torture for the Indians was that they must willfully misunderstand the captive's voluntary and involuntary communication: his pleas and cries of pain are occasions for laughter, his frenzied spasmodic movement is applauded as "dancing," and so on. Likewise the captors must represent their infliction of pain as politeness: Jesuit missionary François le Mercier in 1637 noted how "what was most calculated . . . to plunge [the captive] into despair, was their raillery, and the compliments they paid him when they approached to burn him . . . 'Ah, it is not right . . . that my uncle should be cold; I must warm thee,' and so forth."[6] But it has always been common knowledge among Europeans—one of the major folk images of the Indian, in fact—that there is a semiotics of suffering as well, that there is a communicative choice to be made between singing a boastful and fearless death song (successful performance in the Indian mode); heroic preaching, prayer, and exhortation (success as a martyr in the Christian missionary mode); and "natural" venting of fear and agony (failure in both modes, though more pardonable in the European view).

To date, the best and best-known analyses of the captivity narrative—by Roy Harvey Pearce, Leslie Fiedler, Richard Slotkin, Richard VanDerBeets—have been mythographic in nature, demonstrations of the way the captivity narrative as a genre reinforces preexisting religious, sexual, and political myths. Less attention has been paid to the way in which the captivity experience, for all its physical violence and emphasis on pure survival, is ultimately mediated through language. As Alden Vaughan and Edward Clark note in the introduction to their anthology of Puritan captivities, "The day-to-day struggle with an alien culture is the mainspring of the [captivity] experience and the driving force of the captive's attempt to understand the change he has undergone."[7] This sine qua non of the captivity experience, the encounter with cultural Otherness, is something the captive has in common with the anthropologist or ethnographer, and in fact, as Mary Louise Pratt has written, the captive serves as something of an ideal participant-observer for ethnographic theory, being an "innocent" who is free from complicity in that destruction of native cultures which so haunts the moral imagination of contemporary anthropology. "The experience of captivity," she writes, "resonates a lot with aspects of fieldwork—the sense of dependency, lack of control, the vulnerability to being either isolated completely or never left alone."[8]

There is, of course, a major difference between ethnographer and captive: the former knows in advance that she is going to write up a fieldwork experience; the latter never does. So why do captivity narratives get written? I would suggest that it is precisely because they *are*, at root, ethnographies. By describing and interpreting the experience of captivity, the captive reverses after the fact the "natural" power relations between "savage" and "civilized" that imprisonment has temporarily reversed. The Indian, whatever his actual power during the event, can be captured and tamed once and for all in the written narrative. By transforming her experience into a published account, the author of an Indian captivity is saying, in effect, "Although my body was imprisoned, I remain the master of language; I (unlike my captors) am literate and can give a true account of what happened; I can define my own situation." The captivity narrative's author is always able to counter a physical humiliation with linguistic victory: the captors may have controlled the brute events, but the captive controls the storytelling. Many captives even begin to imagine the possibility of telling their stories while still prisoners, as if the written story they project would be the conclusive evidence of having both survived and emerged with one's selfhood intact. One of the very first European captives in the Americas, Álvar Núñez Cabeza de Vaca, says in introducing his narrative, "My hope of going out from among those nations was always small; nevertheless, I made a point of remembering all the particulars, so that should God our Lord eventually please to bring me where I am now, I might testify to my exertion in the royal behalf."[9] A minority of captives, having the necessary writing materials and permission of their captors, are lucky enough to keep contemporaneous field notes—for example, the journal that Charles Johnston "endeavoured to begin, and intended to keep," using for paper the margins of a stray copy of the Debates of the Convention of Virginia over the adoption of the federal Constitution.[10]

So the captive transforms a brute experience where he was weak and the savage strong into a narrative where the Indian is verbally created, described, and judged, always subject to his former prisoner's interpretation of events. Such a process of reinterpretation corresponds to what Talal Asad calls the "forcible transformation" of a "weak" by a "strong" language in ethnographic description. Asad is addressing himself to the concept of "cultural translation," a central goal of the last generation of social anthropologists, formulated thus by British anthropologist Godfrey Leinhardt in 1954: "The problem of describing to others how members of a remote tribe think . . . appear[s] largely as one of translation, of making the coherence primitive thought has in the languages it really lives in, as clear as possible in our own."[11] But the more culturally or politically powerful the translator's language is seen to be, the less easily will it adapt to the "inferior" language that provides its text.

The writing or dictating of a captivity narrative can in fact serve as proof that the captive, despite his immersion in savagism, has not lost his "strong language." While a few former captives, mostly those who were adopted into tribes or otherwise assimilated, show pride at having mastered Indian languages, for the majority their captivity threatens a lapse into aphasia, as if they were Calibans in reverse, deprived of their human language by their new masters.[12] Perhaps the most dramatic example of a narrative that makes literacy the foundation of civilized identity is that of Father Isaac Jogues, the Jesuit missionary, taken prisoner by Mohawks in 1642. His narrative takes the form of a letter to the provincial of the Jesuits in France, written when he was still a captive, while his Mohawk masters were trading at a Dutch outpost. "I hesitate first in which language to address you," he begins (i.e., whether in French or Latin), "for, after such long disuse, almost equally forgetful of both, I find equal difficulty in each." He goes on to say that he has determined to use the "less common idiom," Latin, in order to be "better able to use the words of Holy Scripture." He prays that his superior "will excuse, in a man for eight years a companion and associate of savages, nay, a savage now himself in form and dress, whatever may be wanting in decorum and correctness" and fears that "wanting in language," he may be "still more so in knowledge"—suggesting a version of the Sapir-Whorf hypothesis whereby his separation from the language of knowledge would have caused him to lose the knowledge it signifies. Ironically, Jogues's modest apology for the loss of language negates itself in the expression, for here he is both writing in (according to VanDerBeets) a "pure and classic Latin" and making use of a classical rhetorical form, a version of the topos of humility. But Jogues's fear of losing the power to write is not groundless, for the Mohawks have been particularly violent in biting, burning, and mangling of his hands and fingers. Providentially, though, while his companion René Goupil has his right thumb amputated, only Jogues's *left* thumb was cut off during his tortures, sparing him from agraphia: "I must thank the Almighty that it was his will that my right should be untouched, thus enabling me to write this letter."[13]

For the Jesuit missionary, what makes Latin or French a "strong" language is its written tradition. The distinction Jogues makes between "language" and "knowledge" corresponds closely to the difference between writing and speech. He has, for example, been making "attempts to study their [the Mohawks'] language," but he asks parenthetically, "What study can there be without writing?" Children and savages learn language orally, civilized men through print. Shortly after his comment about the impossibility of study without writing, Jogues describes how he made his mark, his sign, on the natural environment, thereby simultaneously humanizing and civilizing it: "How often, on the stately trees of the forest, did I carve the most sacred name of Jesus, that, seeing it, the demons might fly, who tremble when they hear it!" To inscribe the trees with the mark of one's faith is already to write a proto-captivity narrative.[14]

Unlike the ethnologist, whose aim is analysis, the captive needs to understand the alien language simply in order to survive. But as James Axtell has noted, the colonists, as opposed to explorers, were less interested in understanding Indian behavior than in predicting it; Christian conversion was desirable because it "substitut[ed] predictable European modes of thinking and feeling for unpredictable native modes."[15] The captivity experience was especially frightening because it exposed the prisoners to what they usually saw as complete unpredictability; narrative after narrative describes the paradox of Indian cruelty followed abruptly by mercy (or vice versa), sudden mood shifts, threats of death that are not carried out, announcements of the killing of family members that turn out not to have been true. As Mary Rowlandson writes, "Sometimes I met with favor and sometimes with nothing but frowns."[16] Because the captives find it intolerable to be governed by language and behavior that are so apparently arbitrary and capricious, their narratives generate theories of Indian language—grammars, if you will—that help make sense of their experience.

In American captivity narratives through around 1800, one finds three basic interpretive strategies for dealing with Indian discourse. First, the author may assume that it is the product of a coherent culture and of humans who are fundamentally like oneself, and may seek to explain it as rationally motivated. Second, it may be viewed as the product of a coherent culture, but one that is perverse, evil, and diabolic and whose motives are therefore unlike one's own. Finally, the captive may deny altogether that Indian discourse *is* a language: instead it is brutish and irrational; it fails to communicate; it is lying, foolish, senseless. To a large extent the strategy adopted in a given narrative corresponds to two factors that scholars of Indian captivity have discussed at length: the ideology (especially religious) of the captive and the degree to which he or she becomes acculturated in Indian society. But the intersection is not systematic. Quaker Elizabeth Hanson consistently discovers a human explanation for Indian behavior; Quaker Jonathan Dickinson finds it mostly incomprehensible. Charles Johnston, who remained with his captors for only five weeks, attributes reasonable motives to them no less than does Colonel James Smith, who lived with Caughnawagas for five years. The one common feature that these three interpretive strategies share is the act of cultural translation itself, the rendering of Indian discourse into an intelligible European narrative form so that it may be categorized, comprehended, or condemned. This structural similarity will be apparent when we look in some detail at four narratives of American captivities that cover a span of slightly over a century, from Mary Rowlandson's of 1682 to Colonel James Smith's 1779 book about his captivity forty years earlier. These four narratives by Dickinson, Hanson, Rowlandson, and Smith display collectively the full range of responses to Indian language.

As is well known, Mary Rowlandson made sense of her captivity by seeing it in typological terms—now as an analogue of the Babylonian captivity, now as God's chastisement for the sins of the Puritan community. But typology also provides her with tools for categorizing Indian discourse. In particular it gives her a means of coping with the lies—or what she takes to be lies—that her captors tell her.

By the 1680s when Rowlandson suffered her imprisonment, the supposed Indian propensity to lie was already a stereotype among the British colonists. This hadn't always been so; in the early years of the Massachusetts colony William Wood had written in *New England's Prospect,* "Nothing is more hateful to [the Indians] than a churlish disposition, so likewise is dissimulation; he that speaks seldom and opportunely, being as good as his word, is the only man they love." According to Wood, the Indians approved of the English because, in their words, "the Englishman all one speak, all one heart."[17] But the colonists soon learned that Indians considered lying a legitimate discursive weapon in times of war or political conflict, and they encountered as well a linguistic practice that would later come to be associated with white frontiersmen: the lie, or tall tale, as a vehicle of group solidarity, used for the ritual testing of outsiders. Early in the nineteenth century the missionary John Heckewelder, in the course of upbraiding his countrymen for their insufficient understanding of Native American languages, would evolve a sympathetic explanation for Indian "falsehood":

> [A]ll that an Indian says is not to be relied upon as truth. I do not mean to say that they are addicted to telling falsehoods, for nothing is farther from their character; but they are fond of the marvellous, and when they find a white man inclined to listen to their tales of wonder, or credulous enough to believe their superstitious notions, there are always some among them ready to entertain him with tales of that description, as it gives them an opportunity of diverting themselves in their leisure hours, by relating such fabulous stories, while they laugh at the same time at their being able to deceive a people who think themselves so superior to them in wisdom and knowledge. They are fond of trying white men who come among them, in order to see whether they can act upon them in this way with success.[18]

Tall tales are a kind of linguistic jujitsu by which the speaker of a "strong" language can be tripped up by his own inquisitiveness and scientific curiosity. In their converse with prisoners, Indians often used lies and even variants of what we might call the "good cop/bad cop" routine as weapons of psychological warfare to demoralize their prisoners, prefiguring the way these techniques have been systematically developed as tools of brainwashing in the twentieth century. Midway into her captivity Mary Rowlandson is confronted with a lie of this unsettling sort:

> I had not seen my son a pretty while, and here was an Indian of whom I made inquiry after him and asked him when he saw him. He answered me that such a time his master roasted him and that himself did eat a piece of him as big as his two fingers and that he was very good meat. But the Lord upheld my spirit under this discouragement, and I considered their horrible addictedness to lying and that there is not one of them that makes the least conscience of speaking of truth.[19]

Shortly afterward she notes the falsehoods that her captors told her about her husband: that he had been killed by Indians; that believing his wife was dead, he had married again. But these lies, says Rowlandson, simply show how "like were these barbarous creatures to him who was a liar from the beginning," the Devil.[20] Not just lies, but Indian irony, jokes, and, above all, inconsistency are evidence for Rowlandson of the fallenness of their language. At one point she gives the Indians some tobacco she had been sent by colonists negotiating for their release:

> [W]hen it was all gone, one asked me to give him a pipe of tobacco. I told him it was all gone. Then he began to rant and threaten. I told him when my husband came I would give him some. "Hang [the] rogue," says he, "I will knock out his brains if he comes here." And then again in the same breath they would say that if there should come a hundred without guns they would do them no hurt, so unstable and like mad men they were.

She concludes by telling how this discourse convinced her that she dared not send to her husband to come to redeem her, since "there was little more trust to them than to the master they served," Satan.[21] Rather than seeking a contextual explanation for lying, Rowlandson gravitates toward an essentialist reading that sees lies as inherent evidence of distance from truth and therefore from God.

"So unstable and like mad men they were." For Rowlandson, as for most captives, inconsistency is the greatest threat, and departures from literal language, which might be acceptable under the head of rhetorical ornament in a Puritan sermon, are sinful when used by savages. Rather than seeing irony and jokes as part of a wide continuum of speech acts available to the Indian community, Rowlandson consistently reads them as tokens of Indian depravity. In the middle of a section complaining of

the hypocrisies and treacheries of the so-called praying Indians—
Christian converts—appears one of Rowlandson's most interesting tran-
scriptions of Indian conversation, used apparently as a self-evident example of how an Indian devil can quote Scripture to his purpose:

> There was another praying Indian who told me that he had a brother that
> would not eat horse; his conscience was so tender and scrupulous (though
> as large as hell for the destruction of poor Christians). Then he said he read
> that scripture to him, 2 Kings, 6:25, "There was a famine in Samaria, and
> behold they besieged it, until an ass's head was sold for fourscore pieces of
> silver . . ." he expounded this place to his brother and showed him that it
> was lawful to eat that in a famine which is not at another time. And now,
> says he, he will eat horse with any Indian of them all.[22]

This is such a fascinating passage because we can hear it easily enough
from the Indian's point of view as a piece of wit: he shows how cleverly
he overturns the objections of his ridiculously devout brother, deflating
his exaggerated piety with the punch line that Rowlandson leaves intact:
"now he will eat horse with any Indian of them all." The praying Indian
has attacked scriptural literalism with its own weapons with a finesse
that would do an English theologian proud. But Rowlandson is apparently scandalized that the praying Indian should quote Scripture with
such levity. Literacy, she seems to feel, is a dangerous thing for Indians;
after all, it is a praying Indian who writes the letter demanding twenty
pounds for her redemption. Literacy, like guns, gives the Indians more
firepower than they can be trusted with. Rowlandson is unwilling to
admit that Indians have legitimate access to anything more than a simple
referential use of language, one in which every natural meaning is linked
to a theological one.

Jonathan Dickinson, a Quaker shipwrecked along the Atlantic coast
of Florida in 1696, finds much of the communicative behavior of his
Jobese captors inexplicable because of the hermeneutic circle he in-
scribes: the Indians are animal-like; therefore their actions and language
are irrational; therefore they are animal-like. The first two Indians Dickinson's party saw came running "foaming at the mouth," and when
given tobacco and pipes, they "greedily snatched" them, "making a
Snuffing noise like a Wild-Beast, turned their Backs upon us and run
away."[23] The first night the English are in an Indian town, when night
came and the moon was up, "an *Indian* who performeth their Ceremo-
nies stood out loocking full at the moon making a hideous noise, and
crying out Acting like a mad man for the space of half an hour; all the

Indians being silent till he had done: after which they all made fearfull noise some like the barking of a *Dogg,* woolf, and other strange sounds.''[24]

Dickinson's Indians act without apparent motivation. At one point they set upon the English party ''with their knives in their hands, ready to execute their bloody design,'' seizing their captives' heads as if to cut their throats, awaiting a signal from their chief:

> In this Posture they seem'd to wait for the *Cassekey* to begin. They were high in words wich we understood not. But on a sudden it pleased the Lord to Work Wonderfully for our preservation, and instantly all these savage men were struck dumb, and like men amazed the space of a Quarter of an Hour, in which time their countenances Fell, and they looked like another People.[25]

Shortly thereafter they cease to threaten the captives, a fact Dickinson can only attribute to divine intervention. It appears not to have occurred to him that in the words that passed among his captors was some command or observation that caused the ''sudden change''; since his working assumption is that Indian behavior is incomprehensible not just to the English but by its very nature, the place to look for explanation of the inexplicable is special Providence.

The comic subplot of Dickinson's narrative—comic to us, dead serious to Dickinson and his fellows—is that since the Indians who hold them are friendly to the Spanish but hostile to the English, the captives must pretend to be Spanish by taking advantage of their captors' limited familiarity with the Spanish language. The English prisoners agree to abstain from speech as much as possible, while one crew member relatively fluent in Spanish is delegated to converse with the principal tribesmen in order to maintain the deception. In this case, mutual comprehensibility becomes a positive threat; the few words of English their captors know are as dangerous as firearms. Once, says Dickinson, when the captives have refused a task the Indians had set them, ''I heard a saying that came from one of the chief *Indians,* thus '*English Son of a Bitch*' which words started me; For I do believe they had some of our Nation in their possession, of whom they had heard such an expression.''[26] Another Indian who had spent time among the English attempted to unmask them by inviting them to eat with him:

> withall asking the name of the *Berries,* Expecting We would call them after the English manner ''Plumbs'': but perceiving his drift, and having learned

the name of them, as the *Spaniard* calls them "Uvaes"; then he would tell us that the *English* called them "Plumbs": such sort of discourse we had at times, Fore he would be striving to trapp us . . . in words.[27]

Dickinson's response to his captors' language forces it into a vicious dilemma; when they use their indigenous tongue, they are irrational, barbaric, and ultimately nonhuman, but when they use a European tongue, they are devious and conniving. In either case Dickinson perceives what amounts to an ontological difference between his own use of language and theirs.

Elizabeth Hanson, another Quaker who spent five months with Indians in 1724, differs noticeably from Dickinson and the earlier Puritan narrators in managing to find some comprehensible motives even for cruelty. Thus her 4-year-old child, who will not stop screaming during the Indians' initial attack, is killed by them "to ease themselves of the noise and to prevent the danger of a discovery that might arise from it" rather than simply out of malice.[28] Describing the captives' arrival at the Indian fort to which the captors had led them, Hanson notes,

> many of the Indians came to visit us and, in their way, welcomed my master home and held a great rejoicing with dancing, firing guns, beating on hollow trees instead of drums, shouting, drinking, and feasting after their manner in much excess for several days together which, I suppose, in their thoughts was a kind of thanks to God put for their safe return and good success.[29]

While she hesitates to accept this clamor as an entirely proper form of thanksgiving, her recognition that it serves a social function is a far cry from simply branding it devil worship, as we might expect one of the Mathers to have done. Hanson is sophisticated, too, at discerning the psychological causes of irrational behavior. For example, she observes that her master has been bad-tempered only when "he wanted food and was pinched with hunger."[30] Likewise, Hanson correctly interprets her master's sadistic teasing as a kind of psychological warfare. He repeatedly threatens to kill and eat her baby when it is fat enough, and at one point he makes her undress the child and fetch a stick that he says he will spit it on; when it is naked, he feels its arms and legs and declares it is not yet fat enough. "Now though he thus acted," writes Hanson, "I could not persuade myself that he intended to do as he pretended but only to aggravate and afflict me," and her interpretation turned out to be the correct one.[31]

Despite her willingness to ascribe human attributes to Indian language and behavior, Elizabeth Hanson could only hypothesize about it from the outside. When we turn from these captivity narratives to one written by someone whose depth of experience led to a high degree of acculturation, their limited, biased, or polemic representation of Indian discourse becomes apparent by contrast. Colonel James Smith, who lived with the Caughnawagas who adopted him (and briefly with other tribes) for five years before returning to an eventual military career with the British and American armies, is fully aware that his task is cultural translation and that there is a tension between the language of his experience and the language of literary description available to him. In his preface he notes that his narrative is based on a journal that he kept during his captivity (the Indians never having prevented him from reading or writing), and although as someone with "but a moderate English Education" he has been advised to "employ some person of liberal education to transcribe and embellish it," he believes that occurrences "truly and plainly stated" make the best history.[32] To resist the stylization and polishing that are a common feature of the captivity genre is already to renounce some of the prerogatives that a "strong" language had in the late eighteenth century, but Smith makes even more explicit his desire that his language serve as a transparent medium between Indian and American reader: "In the different Indian speeches copied into this work, I have not only imitated their own style, or mode of speaking, but have also preserved the ideas meant to be communicated in those speeches.—In common conversation, I have used my own style, but preserved their ideas."[33]

In fact, Smith's narrative comes close to being dialogic; the speech and folkways of the Indians are accorded nearly equal status with his own. So he recalls how a Delaware Indian who "spoke but bad English" yet was "a man of considerable understanding" explained to him the painful ritual of the gauntlet he had just undergone upon arriving at the Indian town: no, Smith was not being punished for having offended anyone; "it was only an old custom the Indians had, and it was like how do you do; after that he said I would be well used."[34] Early in his stay with the Caughnawagas he watched a dance that involved much repetition of the same words. He writes, "This exercise appeared to me at first irrational and insipid; but I found that in singing their tunes they used *ya ne no boo wa ne* &c like our *fa sol la,* and though they have no such thing as jingling verse, yet they can intermix sentences with their notes,

and say what they please to each other.''[35] A little while later the same
Delaware Indian begins to initiate him into the kind of cultural knowledge he will now require as an adopted tribesman, in a passage remarkable both for its depiction of Indian humor and for its careful attempt to
render American Indian Pidgin English:

> On my return to camp I observed a large piece of fat meat: the Delaware
> Indian . . . observed me looking earnestly at this meat, and asked me
> *what meat you think that is?* I said I supposed it was bear meat; he laughed
> and said, *ho, all one fool you, beal now elly pool,* and pointing to the other
> side of the camp, he said *look at that skin, you think that beal skin?* I went
> and lifted the skin, which appeared like an ox hide: he then said, *what skin
> you think that?* I replied that I thought it was a buffaloe hide; he laughed and
> said *you fool again, you know nothing, you think buffaloe that colo?*[36]

Smith admits he has never seen a buffalo, and the Delaware closes the
lesson; it is a buck elk, but Smith will soon see buffaloes at the salt licks
and so learn to recognize them.

The measure of Smith's ability to assimilate into Caughnawaga culture is his willingness to enter into its language. He learns by experience
the virtue of the immersion method. Early in his captivity he goes on a
long hunting trip with an Indian who spoke no English, and recalls, ''I
had to make use of all the Caughnawaga I had learned even to talk very
imperfectly with him: but I found I learned to talk Indian faster this way,
than when I had those with me who could speak English.''[37] Yet it is
significant that the thing that first aroused real affection in Smith toward
the Indians, during the spring some months after his capture, was their
return to him of several books he had lost back in the fall. He uses his
newly acquired Caughnawaga speech to thank the finder. ''This was the
first time that I felt my heart warm towards the Indians,'' he says, the
first time he managed to forgive the tortures he had seen them practice
on captives after Braddock's defeat. No doubt the kindness of the gesture itself was important, but one senses that with the return of the books
Smith is assured he need not lose his civilized identity entirely. Nor does
he; he finally publishes his narrative some forty years after his captivity
primarily to urge upon the American military the advantages of Indians'
mode of warfare. After all, he concludes, ''we are not above borrowing
language from them, such as homony, pone, tomahawk, &c. which is of
little or no use to us.''[38] And this might serve as a summation of all the
captivities' accounts of Indian discourse; whether it is comprehended or

not, respected or not, it is of little conceivable cultural "use" to Americans. The narratives shaped out of their captivity experience *are,* but that is because they share our language.

In the preface to their collection of captivity narratives, Alden Vaughan and Edward Clark imagine a hypothetical category of narratives that "could have been written by those who never returned to their natal culture." We might have a more complete portrayal of Indian life, they add, if "captives who entirely forsook their original environment—who completely transculturated—had written of their experience."[39] But such a narrative is conceptually impossible, a contradiction in terms, and not just because, as Vaughan and Clark remark, such captives were often taken as children and forgot their English. It is impossible fundamentally because the very form of the captivity narrative requires a point of view that makes the languages unequal; the movement of the genre is a descent *down into* the primitive and *back up* into the discourse of civilization. As Talal Asad observes of cultural translation in ethnography, it "is addressed to a very specific audience, which is waiting to read *about* another mode of life and to manipulate the text it reads according to established rules, not to learn *to live* a new mode of life."[40] There can be no written accounts by transculturated captives, in other words, that make visible that imperceptible moment when the Other becomes I, myself, or when the boundaries that have previously separated self and Other are erased. Such narratives may have existed in the living moment of oral storytelling to friends and family, but when, as in the case of Mary Jemison, say, they are transcribed and published by a literate editor, they are transformed into stories of *our* culture. The captivity narrative exists to repair breaches in the palisade of language not by replacing a few logs, but by building, as it always can, a new and larger palisade around the damaged structure.

Notes

1. Richard Slotkin, *Regeneration through Violence: The Mythology of the American Frontier, 1600–1860* (Middletown, Ct.: Wesleyan University Press, 1973), 116.

2. Beverly Flanigan Olson discusses the history of European characterization of Indian English as "broken English" or "bad English." *American Indian English in History and Literature: The Evolution of a Pidgin from Reality to Stereotype.* Ph.D. dissertation, Indiana University, 1981, 1–6. Too often it is forgotten that Europeans, in their turn, generally spoke "broken Indian": Ives Goddard observes that early settlers in the North-

east who thought they were using real Indian language may in fact have been learning forms of pidginized Algonquian. "Some Early Examples of American Indian Pidgin English from New England," *International Journal of American Linguistics* 43 (1977), 41.

3. Roger Williams, *A Key into the Language of America,* ed. John J. Teunissen and Evelyn J. Hinz (Detroit: Wayne State University Press, 1973), 93; Josiah Cotton, *Vocabulary of the Massachusetts (or Natick) Indian Language* (Cambridge, Mass., 1829), 94; Mary Rowlandson, *The Sovereignty and Goodness of God,* in Alden T. Vaughan and Edward W. Clark, eds., *Puritans among the Indians: Accounts of Captivity and Redemption, 1676–1724* (Cambridge: Harvard University Press, 1981), 35.

4. William Fleming, *A Narrative of the Sufferings and Surprizing Deliverance of William and Elizabeth Fleming* (Philadelphia, 1756), 9–10.

5. Fleming, 9.

6. Quoted in Nathaniel Knowles, "Torture of Captives by the Indians of Eastern North America," *Proceedings of the American Philosophical Society* 82 (1940), 183.

7. Vaughan and Clark, 11.

8. Mary Louise Pratt, "Fieldwork in Common Places," in *Writing Culture: The Poetics and Politics of Ethnography.* ed. James Clifford and George E. Marcus (Berkeley: University of California Press, 1986), 38.

9. Álvar Núñez Cabeza de Vaca, *Adventures in the Unknown Interior of America,* trans. Cyclone Covey (New York: Collier, 1961), 25–26.

10. Charles Johnston, *A Narrative of the Incidents Attending the Capture, Detention, and Ransom of Charles Johnston,* in Richard VanDerBeets, ed., *The Indian Captivity Narrative: An American Genre* (Lanham, Md.: University Press of America, 1984), 265.

11. Leinhardt quoted by Talal Asad, "The Concept of Cultural Translation in British Social Anthropology," in Clifford and Marcus, 142.

12. Victor Hanzeli quotes from a letter of the Jesuit missionary Brébeuf to French candidates for North American missions that well expresses this sense of this scandalous muteness: "Il faut faire estate pour gra[n]d maistre et gra[n]d Theologien que bous ayez esté en France d'este icy petit Escolier, et encor ô bon Dieu, de quels maistres! des femmes, des petits enfans de tous les Sauvages, et d'estre expose' à leur risée. . . . [T]out habile homme que vous estes, . . . il vous faut resoudre d'estre assez long-temps muet parmy des Barbares." ("You can be sure that no matter how great a teacher and theologian you have been in France you will be a little scholar here: and good Lord, of what teachers! of all the savages' women and babies, and prone to be their laughing stock. No matter how clever you are, you must make up your mind to be mute for quite some time among the Barbarians.) Victor Egon Hanzeli, *Missionary Linguistics in New France: A Study of Seventeenth- and Eighteenth-Century Descriptions of American Indian Tongues* (The Hague: Mouton, 1969), 47.

13. Isaac Jogues, "Captivity of Father Isaac Jogues of the Society of Jesus, among the Mowhawks," in VanDerBeets, 4, 5, 15.

14. Jogues, 33, 34. When learning Indian languages, the Jesuit missionaries invariably supplemented oral with written instruction. Hanzeli describes the basic procedure all the missionaries used:

> The missionaries sought an informant . . . asked him questions, listened to him talk, and began to record his speech, crudely at first, but realizing that the first record

would need subsequent checks and revisions. . . . Having collected what seemed to be a sufficient number of notes, they proceeded . . . to study them, in order to find the linguistic *oeconomie* or *génie* that could be elicited from these notes. 51

One senses that for the Jesuits Indian language was not "real" until it had been recorded in writing.

15. James Axtell, *The Invasion Within: The Contest of Cultures in Colonial North America* (New York: Oxford University Press, 1985), 42–43.

16. Mary Rowlandson, in Vaughan and Clark, 50.

17. William Wood, *New England's Prospect,* ed. Alden T. Vaughan (Amherst: University of Massachusetts Press, 1977), 91, 92.

18. John Heckewelder, quoted in Wilcomb E. Washburn, ed., *The Indian and the White Man* (Garden City, N.Y.: Doubleday Anchor, 1964), 70–71.

19. Rowlandson, 52. Her son was in fact alive and well.

20. Rowlandson, 53.

21. Rowlandson, 62.

22. Rowlandson, 62.

23. Jonathan Dickinson, *God's Protecting Providence Man's Surest Help and Defence* (Philadelphia, 1699), 5, 6.

24. Dickinson, 14.

25. Dickinson, 8.

26. Dickinson, 16.

27. Dickinson, 48–49.

28. Elizabeth Hanson, *God's Mercy Surmounting Man's Cruelty,* in Vaughan and Clark, 232.

29. Hanson, 236.

30. Hanson, 237.

31. Hanson, 239.

32. James Smith, *An Account of the Remarkable Occurrences in the Life and Travels of Col. James Smith . . . during His Captivity with the Indians* (Lexington, 1799), [3].

33. Smith, [3].

34. Smith, 7–8.

35. Smith, 12–13.

36. Smith, 13. For a discussion of the linguistic features of this passage see Olson, 103–4.

37. Smith, 16.

38. Smith, 88.

39. Vaughan and Clark, 16.

40. Asad, 159.

3

John Williams's Captivity Narrative: A Consideration of Normative Ethnicity

Rosalie Murphy Baum

Most studies of early captivity narratives have considered only New England, usually Puritan, narratives of the seventeenth and eighteenth centuries and have focused on the archetypal structure of the form. Richard VanDerBeets, for example, describes "the most compelling pattern" as that of a hero "who engages in an archetypal journey of initiation, a variation of the fundamental Death-Rebirth archetype." Such an archetypal hero experiences "Separation (isolation from one's culture and symbolic death), Transformation (a series of excruciating ordeals in passing from ignorance to knowledge and maturity, accompanied by ritualized adoption into a new culture), and Return (symbolic rebirth with a sense of moral or spiritual gain)."[1] Louise K. Barnett suggests that Cotton Mather's accounts of the captivity of white settlers by Indians in *Decennium Luctuosum* (1699) define the captivity narrative as "the central experience of white-Indian relations" and the "prototype for countless early nineteenth-century novels," with the satanic Indian as "gratuitous persecutor of whites, perpetrator of numberless atrocious deeds which provoked pity for his victims' suffering and admiration for their endurance."[2] Richard Slotkin asserts that "almost from the moment of its literary genesis, the New England Indian captivity narrative functioned as a myth, reducing the Puritan state of mind and world view, along with the events of colonization and settlement, into archetypal drama."[3] In this drama, "the hero was the captive or victim of devilish American savages and . . . his (or her) heroic quest was for religious conversion and salvation''; this structure, he recognizes (as does VanDerBeets), is simply ''a variation of the initiation into a new life or a higher state of being or manhood that is a myth-theme as old as mankind.''[4]

Alden Vaughan and Edward Clark's introduction to *Puritans among the Indians,* while recognizing (and expressing reservations about) the archetypal structure identified by other critics, views the captivity narrative that emerged ''as a separate and distinct literary genre'' in the late seventeenth century as a much more complicated discursive form. Vaughan and Clark suggest that these ''unpolished but intense religious statements'' blended the impulse and techniques of the spiritual auto-biography, the sermon, and the jeremiad with ''an element of pathos that appealed profoundly to a society which placed unusual emphasis on family ties and responsibilities.'' They also point to the importance of these accounts, for the modern reader, as anthropological records and ethnological histories and divide the New England narrators of these accounts into three groups: those like Mary Rowlandson who indicate they have not ''substantially changed'' from the experience; those like John Gyles who ''gained empathetic insight into Indian culture''; and those like James Smith who ''had difficulty adjusting to their natal culture after long exposure to Indian life.''[5]

My own readings suggest that it is time now for a more careful examination of the nature of these *apparently* archetypal dramas, with their requirement not simply of an ethnic Norm and an ethnic Other but also of victims and victimizers; it is time to consider the degree to which paradigmatic expectations defined the Other and, in so doing, further clarified the nature of the ethnic Norm.[6] It is also time for an emphasis upon the differences that exist among captivity narratives, including religious differences (e.g., Puritan, Catholic, Quaker, Baptist), ''racial'' or ''national'' differences (e.g., white and black, English and French), and gender differences.[7] We need to compare narratives in which the ethnic Norm and ethnic Other are reversed; after reading narratives in which the English view the French as Other, we need to read accounts in which the French portray the English as Other. Above all, we need to consider the degree of cultural mediation that occurs along with the multicultural contact occasioned by these experiences and their descriptions.

That significant differences exist is hardly surprising, given the nature of this particular genre grounded in conflicts, both physical and spiri-

tual, which thus offers an especially rich source for the study of disparate personal and cultural paradigms, disparate worldviews. Nowhere is
Northrop Frye's "horizontal bar" better represented: that is, the writer's
"historical and cultural situation, the assumption that he was bound to
make as man of his time, the ideology he was bound to reflect when he
wrote."[8] Nowhere do we become more aware, as William H. McNeill
points out, that "the same words that constitute truth for some are, and
always will be, myth for others, who inherit or embrace different assumptions and organizing concepts about the world."[9] Nowhere can we
be more certain of finding the pluralistic historical narration called for by
Hayden White and Dominick LaCapra. Most significant for this particular collection of essays on ethnicity, nowhere do we become more aware
of the writer's *opportunity* to assume or discover his or her group(s) as
the normative ethnicity against which the Other(s), often declared "savage," is (are) defined.

Even a cursory look at some of the captivity narratives written in the
last quarter of the seventeenth century and the first quarter of the eighteenth century makes obvious how "author-saturated," rather than
"author-evacuated," they are and thus should caution against any impulse to consider them models of representation of either ethnic Norm or
ethnic Other.[10] Rather, the narratives of such writers as Mary Rowlandson, Quentin Stockwell, Father Pierre Millet, John Gyles, Hannah
Dustan, John Williams, and Elizabeth Hanson should be valued as "partial descriptions" that "always exclude a great many other kinds of
important information" and offer not "a *single* correct view" but only
one of "*many* correct views, each requiring its own style of representation."[11] Above all, they are telling examples of the very human tendency (of both writers and literary critics?) to think in terms of the
archetypal pattern of ethnic Norm and Other while often unconsciously
revealing a pattern of cultural mediation.

A consideration of only one of the above narratives—that of John
Williams—in the context of contemporaneous captivity narratives, especially those of Mary Rowlandson, Father Millet, and Quentin Stockwell, suggests that the existence of very different "correct views" may
require that we rethink the archetypal designation that required ethnic
Norm and ethnic Other, victim and victimizer, and a pattern of
Separation-Transformation-Rebirth. Both the apparently coherent pattern of the past, eloquently supported by Williams, and the orderly
archetypal pattern asserted by recent critical studies of captivity narra-

tives need to be scrutinized with the kind of critical historiography being urged by White and LaCapra. Although Williams's narrative posits a clearly defined, even revealed, ethnic Norm and displays the ethnic Norm/ethnic Other dichotomy found in most captivity narratives, it does not follow the Separation-Transformation-Rebirth pattern expected of the Puritan captivity experience and thus questions the very nature of one of the supposedly more established ethnic Norms of the period.

The first consideration in examining any one of these "partial descriptions," of course, is the narrator himself or herself who in narrating defines the cultural meanings that underpin his or her captivity story. In all of the captivity narratives, the "implied author" or "second self" appears synonymous with the first-person narrator; but the first-person narrators vary significantly in their relationships to what could be loosely described as a normative ethnicity and therefore have very different perspectives on what they designate as an Other.[12] In addition, in the cases of Quentin Stockwell, Hannah Swarton, and Hannah Dustan, a second narrator (Increase or Cotton Mather) has stepped in to further clarify the coherent "Puritan state of mind and world view."[13]

The voice of John Williams speaks for a normative ethnicity privileged for centuries by historians and literary critics—Puritan, English, male, husband, father—and largely defined by marginal Other(s)—Indian, French, Catholic, female, child. His voice most clearly sustains the ideology of power and privilege. The voice of Father Millet also defines a normative ethnicity—Catholic, French, male—but from the perspective of an individual whose religious commitment defines as marginal many areas of primary definition (e.g., husband, father) for most males. The voice of Quentin Stockwell is also a clarion of normative power and privilege but lacks the supernatural/religious dimension of absolute power (despite Increase Mather's attempt to provide it) and omits the marginal Others of female and child in order to fully define patriarchal privilege. The voice of John Gyles is a complex study in perspectivism as the 56-year-old man draws upon his private memoirs in order to merge the marginal voice of a child and the privileged voice of the Puritan-English-male-husband-father. Within the normative ethnicity of the English heritage and of Puritanism and Quakerism the strikingly different marginal voices of Rowlandson, Swarton, Dustan, and Hanson become in their narratives voices of power and privilege as defined by the Otherness of the Indians and, in some cases, of the French. Thus, even for those whose shared geographic location, institutional church, and national heritage might suggest similarities in perspective, the details and shading of the ethnic Norm vary considerably—even question the existence of *an* ethnic Norm—and, obviously, affect the observation and definition of the Other. The comments added by Increase and Cotton Mather to the narratives of Stockwell, Swarton, and Dustan are clearly intended to compensate for the narrators' inadequacies in presenting the privileged Puritan perspective.

All of these narrators, except Quentin Stockwell, see the world "as a whole, a totality, a system, instead of as a sum of self-contained societies and cultures."[14] They define their own cultures as well as the strange and hostile cultures they encounter in terms of that totality, their own culture, of course, being assumed as the ethnic Norm. But, as the descriptions in the previous paragraph suggest, their differing definitions of their own cultures insurmountably confuse the definition of the ethnic Norm even for those who share, for example, the Puritan worldview. (Thus we might better speak of a personal/cultural ethnic Norm.) Further, these narrators "anatomize codes" of the Other, especially at the beginning of their experiences—unable to offer indigenous readings of native culture or of a different European culture and unaware, in varying degrees, of the possible value of imaginative attempts to reconstruct the cultural ideology of the Other (much less of the many Others within the ethnic Other).[15] As their captivities continue, however, they begin in their own ways to convey what Clifford Geertz calls "the structure of action" of the Other, although they seldom attempt the Other's "structure of thought."[16] By the end of all of the accounts, areas of the ethnic Norm and of the Other have merged—especially in the areas of communal sharing, kindness, and courtesy—so that at least the experience of the ethnic Other varies from the original concept, with only Williams not explicitly acknowledging this change.

Given the similar perspective of the world as "a totality, a system," even if not the same totality or system, it is not surprising that such narratives appear to yield to the archetypal paradigm described by VanDerBeets, Barnett, Slotkin, and Vaughan and Clark. Very simplistically, God's in his heaven, all's right in the world, even though certain chosen ones may be suffering at the hands of ethnic Others stages of separation, transformation, and rebirth in order to be worthy of their eternal destinies. As believers in *the* Truth (but a variable truth, depending upon the narrator), these chosen ones can expect their ephemeral lives within a culture (an *apparent* ethnic Norm) to serve as testing grounds for the eternal life that gives ultimate meaning to the system. No Other/outsider can harm or help a chosen one/insider except as part of the total divine plan. No one English can harm or help a French person; no one French can harm or help an English man or woman; no Indian can harm or help an English or French person without the direct consent and intention of God.

But within such a structure, at once theological, philosophical, and fictive, different kinds of internal tensions appear in the texts. As La-Capra explains, "A text is a network of resistances, and a dialogue is a two-way affair; a good reader is also an attentive and patient listener."[17] Although these narrators define the Other from the perspective of their personal/cultural ethnic Norm in significantly consistent, coherent ways, "submerged voices," not only voices of the Other but sometimes even the voice of the narrator or those with whom he or she identifies within the ethnic Norm, contest that reading.[18] These narrators may have the unified closures necessary for "moral meaning," but a clear disjunction often exists between the words of the text and the experiences being described.[19] This disjunction is clearest in the narrators' inability to understand the Other(s) and in their unawareness, sometimes partial, sometimes total, of the cultural mediation that occurs between what they regard as the ethnic Norm and the ethnic Other.

John Williams's *The Redeemed Captive* (1707) is one of the New England Puritan accounts that is considered an example of the archetypal form, offering a highly consistent, coherent view of ethnic Norm and ethnic Other. Like Mary Rowlandson and Hannah Swarton, Williams, minister to the Deerfield community, experiences many losses of family members, friends, and home. Like Rowlandson, Swarton, and John Gyles, he thinks of himself as being carried "from God's sanctuary to . . . a strange land," and like Rowlandson and Gyles, he refers to the land of captivity as a "wilderness," even though in fact most of his captivity is spent in Montreal, Quebec, and Chateau Richer.[20] Like Gyles and Swarton, he fears his captivity with the French Other, where he is under spiritual pressure to convert to Catholicism, more than he does his captivity with the Indian Other, where his sufferings are physical rather than spiritual.

Like Rowlandson and Swarton, Williams clearly sees his captivity as the will of God rather than, as Stockwell does, one possible and natural outcome of the ongoing warfare between the Indians, supported by the French, and the English. In jeremiad fashion, he sees his captivity as a way of God's admonishing His people and explains that his narrative is to prove to his people "that days of fasting and prayer, without *reformation* [italics mine], will not avail to turn away the anger of God from a professing people" (43). Reformation includes, of course, complete yielding of one's own will to God's. In the first incident of the narrative, in fact, Williams acknowledges that his life is saved because his attempt to shoot an Indian is foiled by his pistol's not firing, one of many instances, he writes, in which he has "found it profitable to be crossed in my own will" (45). Later in the narrative, he, like Mary Rowlandson, will not consider rescue until "God's time of deliverance" (78) has come. In addition, like Rowlandson, Swarton, and Gyles, Williams clearly stresses that the Indians can "act nothing against us but as they were permitted of God" (50–51) and acknowledges both the mercy and many kindnesses of God during his captivity. Some of these kindly providences come directly from God, as when He "wonderfully" supports Williams and renews his strength "to admiration" as he travels on "tender, swollen, bruised" feet (56). Most of them are indirect, however, humane actions of the Indian/Other that Williams does not consider to be natural or decent parts of the Indian culture but providential dispensations. For example, he writes that "God made the heathens so to pity our children" that they carried them "upon their shoulders and in their arms" (47).

By attributing the mercy and kindnesses of the Indians, in his case the Mohawks and Abenakis, to God rather than to the Indians themselves, Williams is, of course, revealing the typological conceptualization of the Puritans as Israelites, the Indians as heathen, ethnic Other. And a more foreign Other could hardly be conceived in dress, language, religion, social and political organization, and customs. The Indian existed in a state of "typological disorderliness: he was nomadic, a beast, a mere body without a soul," part of a wilderness that had to be tamed.[21] How then could such a creature display qualities of decency, morality, or civilization? Thus, Williams explains that it is "by the goodness of God" that his Indian master always shares "the best he had to eat" (55) with him and gives him a Bible. Mary Rowlandson, among the Narragansetts, describes the graciousness of the Lord in motivating the mistress/owner of her 13-year-old son to travel six miles to bring the boy to visit her and rejoices that the "wonderful mercy of God" inspires an Indian warrior to give her a Bible found in the plunder from Medfield.[22] Neither Williams nor Rowlandson could attribute such gestures to the

Indians themselves, since their kidnappers are clearly "murderous wretches," "bloody heathen," "ravenous bears," "barbarous creatures," and "black creatures in the [hellish] night."[23]

However, the perception of Otherness was not always as harsh as that of Williams and Rowlandson. Father Millet—like Swarton, among the Abenakis, and Stockwell, also among the Algonquians—sees the Indians who capture him more as enemies who have very different manners and ways of life than as simply "cruel and bloodthirsty savage[s]" (49). In fact, Millet assumes that any ill-treatment he receives is largely because of the English influence on the Indians. (The English have already burned him in effigy.) He prays that God will reward the Indians who are especially helpful to him and at one point exclaims that he can "scarcely restrain . . . tears on beholding the Charity and Heart of these poor Indian Christians."[24] Father Millet's position, of course, is completely different from that of Williams; he has been a missionary to the Indians for many years and has respect and affection for them. Further, like many Jesuit missionaries, he will welcome martyrdom if such is the will of God. The Indians for him are a kind of modified Other: even after his kidnapping he continues to learn their language, convert them to Roman Catholicism, and modify institutional structures and customs that are inconsistent with Catholicism. In fact, Millet notes that "the Irroquois, when They Are not Intoxicated, Seem much more reasonable" than the English.[25] He is eventually adopted and naturalized by the Iroquois, but that they always remain Other is clear from his recurring designation of them as "Savages."[26] Thus, despite the fact that, as Werner Sollors argues, "the achievement of A Christian and American selfhood was always part of the struggle against a heathenish, ethnic 'Otherness'," the attitude toward and appreciation of that Otherness varied immensely.[27]

Although Williams's attitude toward the Indians is characteristic of many captivity narratives, in other significant ways affecting an ethnic and archetypal reading of the genre, Williams's captivity narrative is unique among contemporaneous accounts. To begin with, the narrative is prefaced with a dedication to Joseph Dudley, "Captain-General and Governor-in-Chief" (39), making it something of a political document. It is true that the dedication opens with the strong statement that a lack of gratitude to God for "the signal favors of heaven" is "criminal and unpardonable" (39) and that the narrative intends "to preserve the memory" of the many "wonders of divine mercy" (40) experienced during captivity. By analogy, then, as well as the view of correspondence between the heavenly ruler and the earthly ruler, one could argue that it is only appropriate that Williams should in the fourth paragraph of the dedication offer thanks to Dudley as "the prime instrument in returning our captivity" (40). But, in a narrative like that of Rowlandson, Gyles, or Swarton, those involved in redeeming the captives are mentioned almost casually at the end of the account, because the focus is upon the religious experience. Thus, the intensely religious intention of Williams's account is certainly tempered by his dedication. Williams's words in praise of Dudley—sagacity, prudence, vigor, persistence—are very strong as he describes Dudley's "uncommon sympathy with us, your children." And his statement that "all your [Dudley's] people are cherished under your wings, happy in your government, and are obliged to bless God for you" (40) is puzzling given our awareness that Dudley was so disliked by many prominent Puritan families (e.g., the Mathers and the Sewalls). The dedication appears to be a very *worldly* opening, even a politically expedient opening to a religious narrative.

Only Stockwell's account is as secular as Williams's opening, but Stockwell's account never becomes a religious narrative as does that of Williams. It is Increase Mather, in *An Essay for the Recording of Illustrious Providences* (1684), not Stockwell, who describes the narrative as an account of "Captivity and Redemption, with the more notable Occurrences of divine Providence attending him in his distress."[28] It is also Increase Mather who adds at the end of the account that "in God's good time" Stockwell was freed and gave this account of "the changes of Providence which passed over him."[29] Stockwell himself does not mention Providence or God. The only time he mentions praying is when the Indians request the English to pray for a good hunt or to give a blessing at mealtime. Yet his account abounds with occasions where one would expect a good Puritan to acknowledge the direct hand of God in the experience he has; for example, Stockwell describes the kindness of the Indian captain, Ashpelon, and the occasion when old war wounds so cripple him that he cannot travel, until "[his] pain was suddenly gone and [he] was much encouraged again."[30] But, for reasons not clear from the narrative, this apparently "ordinary" Puritan of Deerfield, neither minister nor priest, perhaps not husband or father, does not describe the active hand of God in his life during his captivity as do Williams, Rowlandson, Swarton, Gyles, Hanson, and Millet.

The perspective, tone, and incidents of Williams's narrative also are very different from those of other captivity narratives and do not suggest a *personal* archetypal journey of separation, transformation, and return. (Millet's experience, of course, offers two possibilities of rebirth: increased spiritual growth in this world and the sanctity of martyrdom.) One significant difference is that Williams and his Deerfield congregation, warned by other recent attacks along the frontier, are somewhat prepared—spiritually at least—for the experience they have. Not long before the attack, Williams and a group of parishioners have prayed together to ask God to grant them the ability to deal with whatever "public calamities" (43) may befall them. As a group they realize that "days of fasting and prayer, without reformation" (43) will not turn God's anger from His people, and thus they gather to pray together that they may have the "right Christian spirit" to handle whatever hardships a God both merciful and judging may decide to afflict. This is not a group of people, then, who need—as Rowlandson and Swarton said they needed—to be reminded of the power of God and their dependence upon Him or of the temporal nature of earthly comforts. Rather, Williams suggests that his worthy people, after their captivity and rescue, have a relationship with God like that of Jacob: they "have striven with God and with men, and have prevailed" (120).

Williams's account of his captivity also does not suggest a *personal* archetypal journey in the manner in which it blends the predominant description of his public or pastoral role with his personal experience as husband, father, and individual. Thus, the always accepting tone seldom shifts from the consoling and sometimes almost clinically formulaic to the intimate and painful during the period Williams is with the Indians. When he arrives among the French, eight weeks after his capture, his voice becomes primarily a public one as he serves as spokesman for the true faith and attempts to guide his people, even though the French actively work to prevent communication between the minister and members of his congregation. Only Stockwell's narrative reveals equally little of his inner life; the other narrators' accounts either dwell on their reactions or at least balance events and emotional responses.

Williams himself never seems to think of his captivity as a particularly personal event in his life. He never thinks of himself as having been captured because of his own iniquities, as do Rowlandson and Swarton. Rather, he seems to see himself as one of a group who have been captured because of the iniquities of humanity in general. In addition, Williams, like Millet, never wonders, as do Rowlandson and Swarton, if his God has forsaken him, and he appears less capable than the other narrators of seeing rather than seeing through the ethnic Other.[31] Instead of using the occasion of captivity to confront challenges to his own ethnic identity, Williams describes himself enacting the pastoral role that he had anticipated when he prayed with a group from his community before the attack and capture. And with that pastoral role comes a certitude, both nationalistic and religious, which none of Williams's experiences apparently cause him to question or modify. He continues to see the Indians as the Other "who delightfully inbrued their hands in the blood of so many of His people" (50); he is horrified by the change in dress and manners of assimilated English children. When the Jesuits suggest to him that the Indian cruelties are justified by the cruelties of the English against the Indians for decades, Williams states that the Indians are lying because he "well knew the English were not approvers of inhumanity or barbarity towards enemies" (59). And when the Jesuits ask Williams to attend one of their services just as they would attend one of his if they were in New England, Williams responds that indeed it would be quite all right for the Jesuits to attend his services, since there is nothing "as to matter or manner of worship but what was according to the word of God" in his church. However, he cannot attend a Catholic service because of the "idolatrous superstitions in worship" (60) of Catholicism. Thus, Williams in no way fulfills VanDerBeets's formula for the archetypal hero who passes from "ignorance to knowledge and maturity."[32] Unlike Millet, who also experiences no spiritual struggle, he does not appear to grow emotionally or spiritually or to gradually perceive the cultural ideology of the Other. Rather, as an archetypal figure, he is something of a Nestor—a man understanding what is true, right, and just—accompanying his people on their journey.

Even at the time of the attack, Williams speaks more for the group, as their minister, than for himself. He declares that "God beyond expectation made us in a great measure to be pitied" (45); he exclaims, "Who can tell what sorrows pierced our souls when we saw ourselves carried away from God's sanctuary" (46); and he describes the people of Deerfield standing together on a mountainside as they behold "the awful desolations of our town" (47). In fact, Williams's pastoral and governing role is so strong that his first observation about the attack is that the enemy has been able to come "like a flood upon us" because the watch was "unfaithful." Not even the bloody attack with its fatalities and the subsequent captivity of the survivors can distract Williams from his role as teacher: before proceeding to describe the attack, he admonishes all watchmen to avoid such negligence in the future lest they also "bring the charge of blood upon themselves" (44). On the second day, when Williams is permitted to speak to his faltering wife for the first time since the attack and the deaths of two of their children, his account of their conversation reads like a deeply religious exchange between a minister and member of his congregation, not one between husband and wife.

Williams's attitude toward the Indians, the savage Others embroiled in a struggle with the Chosen Ones, and his public/pastoral role appear to prevent any significant cultural mediation from occurring during his short stay with the Abenakis and Mohawks. Williams experiences a number of physical hardships, especially hunger, lice, and frostbite, and he describes good treatment by both the Indians and the French (thanks to the will of God), but he does not indicate that his view of the situation or of either of the ethnic Others he lives among changes through the months. In fact, Williams's captivity narrative makes of history a lesson in theology and is an excellent example of the tendency of "ethnic narrators to mimetically ransack their respective cultural warehouses."[33] Certainly this minister is not going to be affected by the remarkable efforts of the Indians to integrate the captives into their kinship structure or social life, by the Indians' impressive technological adaptation to their environment (e.g., moccasins, canoes), or by their respectful treatment of women and children. Rowlandson, on the other hand, is conscious of changing while she is among the Narragansetts. She comes to understand enslavement from the perspective of a slave. (Williams actually owned two slaves before his capture, but there is no indication that he sees any similarities between his condition among the Indians and that of his African-American slaves.) She overcomes her inability to stay in the room with a dead person; develops a very different appreciation of food; gains power over smoking, a habit she had unsuccessfully struggled against for many years among her own people; begins to regard material objects and vanity differently after viewing both deprivation and vanity among the Indians; and even comes to believe that the Indians are mistreated by the English. Both Rowlandson and Millet begin to see the Indians individually, as they witness the conflicts and factionalism within the tribes.

Millet's concepts of generosity and appreciation are modified by the depth of these virtues in the Indians despite their own needs or the dangers they risk in assisting him. He is overwhelmed by the deep faith of the Christian Indians and the strong aversion to war of many in the tribe. Stockwell is impressed by the Indian efforts to assimilate the captives into their tribe and by their sharing equally with their captives whatever food or comforts they have. He learns enough of the language to understand the Algonquian fear of the Mohawks, to appreciate the reasons they stake their captives to the ground at night (so "we should be out of our knowledge" of English ways), and to realize that the sporadic harsh treatment of the captives is in response to outrages the Indians have received from the English.[34] Gyles admires many Indian skills—in hunting and preserving food, for example—and develops such an affectionate relationship with one of his masters that the Indian visits him some twenty years after his ransom. Rowlandson, Millet, Stockwell, and Gyles, although they continue to regard the Indians as Other, learn to see differently as a result of their experiences and redefine, to varying degrees, both ethnic Norm and ethnic Other. Williams, as he recounts his experience two years after his capture, presents the perspective of a person who sees at the end of his experience what he had seen at the beginning: the typology of the Puritans as Israelites, the Indians and French as heathen and ethnic Other.

The French and the Indians themselves acknowledge Williams's public/pastoral relationship to his people from the very beginning. When John Alexander escapes the first night, the French commander instructs Williams to tell the English that if there are any more escapes, the rest of the captives will be burned. And during the period when the captives are marching to Canada, Williams is allowed great freedom as mentor and minister. On the Sabbath, five days after their capture, he is allowed to pray and preach to his congregation. Two days later he prays with Mary Brooks, who has suffered a miscarriage and assumes, correctly, that the Indians will kill her that day. Two days after that, he again prays with the captives, and they sing a Psalm together. When Williams and many of the other captives reach Canada, however, he is not allowed to pray or preach to his people. In fact, as the French try to convert the captives to Roman Catholicism, they refuse to allow Williams to visit any of his townspeople.

The passages revealing a more intimate side to Williams are few and, except for two short periods of personal weakness, concern his wife and son Samuel. At the time of the attack Williams describes his "distressing care" (45) for his wife, who is weak from childbirth. (He expresses no emotion when his two children are killed or when the attackers set fire to his house and barn.) As he anticipates the death of his wife, he speaks of her as "the desire of [his] eyes, and companion in many mercies and afflictions" (48); later he describes her death as a "great" loss (49). During the first weeks of captivity Williams experiences two moments of personal weakness. Nearly two weeks after being captured, Williams is separated from all members of his congregation and approaches despair. He writes, "My spirit was almost overwhelmed within me at the consideration of what had passed over me and what was to be expected, I was ready almost to sink in my spirit" (53). Several weeks later, after Williams's feet have been bleeding and frostbitten for days, he once describes their condition in other than matter-of-fact terms. In crossing Lake Champlain, he writes, "the ice was very rough and uneven, which was very grievous to my feet that could scarce endure to be set down on the smooth ice on the river." At this point he cries "to God in ejaculatory requests that He would take notice of my state and some way or other relieve me" (56). (Shortly afterward moist snow begins to fall to cover the ice.) Except for these two passages, Williams's personal reactions tend to be very subdued. For example, when he discovers that two of his children are safely at Montreal and many of the captives have arrived in Canada before him, he merely says, "Mercy in the midst of judgment!" (57). When he sees "several poor children" dressed and acting "very much like Indians," he calls it "a sight very affecting" (58).

Williams's impersonality sets his narrative apart from those of Rowlandson, Millet, Swarton, Hanson, and Gyles; of those mentioned for comparison, only Stockwell's shares this quality to any appreciable degree. Such impersonality does not, however, arise from the same roots, and in Williams's case personal feelings seem to be subsumed by his public role. It is in Williams's relationship with his son Samuel that he reveals himself most personally and, I would suggest, also establishes a yet unrecognized archetype of the captivity narrative. Further, his interaction with his son suggests the strength of Boelhower's claim that "the impulse to recover, rebuild, and maintain an ethnic *imago mundi* and an ethnic community is nothing but the genealogical principle itself." Williams's great anguish in dealing with his son is the problem of "lost authority" (96), both ethnic and personal.

About two years later into his captivity, Williams receives word that his son Samuel, held in Montreal, has embraced Catholicism. His reaction is intense—"sorrow and anguish took hold upon me" (91)—and he comes close to despair in reviewing the afflictions of the last two years, with the apostasy of his son being the worst. In a short letter to his son, which he knows may not be delivered, he pours out his grief:

> Oh! I pity you; I would mourn over you day and night! Oh, I pity your weakness that through the craftiness of man you are turned from the simplicity of the gospel! I persuade myself you have done it through ignorance. Oh! Why have you neglected to ask a father's advice in an affair of so great importance as the change of religion! . . . Oh! Consider and bethink yourself what you have done! . . . Let a father's advice be asked for the future in all things of weight and moment. (92)

Several weeks later he writes a much longer letter to his son, continuing in the vein of any father who has raised a son to follow one path and discovers he is following another. Aggrievedly, he explains that he is writing a second time because Samuel has neglected to write to him, just as he "neglected to take any advice or counsel" (93) from his father when he changed religion. He then argues his own case and demolishes his son's before closing with "I am your afflicted and sorrowful father" (105). Thus, Williams's captivity narrative—unlike any of the other early captivity narratives—establishes a pattern in which the archetypal journey of initiation is that of the son, who is, so to speak, offstage. And the son's archetypal journey of initiation is in defiance of his father. Two new archetypal patterns, then, emerge: Williams as Nestor figure to his Jacob-like congregation (including the son) and Williams as aggrieved father in response to his rebellious son. Further, in his son's case multicultural contact has defeated the ethnic Norm. The "submerged voices" of Indians and Frenchmen breaking out of the paradigms imposed upon them and of some English captives understanding or adopting Indian and French ways have become one loud declaration that the ethnic Other is not Other, with eternity and salvation at stake.[35]

Williams's second letter to his son (more than 3,600 words long) is also an unusual feature in the captivity narrative. References to exchanges of letters appear in other narratives—for example, Mary Kinnan and her brother correspond for almost six months in 1794 before she is rescued—but the letters are not included in the narratives. Williams's second letter is a valuable document in and of itself, offering a lengthy and clear explication of the differences between Protestant and Romish faiths from a Puritan point of view. Those religious differences are the essential element of Williams's condemnation of the French as ethnic

Other that culminates in these letters. Despite the fact that a very real material problem between the English and French was land, nationalistic and political differences are for Williams less the stuff of a boundary-constructing response than are religious differences.

Interestingly enough, although Williams's fear of the French is of a very different order than his fear of the Indian, the language of the Other remains similar. He describes the French as "Romish ravenous wolves" (71), notable for their "heathenish cruelty" and "crafty designs" (77), thus indicating that for him such vocabulary is not limited to an apparently primitive way of life but indicates a more inclusive state of Otherness. Williams also details the crimes the French, especially the Jesuits, commit in the interests of their false religion: without parental consent they baptize all of the captured English babies; offer various kinds of bribes to the captives to seduce them into Catholicism; and send the Indians to "commit outrages against the English" (75), both murders and kidnappings. Among the "idolatrous superstitions in worship" (60) of this false religion that Williams discusses are the papist belief in seven sacraments; the withholding of wine in the Lord's Supper and the belief in transubstantiation; the saying of the Mass; the office of the pope and the heirarchy of the priests; the practice of praying to the Virgin Mary and the saints; the belief in purgatory and prayers for the dead; and the common use of statues, pictures, and other ceremonials.

Swarton, Gyles, and Hanson also fear the French, since they object to the same beliefs and practices Williams discusses and view becoming papists as worse than death. They do not, however, describe the French with the terminology of savagery they sometimes use for the Indians, and they speak more restrainedly of the pressures brought upon them to convert, emphasizing primarily the kindnesses of the French. Swarton writes, "I must speak it to the honor of the French, they were exceeding kind to me at first, even as kind as I could expect to find the English," although she later feels oppressed by the "zeal, love, entreaties, and promises" as well as threats and "hard usages" of their efforts to convert her.[36] Gyles mentions only a few occasions when he is pressured to participate in papist services. Stockwell, of course, does not even mention conversion, since he does not mention any religious beliefs in his account. He does reflect the tension in loyalties that exists among the three groups in his description of an argument that breaks out between the Indians and the French one morning when the Indians contend that the French love the English "better than the Indians."[37]

Hanson's account is particularly interesting because her baby, taken captive at fourteen days of age, is one of the infants baptized by the French so that it will not be damned. The successive versions of her narrative (1728, 1754, 1769), however, indicate the increasing hostility between the English and the French. For example, the version of 1754 reads that the Indians take scalps "for a testimony and evidence that they have killed so many, receiving sometimes a reward for every scalp." The 1760 version explicitly states that the French give "the Indians a pecuniary reward for every scalp they brought to them."[38] Compared with Williams narrative, all of these accounts reveal a considerably more flexible and shifting ethnic boundary in which religious differences are relatively less important.

Writing his narrative from the other side of the boundary, Father Millet shows feelings against the English certainly as strong as Williams's against the French but for very different reasons. Millet expresses no concern about the beliefs of the English; he is disturbed by their brutality toward the missionaries and their encouragement of the Iroquois in their warfare against the French. During his captivity he is considered "a great Iroquois and english State Criminal," as "a great criminal and great deceiver, who caused their [the Iroquois's] fellow-countrymen to be seized under pretext of a st. John's day festival." When the Christian Indians succeed in saving his life and he is adopted by the Onneiouts ("for one called Otassete"), the English are very angry and solicit the assistance of neighboring tribes in overturning the decision.[39]

In some respects it would seem that cultural comprehension could occur more easily between the English and the French than between the Europeans and the Indians. However, Millet's situation does not allow for cultural mediation with the English; that is, he is not among them and experiences their presence only in the intrigues that occur among the Indians themselves. Williams's situation could allow cultural mediation, and in a sense it does, as Williams shares the kinds of meals and conversations with the French, especially the governing officials, that only European civilization offered at that time. However, Williams's rigidly doctrinaire religious position prevents any kind of religious comprehension from occurring, even within the areas in which the French beliefs allow some flexibility. The French may believe that the Puritans are misled and that only Catholics will be saved, but Williams believes the papists are Satanic followers of the anti-Christ. Thus, Williams acknowledges the topographical divisions of wilderness (Indian) and Canada (French), but his own movement through these localities and therefore into different cultural paradigms does not affect the Puritan model of "a totality" with Norm and Other, Insider and Outsider. As Boelhower suggests of so many colonists and explorers, Williams does not so much see the French or the Indians as see through them into his own self-constructed system of symbols and types.[40] Adoption was never a possible solution for him.

With Stockwell, however, multicultural contact does become cultural comprehension. He shows great respect for the French and for the Indians as well as gratitude for their kindnesses. His "Relation" comes close to offering a worldview in which self-contained cultures may sometimes interact cruelly in warfare but also retain valuable intrinsic attributes away from the battlefield and even respect wartime obligations to each other. For example, the ownership of the English captives by the Indians is respected by both the French, who may, however, try to buy them from the Indians, and the English, who ransom them. Examples of cultural mediation such as those in Stockwell's narrative suggest more numerous and complex ways of confronting the ethnic Other than John Williams's rigid construction of boundaries.

Of equal interest in a consideration of cultural mediation are the captives' children who adopt the French or Indian ideology and culture, creating a situation in which the ethnic Other becomes the ethnic Norm. Hanson's oldest daughter (16 when captured) becomes a Catholic and marries a Frenchman; Swarton's daughter Mary (17 when captured) converts and marries an Irish Canadian. As discussed earlier, Williams's son Samuel (15 when captured) converts to Catholicism for a short time, and Williams's daughter Eunice (7 when captured) not only becomes a Catholic but marries an Indian. None of her father's pleas—even after he is ransomed and returns to Canada for her—can persuade her to leave her Indian life in Canada. It is very possible that such decisions on their children's part, especially with the older children, account in part for the tendency in their parents to emphasize ethnic Norm and ethnic Other in their narratives even when their very accounts, or at least the submerged voices in them, suggest a much more complex cultural interaction. Obviously the way of life of the ethnic Other, Indian or French, is an active threat to their own authority and elaborate cultural system. Given the significant differences between the apparently primitive Indian life and the civilized Indian life, the Puritan and Quaker religions and Catholicism, a child's decision to make the ethnic Other the ethnic Norm becomes a shattering rejection of both cultural and parental authority in a world that insists upon a privileged genealogical principle and dichotomous cultures.

The early captivity narratives describe experiences whose subjective comprehension and rendering of "many correct views" become crucial in an understanding of an "Americanness," both one and divisible, myth and reality. As Boelhower points out, "a sign is only ethnic if it is produced or interpreted as such by an intending subject."[41] Since each writer of these narratives assumes the stance of a defining presence, he or she offers versions of ethnic Norm and ethnic Other by assigning both distinctive characteristics and the absence of such characteristics. The process, more often reactive than proactive—even in the case of Williams—places the self and its extension in a familiar community in the Normative role and works to marginalize characteristics seen as opposed, alien, or valueless. The Other becomes "bad" or less desirable rather than Other as source of possibility or enrichment or, simply, the yet unknown. Williams's narrative with its privileged voice is an especially powerful example of this process, given his position as interpreter or exegete of revealed truth, revealed paradigms, which lead to archetypal readings. The other narratives, written by more marginal voices, suggest on the other hand very personal/cultural ethnic Norms and a process of formation of the ethnic Norm and Other that is much more relational, not quite fulfilling a monocultural or multiethnic paradigm. It appears uncomfortably clear that the relational capacities of the narrators who are young (Gyles), ordinary (Stockwell), and female (Rowlandson, Swarton, and Hanson) are far greater than the relational capacity of a man like Williams who is the only narrator in a position of significant influence in his community. It is also uncomfortably clear that the relational potential and actuality expressed in these narratives have not, until very recently, been noted in studies of the captivity narratives or of early American literature in general. For too long the adult public and occupational world, the "affect-denying world of alienated work," has not only suppressed relational capacities and repressed relational needs but also prevented an awareness of this curtailment.[42] Reading John Williams's construction of ethnic Norm and ethnic Other against the differing understandings of those such as Rowlandson, Gyles, Stockwell, and Hanson is a step toward letting the submerged voices speak.

Notes

1. Richard VanDerBeets, *The Indian Captivity Narrative: An American Genre* (Lanham, Md.: University Press of America, 1984), x.

2. Louise K. Barnett, *The Ignoble Savage: American Literary Racism, 1790–1890* (Westport, Ct.: Greenwood Press, 1975), 4. Although Werner Sollors points out in *Beyond Ethnicity: Consent and Descent in American Culture* (New York: Oxford University Press, 1986) that "it has become de rigueur in ethnic criticism to refer to the original inhabitants of the American continent as 'Native Americans' in order to avoid the, not slur, but misnomer 'Indians'" (27), I have followed his and William Boelhower's example and used the word "Indians." This usage is less disruptive in the text since both the captivity narratives and criticism of the genre use the term "Indians."

3. Richard Slotkin, *Regeneration through Violence: The Mythology of the American Frontier, 1600–1860* (Middletown, Ct.: Wesleyan University Press, 1973), 94.

4. Slotkin, 21, 22.

5. Alden T. Vaughan and Edward W. Clark, ed., *Puritans among the Indians: Accounts of Captivity and Redemption, 1676–1724* (Cambridge: Harvard University Press, 1981), 2, 3, 10, 14, 15. The authors also identify a fourth category, a "hypothetical" one that "could have been written by those who never returned to their natal culture" (16).

6. William Boelhower discusses the difficulty of identifying the components of ethnicity, citing Thomas Sowell's statement that "ethnic identity has been a complex and elusive phenomenon." He notes the attempts of Joseph Rothschild ("race, consanguinity, religion, language, customs and practices, regionalism, and political experience") and Anthony Smith ("common origins, . . . shared and distinct historical past and destiny, . . . one or more distinguishing cultural attributes . . . sense of collective unity and solidarity") to define such factors and lists the sixteen "control features" in the *Harvard Encyclopedia of American Ethnic Grops:* "origins, migration, arrival, settlement, economic life, social structure, social organization, family and kinship, culture, religion, education, politics, intergroup relations, group maintenance, individual ethnic commitment." *Through a Glass Darkly: Ethnic Semiosis in American Literature* (New York: Oxford University Press, 1987), 31–32.

7. Because the scope of this paper is already considerable and the subject of gender differences is highly complex, I shall not consider it as such in this essay.

8. Northrop Frye, "Framework and Assumption," *Northrop Frye Newsletter* (Fall 1968), 6.

9. William H. NcNeill, *Mythistory and Other Essays* (Chicago: University of Chicago Press, 1986), 19.

10. Clifford Geertz, *Works and Lives: The Anthropologist as Author* (Stanford: Stanford University Press, 1988), 9.

11. Lloyd S. Kramer, "Literature, Criticism, and Historical Imagination" in Lynn Hunt, ed., *The New Cultural History* (Berkeley: University of California Press, 1989), 118; Hayden White, *Tropics of Discourse: Essays in Cultural Criticism* (Baltimore: Johns Hopkins University Press, 1978), 46.

12. Wayne Booth, *The Rhetoric of Fiction* (Chicago: University of Chicago Press, 1961), 71; Kathleen Tillotson, *The Tale and the Teller* (London: Rupert Hart-Davis, 1959), 22.

13. Slotkin, 94.

14. Eric R. Wolf, *Europe and the People without History* (Berkeley: University of California Press, 1982), 385.

15. Clifford Geertz, *Local Knowledge: Further Essays in Interpretive Anthropology* (New York: Basic Books, 1983), 183.

16. Clifford Geertz, *Negara: The Theater State in Nineteenth-Century Bali* (Princeton, N.J.: Princeton University Press, 1980), 135.

17. Dominick LaCapra, *Rethinking Intellectual History: Texts, Contexts, Language* (Ithaca, N.Y.: Cornell University Press, 1983), 64.

18. Kramer, 103.

19. Hayden White, *The Content of the Form: Narrative Discourse and Historical Representation* (Baltimore: Johns Hopkins University Press, 1987), 21.

20. John Williams, *The Redeemed Captive, Returning to Zion,* ed. Edward W. Clark (Amherst: University of Massachusetts Press, 1976), 46, 44. Subsequent references to Williams will be identified parenthetically in the text.

21. Boelhower, 61.

22. Rowlandson, *The Narrative of the Captivity and Restoration of Mrs. Mary Rowlandson* (Boston: Houghton Mifflin, 1930), 19.

23. Rowlandson, 4, 5, 9, 10.

24. Pierre Millet, "Lettre a Quelques Missionaires due Canada," in *The Jesuit Relations and Allied Documents,* tr. Percy Favor Bicknell, Crawford Lindsay, and William Price (New York: Pageant, 1959), Vol. 64, p. 79.

25. Millet, 99.

26. For example, Millet, 79.

27. Sollors, "Literature and Ethnicity," in *Harvard Encyclopedia of Ethnic Groups,* ed. Stephen Thernstrom, et al. (Cambridge: Harvard University Press, 1981), 654.

28. Quentin Stockwell, "Relation of His Captivity and Redemption," 80.

29. Stockwell, 89.

30. Stockwell, 82–83.

31. Cf. Boelhower, 48.

32. VanDerBeets, x.

33. Boelhower, 95.

34. Stockwell, 82.

35. Kramer, 103.

36. Swarton, "A Narrative . . . Containing Wonderful Passages Relating to Her Captivity and Deliverance," in Vaughan and Clark, 153–54.

37. Stockwell, 87.

38. Hanson, "God's Mercy Surmounting Man's Cruelty," in Vaughan and Clark, 232; for the 1760 version, see Richard VanDerBeets, ed., *Held Captive by Indians: Selected Narratives, 1642–1836* (Knoxville: University of Tennessee Press, 1973), 133. See also VanDerBeets's comments on stylistic change in the versions, 130–31.

39. Millet, 73, 90–91, 101.

40. Boelhower, 48.

41. Boelhower, 38–39.

42. Nancy Chodorow, *The Reproduction of Mothering: Psychoanalysis and the Sociology of Gender* (Berkeley: University of California Press, 1978), 207.

4

The American Indian as Humorist in Colonial Literature

Luise van Keuren

If, at some distant time, our probings of outer space reach another planet sustaining flora, fauna, and an unknown race of people, the imagination of our earthly globe with be galvanized. Curiosity afire, writers of every description will hasten to record the story. One can scarcely imagine the media coverage! The entrepreneurs among us might await word of deposits of oil, gold, diamonds, or uranium. For most of us, however, the richest vein of interest would be the people of this newfound planet. What extraordinary light such a new race might shed on the mystery of our own existence.

In the centuries following Columbus's enduring contact with the New World at the turn of the sixteenth century, the eager curiosity of the Old World focused on the New. The natives of this continent were of intense interest. As explorers and settlers reached this hemisphere, their compatriots across the Atlantic hungered to hear every detail of the native cultures. On the freshness and vigor of this interest depends the ethnic presence of the American Indian in colonial literature. With the passing years, as the settler's status and goals changed, so did attitudes toward the Indian. To a later age, drunk with the dream of manifest destiny, early interest in the Indian was scarcely comprehensible.

Thus it is that Moses Coit Tyler writes of the Indian from the vantage point of 1878:

> Furthermore, those uncouth dusky creatures, the savage proprietors of the continent, whom, both in friendship and in hostility, the colonists at once came in contact with, for a long time seemed to our ancestors to be most mysterious beings, and were the objects of an unspeakable interest in

77

England as well as here. . . . To us, of course, the American Indian is no
longer a mysterious or even an interesting personage—he is simply a fierce
dull biped standing in our way; and it is only by a strong effort of the
imagination that we can in any degree reproduce for ourselves the zest of
ineffable curiosity with which, during most of the seventeenth century, he
was regarded by the English on both sides of the ocean. Scarcely a book
was written here on any subject into which he was not somehow introduced.[1]

Along with its startling bias, Tyler's observation conveys the great
changes that had occurred in the Indian image in American literature
since the colonial era. Indeed, the ethnic presence of the Indian is never
so strong, so detailed, so varied as in the early period. Here the white
settler is a listener, an observer, and sometimes a companion of the
native. There are few stereotypes, and the variety of characteristics is
broad.

One of the most fascinating ways to explore this complex portrait is to
examine the humor involving Indians in this period. A sense of humor is
not a salient feature of the nineteenth-century literary Indian, but in the
colonial era the Indian is often shown as wit, satirist, ironist, and joke-
ster.

It is true that the colonial writers who portray these Indian humorists
are influenced by several motives. The disillusioned misfit or bitter critic
of contemporary society found a suitable mouthpiece for his views in a
satirical Indian. Irish-born trader and adventurer James Adair thought
himself ill-used by the authorities from whom he had hoped for reward
and advancement. In his *History of the American Indians,* he is therefore
quick to channel criticism of white society through Indian humor. Naturally, the suffering captive of Indians Mary Rowlandson, from
seventeenth-century Massachusetts, writes of Indian humor of the
bitterest sort. But Moravian missionaries Christian Post and John
Heckewelder are much more sympathetic listeners. They are also interested in inspiring support of their missionary efforts to convert natives in
Pennsylvania, Ohio, and New York. A writer's circumstances, religion,
occupation, and character all color his or her writing on this as on any
other topic. A reader might expect the generous spirit of Quaker natural-
ist William Bartram to describe the charming playfulness of the Cherokee maidens in their strawberry fields, but John Underhill, Indian
fighter in the Pequot War, is understood to be impervious to native
charm. It is impossible to separate the authentic from the fictive in this

ethnic portrait. Yet the sheer volume of Indian humor, its consistency, and its repetition of themes and viewpoints testify to its significance as signs of an ethnic interaction that was neither merely mysterious nor dull, to use Tyler's polar terms.

There is no better example of the place of Indian humorists than the Indian anecdote typically found in Franklin's work. In several instances, Franklin embellishes a verifiable germ of Indian humor, heightening its satirical power. Though the result may be inauthentic from the social scientist's view, Franklin shows us that by his own day the Indian was recognized as a perfectly appropriate vehicle for humor. A humorous comment appears, for example, in the Lancaster treaty records for July 1744. The incident was later used by Benjamin Franklin in his "Remarks Concerning the Savages of North America" (1789). The original occurrence began when Governor George Thomas and his commissioners offered rum to the Indians in small glasses that had been captured from the French. This took place on July 3 at the close of the day's negotiations. Toward the end of the next day's proceedings the Onondaga chief Canassatego remarked: "We mentioned to you Yesterday the booty you had taken from the *French,* and asked you for some of the Rum which was supposed to be Part of it, and you gave us some; but it turned out unfortunately that you gave it to us in *French* Glasses, we now desire you will give us some in *English* glasses."[2] Evidently, Canassatego's wit was not lost on Governor Thomas, for the record shows that rum was served in "middle sized Wine Glasses."

Lawrence C. Wroth and Constance Rourke both discuss Indian wit and humor in the treaties, and they point out that the Indians provided a model for the style and organization of the treaty negotiations. Constance Rourke notes that "Indian speech was characteristically grave and rhythmic, but it attained a sharp and witty realism in the discussion of rum, traders and white trickery. The Indian style of address was generally accepted and used by the white men, even to the sly introduction of humor."[3]

Indian humor becomes one means of resistance to European domination of the language and procedures of treaty negotiation, suggesting that this scene of ethnic interaction involved rhetorical manipulation and control on both sides of the council fire. The lessons of Indian humor, grounded in the ethnic construction of the treaty process, in turn became useful to the white colonists in their negotiations across their Atlantic frontiers. Franklin evidently enjoyed the affair of the French glasses, and he uses it nearly intact in his "Remarks," transferring it from a representation of the meeting of European and Native Americans to a representation of the New World for the Old.

His use of another incident at the same treaty negotiation is broadly embellished. On July 3, 1744, the colonial authorities offered to educate a group of Indian youths at the college in Williamsburg, Virginia. The purpose of this project was to train boys to serve in the interpreter/ emissary role so well performed by Conrad Weiser at the time. Weiser himself served as interpreter at the conference. When Weiser died in 1760, Indians and whites alike felt the loss. In 1761, at a treaty conference, the Indians lamented Weiser's absence, saying, "We . . . sit in Darkness, as since his Death we cannot so well understand one another."[4] Weiser's place was taken, not by a college-trained Indian youth, but by Samuel Weiser, his son. At the Lancaster treaty negotiations of 1744, the colonial officials made their offer to educate the Indians. In correct Indian form, a decision was delayed until the following day when Canassatego gratefully refused the proposal on the grounds that the Indian people were much too loving parents to send their children so far away. The theme of his reply suggests that different nations have different customs, and these differences should be accepted.

Franklin alters the original incident to heighten the criticism of the colonial concept of civilization. Alfred O. Aldridge notes that Franklin—who printed this treaty—was impressed enough with the incident at Lancaster to share its details with Peter Collinson in a letter dated May 9, 1753.[5] In that letter, as in the "Remarks," Franklin includes his own version of the incident. Franklin first adds the results of a supposed experiment in educating Indian boys at an earlier date. His Canassatego declines with thanks, explaining:

> Several of our young People were formerly brought up at the Colleges of the Northern Provinces; they were instructed in all your Sciences; but, when they came back to us, they were bad Runners, ignorant of every means of living in the Woods, unable to bear either Cold or Hunger, knew neither how to build a Cabin, take a Deer, or kill an Enemy, spoke our Language imperfectly, were therefore neither fit for hunters, Warriors, nor Counsellors; they were totally good for nothing.

Then Franklin adds an ironic stroke in the form of a counteroffer made by the Indians. The chief continues after his refusal:

> We are however not the less oblig'd by our kind Offer, tho' we decline accepting it; and, to show our grateful Sense of it, if the Gentlemen of Virginia will send us a Dozen of their Sons, we will take great Care of their Education, instruct them in all we know, and make *Men* of them.[6]

There are other instances of this type in Franklin's work. They demonstrate the recognition of the Indian humorist in actual life and the potential of this humor for the purposes of the colonial writer. Franklin's empowerment of native voices, for instance, implicitly justifies the possibility of an argument that the white colonists ought to educate their own sons at home rather than sending them back to England, as some "Gentlemen of Virginia" did.

Naturally, the Indian humor thrives, both in clearly fictional and more straightforward renderings, on the clash of cultures. In some cases, humor arises from simple and harmless contrasts in custom. Leslie Wardenaar, in his discussion of promotion tract humor, points out the prominent and complex role of the Indian in this variety of humor.[7] To the colonists, the Indian methods of performing daily tasks and their codes of manners seemed absurd at times. The feeling was mutual, as the Indians observed the colonists. Robert Beverley in *The History and Present State of Virginia* (1705) describes the difference in the sizes of Indian and English spoons: "the spoon which they eat with, do generally hold half a pint; and they laugh at the *English* for using small ones, which they must be forc'd to carry so often to their Mouths, that their Arms are in danger of being tir'd, before their Belly."[8]

Adventurer and surveyor John Lawson in North Carolina notes that the natives kept their fingernails long. The Indians, he writes, "laugh at the *Europeans* for pairing theirs which they say disarms them of that which Nature design'd them for."[9] Planter-aristocrat William Byrd II of Westover, Virginia, in his "Journey to the Land of Eden," notes that the Indians went hunting on Sundays despite the English custom of resting on the Sabbath, and they "laughed at the English for losing one day in seven."[10] James Adair's Indian friends mock the idea of monogamy and "ridicule the white people, as a tribe of narrow-hearted, and dull-constitutioned animals, for having only one wife at a time."[11] Criticizing the boiled eggs the natives offer him, Adair says his teeth are not equal to chewing bullets. The Indians reply that "they could not suck eggs after the manner of the white people, otherwise they would have brought them raw."[12] The Indians argue with him about the correct way of mounting a horse, they preferring to mount from the right and the colonists from the left. "They carried it against me," Adair writes, "by a majority of voices, whooping and laughing."[13]

In some cases, the contrast denotes the Indians' wise perception that the colonists had brought with them a host of customs inappropriate to their circumstances in the New World. Of course, the most famous instance of this is the contrast in fighting techniques. The Indians' guerrilla tactics, well suited to small bands fighting in the wilderness, must have been a startling contrast, indeed, to the Old world style of assembling in regulation array in an open field. The sight of the Old World military tactics may well have seemed ludicrous to the Indians. Missionary Christian Post tells how the Indians mocked English soldiers. They told Post, "The *English* people are fools; they hold their guns half man high, and let them snap: We take sight and have them at a shot. . . . We take care to have the first shot at our enemies."[14]

The colonial farmer earned the mockery of southern Indians, Adair writes, for fencing in his crops, a puzzling precaution to the Indians who farmed "without wasting their time in fences and childishly confining their improvements, as if the crop would eat itself."[15]

Of course, the colonials adopted much from Indian military tactics and agricultural methods, just as they did with Indian clothing. The coonskin cap, leather britches, and generally simple, durable clothing, so practical in rough country, became part of the American style. Initially, however, Old World dress was a natural subject for humor. Men's breeches were frequently ridiculed. Adair writes:

> They have a great aversion to the wearing of breeches; for to that custom, they affix the idea of helplessness, and effeminacy. I know a German of thirty years standing, chiefly among the Chikkasah Indians, who because he kept up his breeches with a narrow piece of cloth that reached across his shoulders, is distinguished by them, as are all his countrymen, by the despicable appelative, Kish-kish-Taraksha, or *Tied Arse*.[16]

In the Pequot War, John Underhill observed how the hostility of native opponents was demonstrated through the mockery of English clothing. Indians put on the clothing of slain soldiers and jeered at English forces, daring them to retrieve the garments. Later the Indians passed the English camp in a canoe, accompanied by captive colonial women: "having put poles in their Conoos, as we put Masts in our boats, and upon them hung our English mens and womens shirts and smocks, instead of sayles, and in way of bravado came along in sight of us as we stood upon Seybrooke Fort . . . in such a triumphant manner.''[17]

Even in these instances of the mockery of everyday things, the intent of the humor is social criticism. This is the primary function of the humor. In some cases, this criticism uncovers serious themes. William Wood, in his seventeenth-century work *New England's Prospect*, an Indian disapproves of a timid, henpecked husband. The colonial husband will not stand up to his complaining wife. The Indian man says the husband was a great fool ''to give her the audience and no correction for usurping his charter and abusing him by her tongue.'' He mimics the woman's shrewish speech, crying out *''Nannana, Nannana, Nannana, Nan.''*[18] The criticism cuts more deeply than marital relations in an incident in Franklin's ''Remarks Concerning the Savages of North America.'' The episode is based on information provided by Conrad Weiser, and its point is the hypocrisy of the ''Christian'' colonials who do not scruple to cheat Indians for lands and furs. A man of the cloth explains to Chief Canassatego that the Sabbath is the day people go to church to learn the good things. The chief replies by relating how he had gone to trade on the Sabbath and was given a certain price for his beaver pelts by a ''man in black.'' The negotiations were postponed when the man left for church services. When he returned, the man gave Canassatego an even lower price for the pelts. So the chief concluded that the ''good things'' taught in church were merely the best ways of cheating Indians.[19]

A serious criticism is also behind the response James Adair received when he related colorful accounts of the Hottentots in Africa to his Indian companions. Perhaps the Indian who commented on these tales was reminded of the misconceptions the colonists often had about Indians, for he rejected this supposedly true account: ''[He] laughed, and said there was no credit to be given the far-distant writers of those old books, because they might not have understood the language and customs of the people.''[20] Other examples show that the Indians could laugh at their own folly, too. On a diplomatic tour to the Ohio River region in 1748, Conrad Weiser was required to respond to complaints about rum traders selling liquor to the natives. Weiser listened to the Indians' grievances and answered that government regulation on this issue was futile, since the natives themselves were active in liquor trade:

"beside this you never agree about it—one will have it, the other won't (tho' very few), a third says we will have it cheaper; this last we believe is spoken from your Hearts (here they Laughed)."[21]

A rude Chocktaw man, described by James Adair, earned the laughter of his native companions—and even laughed himself, when his violation of the Indian etiquette demanding civility in speech was roundly punished by an Englishman. The Englishman was a visitor at a Frenchman's house. Adair writes:

> On the Spanish side of the river, a very lusty Choktah called there, in company with others upon a hunt. As the French Choktah was desirous of ingratiating himself into the favour of the host, he began to ridicule my friend with gestures, and mocking language: the more civilly the Englishman behaved, so much the more impudently the savage treated him. At length, his passions were inflamed, and he suddenly seized him in his arms, carried him a few steps off, and threw him down the bank into the Mississippi. The laugh now turned against him loud; for if the Indians saw their grandmother break her neck by a fall from a horse, or any other accident, they would whoop and halloo. The Baptist, or dipped person, came out ashamed, but appeared to be very good-humoured after his purification, as he found he had not one of the French wood-peckers to deal with.[22]

Perhaps, the anecdote shows, too, that Adair could not have taken the comedown of his own fellows with the humor the Indians displayed toward their own comrade. To them if the jest was well deserved, they were not prevented by pride from laughing.

The ethnic portrait drawn by this humor reveals an Indian with wit, perception, and pluck. The observer also sees at once that this portrait is a two-way mirror, telling as much about the colonist as about the native. The colonial portrait is also distinctive. Here the colonist is a greenhorn, equipped with an array of possessions but still a naive bumbler in an Indian world. Ineptness is a key theme in the colonial greenhorn anecdote. At times the humor is cruel. As one would expect, this is often the case when the Indians involved are losing the battle against the encroaching settlers. Captive Mary Rowlandson was laughed at by Indians as she fell from her horse with her dying child in her arms.[23] Unused to the rigors of the outdoor life, she staggers, weary and hungry, along the road and is laughed at by her captors.[24] Florida captive Jonathan Dickinson also commented on the Indians' mockery of two other captives stricken with fever.[25] Here the humor masks Indian anger and desperation, even as the colonist writers' rejection of the possibility of humor unmasks their own anger.

The taunting, scoffing ridicule in the captivity narrative becomes part of the captive's ordeal. An insight into this type of humor as a facet of Indian character is shown in a passage from John Gyles's captivity narrative. In this incident Maine Indians laugh not at the pitiful but at cleverness and spunk exercised in adversity. These Indians laugh with delight and admiration. In Gyles's account, the captive approaches a cluster of Indians, and "hearing them laugh merrily," he asks what has caused their mirth. He writes:

> They showed me the track of a moose, and how a wolverene had climbed a tree, and where he had jumped off upon a moose. It so happened that after the moose had taken several large leaps, it came under the branch of a tree, which striking the wolverene, broke his hold and tore him off; and by his tracks in the snow it appeared he went off another way, with short steps, as if he had been stunned by the blow that had broken his hold. The Indians imputed the accident to the cunning of the moose, and were wonderfully pleased that it had thus outwitted the mischievous wolverene.[26]

Here are the qualities the Indian humor applauds: spirit, cunning, a stubborn resourcefulness equal to one's circumstances. It may well be that cruel gibes directed toward the suffering captive mock the lack of stoicism and resilience so admired in many native cultures.

The many examples that describe Indians laughing at the colonial greenhorn are always measuring the Indian way versus the colonial. To the Indian, the newcomer is lazy. William Byrd in Virginia describes how the Indians, who commonly walked great distances on foot, mocked the English dependence on horses: ". . . very often they laugh at the English, who can't stir to a next neighbor without a horse, and say that two legs are too much for such lazy people, who can't visit their next neighbor without six."[27]

James Adair is laughed at by his Indian friends when he imprudently tries to eat a milky mash called "hiccory milk" with his hands instead of properly supping it up with bread.[28] Similarly, surveyor John Lawson inspires merriment when he tries to butcher and pluck a fowl, complaining that the Indians did not do a clean enough job of it. The animal struggled so that Lawson had a difficult time of it, and the onlookers laughed at his awkwardness.[29] Lieutenant Henry Timberlake labored vigorously as he poled his craft along the Tennessee River, knowing that he "had to keep pace with the Indians, who would otherwise have laughed at us."[30]

The famed botanist John Bartram tells a notable story of the Indians' good-humored enjoyment of the white man's ineptness. At treaty conferences, the Indians used various shouts to signify their reception of proposed measures in the negotiations. The *Yohay* was the shout that signified approbation among Indians in the middle colonies. Bartram describes the Yohay as "very difficult for a white man to imitate well."[31] The unfortunate interpreter on this occasion was to give the Yohay at the appropriate moment in the negotiations. When he mistakenly gave the war shout, the surprised Indians laughed.[32]

A striking symbol of the colonial greenhorn is seen in a tale told by William Wood about a spring trap. This trap, designed to catch deer, used ropes to hold down a young and supple tree. A snare on the ground caught the deer's feet, set off the trap, and hoisted the deer into the air. One morning the Indians discovered to their rich amusement that they had caught an unusually "long-scuttled deer in their merrytrotter," that is, a very long tailed deer in their seesaw.

> they bade her good-morrow, crying out, "What cheer, what cheer English-man's squaw horse,"—having no better epithet than to call her a woman's horse. But being loath to kill her, and as fearful to approach near the friscadoes of her iron heels, they posted to the English to tell them how the case stood, or hung, with their squaw horse.[33]

For these natives the poor horse is an appropriate emblem for the lubberly colonist. It is an emblem of a foolish creature falling into a simple snare, a symbol at once pretentious in its refinement—a squaw horse—and laughably clumsy. This is the heart of the Indian humor: a recognition of the colonial as a naive wanderer in an Indian world. The New World was the Indian's habitat, and its hardships his briar patch. The humor contains an implicit message: if the colonist is to thrive, he must Indianize himself. The greenhorn humor relishes that idea that the colonist, despite all his fancy gadgets and sophisticated knowledge of the world, is bumbler in his newfound land. This can be seen from the first examples of Indian humor. Writing in 1612, William Strachey tells how Virginia Indians made a fool of a group of hostile Englishmen. The incident begins when a false-bargaining werowance, who had been captured by the English, leaves a "nephew" as a hostage so that he himself can be at liberty to carry out the terms of his release. The "nephew" soon leaps overboard, although his feet are bound. The English cannot determine if the hostage reaches shore or not, but, Strachey says, "the Indyans of Warraskoyack would oftentymes afterwards mock us, and call to us for him, and at length make a great laughter, and tell us he was come home."[34]

The development of the American tall tale may well owe much to the Indian-colonist relationship in these humorous accounts. William Byrd II ascribes to his "merry Indian" guide a story that claims remarkable skills for the bushy-tailed squirrel. According to the guide, Byrd relates, "whenever this little animal had occasion to cross a run of water, he launches a chip or piece of bark into the water on which he embarks and, holding up his tail to the wind, sails over very safely."[35] John Heckewelder, a missionary in Pennsylvania, agreed that much Indian humor intended to expose colonial naiveté through the telling of tall tales:

> when they find a white man inclined to listen to their tales of wonder, or credulous enough to believe their superstitious notions, there are always some among them ready to entertain him with tales of that description, as it gives them an opportunity of diverting themselves in their leisure hours, by relating such fabulous stories, while they laugh at the same time at their being able to deceive a people who think themselves so superior to them in wisdom and knowledge. They are fond of trying white men who come among them, in order to see whether they can act upon them in this way with success.[36]

Part of a greenhorn's vulnerability concerns his notions about the Indians themselves. Certainly the quintessential episode of this variety comes from Crèvecoeur's *Letters from an American Farmer*. The anecdote involves a newly arrived Scots immigrant, Andrew the Hebridean. In the employ of a Quaker farmer, Andrew is left at home one Sabbath morning while the family goes to meeting. As he sits reading his Bible at the front door, Andrew is surprised by nine Indians who have come, as usual, to trade with the master of the house. From their appearance, "the honest Hebridean" takes them for a lawless band come to rob his master's house. He rushes inside, attempting to jam the door shut with his knife. Nevertheless, the Indians, accustomed to the hospitality of the master, force their way in, sit down, and help themselves to some food. Meanwhile, Andrew flees upstairs to fetch his broadsword, an implement he had brought with him from his homeland. As the Indians sit, enjoying their meal, Andrew

with his broadsword in hand, entered the room; the Indians earnestly looking at him, and attentively watching his motions. After a few reflections,
Andrew found that his weapon was useless, when opposed to nine toma-
hawks; but this did not diminish his anger, on the contrary; it grew greater
on observing the calm impudence with which they were devouring the
family provisions. Unable to resist, he called them names in broad Scotch,
and ordered them to desist and begone; to which the Indians (as they told
me afterwards) replied in their equally broad idiom.

Finally, Andrew makes the mistake of seizing one native to toss him out
of the house, for which he is treated with a pantomine of the scalping he
will receive if he persists. This threat sends Andrew rushing off to seek
his employer. Later, one of the natives says that "he never laughed so
heartily in all his life" as when he watched Andrew fleeing into the
woods. Andrew's employer assures him that the natives are not "mon-
sters," but friends, and "the Indians renewed their laugh" and invited
the Hebridean to smoke a peacepipe with them.[37]

In the Carolinas John Lawson is himself often the main character in
various greenhorn anecdotes he relates. In Lawson's case one sees a
chief feature of this type of humor: the colonist is often able to share in
the laugh himself, acknowledging his own innocence. It is ironic that
Lawson finally met his death at the hands of the Indians, and that may
point out another feature of the humor. It can often display a warm
exchange of mutual enjoyment. In its happiest moments it implies a
mutual liking and even trust. Lawson eventually lost the trust of Carolina Indians when he became involved in land schemes to develop the
wilderness schemes that increasingly threatened the Indian territory. It
may well be that in its most good-natured moments, the humor captures
a fleeting historical moment when peaceful coexistence seemed possible
between the native and the European immigrant. The Indians feel the
assurance of their greater expertise in the New World, and the colonist
accepts his need to learn. Both the Indian with his puckish relish of the
upper hand and the bungling greenhorn enjoy the joke.

In one such anecdote from Lawson's account, the surveyor-adven-
turer is shaken to the core by ferocious roaring from some unknown
source outside his cabin. He even suspects the Indians of "some Piece of
Conjuration." Unaware that this roaring is simply a feature of the alliga-
tor mating season, he is enlightened by an Indian friend who returns to
the cabin. Lawson explains, "When I had the Story, he laugh'd at me,

and presently undeceiv'd me, by telling what it was that made that Noise.''[38]

But the Lawson tale that creates the most picturesque figure of the greenhorn is the story of the Winchester wedding. This episode shows all the richness that is to be found in Indian humor and the merit of this aspect of colonial literature as it creates a distinctive ethnic portrait. It contains the typical elements of the greenhorn humor in particular: the view of the European American from another vantage point, the sharing of the eventual hilarity, and the colonist's acknowledgment of his own folly. The larger outlines of the Indian as humorist are here, too. The natives are clever and buoyant, perceptively recognizing the colonist's cocksureness as an Achilles' heel. As elsewhere in these selections, we find that the process of forging an American identity from both Indian and Old World elements is foretold. Moreover, it is significant of the Winchester wedding anecdote that, indeed, it is not unique in its portrayal of the American Indian. This is but one of numerous accounts that together describe the Indian sense of humor. The samples in this essay include but a portion of the examples; these alone cover colonies from Maine to Georgia from the early seventeenth century to the later eighteenth century. It is clear that John Lawson's Indian friends and acquaintances evinced a sense of humor common among many native cultures of the era. It is, however, true that this selection contains one of the most delightful pictures of the butt of the joke: the colonial American. In the story, a companion of Lawson's in the wilds of North Carolina thinks himself a crafty negotiator for obtaining a female Indian companion for the night. He arranges what is known as a ''Winchester-wedding.'' By hindsight, Lawson describes the woman as ''No Novice at her Game.'' Requiring payment for her company in advance, she receives a few of the man's trade goods. Lawson eloquently describes the aftermath:

About an Hour before day I awak'd, and saw somebody walking up and down the Room in a seemingly deep Melancholy. I call'd out to know who it was, and it prov'd to be Mr. Bridegroom, who in less than 12 Hours, was Batchelor, Husband, and Widdower, his dear Spouse having pick'd his Pocket of the Beads, Cadis [cloth], and what else should have gratified the *Indians,* for the Victuals we receiv'd of them. However that did not serve her turn, but she had got his shooes away, which he had made the Night before, of a drest Buck-skin. Thus dearly did our Spark already repent his new Bargain, walking bare-foot, in his Penitentials, like some poor Pilgrim

to *Loretto*. After the *Indians* had laugh'd their Sides sore at the Figure Mr.
Bridegroom made, with much ado, we muster'd up another Pair of Shooes,
or *Moggisons,* and set forward on our intended Voyage.[39]

In this incident, with all of its humor, we may also find the key to the
disappearance of the Indian humorist as an ethnic type: the day was
approaching when the colonist would no longer accept a portrait of
himself as a poor, barefoot pilgrim to Loretto.

Notes

1. Moses Coit Tyler, *A History of American Literature, 1607–1765* (Ithaca, N.Y.:
Cornell University Press, 1949), 9.

2. Conference at Lancaster, Pa., July 4, 1744, in *Indian Treaties Printed by Benjamin
Franklin, 1736–1762* (Philadelphia: Historical Society of Pennsylvania, 1938), 78.

3. Lawrence C. Wroth, "The Indian Treaty as Literature," *Yale Review* 17 (1928),
749–66; Constance Rourke, *The Roots of American Culture and other Essays,* ed. Van
Wyck Brooks (New York: Harcourt, Brace 1942), 62–63.

4. Conference at Easton, Pa., August 3, 1761, in *Indian Treaties Printed by Benjamin
Franklin, 1736–1762* (Philadelphia: Historical Society of Philadelphia, 1938), 248.

5. Alfred O. Aldridge, "Franklin's Deistical Indians," *Publications of the American
Philosophical Society* 94 (1950), 399.

6. Benjamin Franklin, "Remarks Concerning the Savages of North America," in *The
Writings of Benjamin Franklin,* ed. Albert H. Smyth (New York: Macmillan, 1907), X,
98–99.

7. Leslie A. Wardenaar, "Humor in the Colonial Promotional Tract: Topics and
Techniques," *EAL* 9 (1975), 286–300.

8. Robert Beverley, *The History and Present State of Virginia,* ed. Louis B. Wright
(Chapel Hill: University of North Carolina Press, 1937), 182.

9. John Lawson, *A New Voyage to Carolina,* ed. Hugh T. Lefler (Chapel Hill: University of North Carolina Press, 1967), 176.

10. William Byrd II, "Journey to the Land of Eden," in *The Prose Works of William
Byrd,* ed. Louis B. Wright (Cambridge: Harvard University Press, 1966), 391.

11. James Adair, *History of the American Indians,* ed. Sanuel Cole Williams (Johnson
City, Tenn.: Watauga Press, 1930), 145–46.

12. Adair, 422.

13. Adair, 457–58.

14. Christian Frederick Post, "Two Journals of Western Tours," in *Early Western
Travels,* ed. Reuben G. Thwaites (Cleveland: Arthur Clark, 1904), I, 231.

15. Adair, 436.

16. Adair, 8–9.

17. John Underhill, *Newest from America* (1638; facsimile reprint, New York: DaCapo
Press, 1971), 16, 18.

18. William Wood, *New England's Prospect,* ed. Alden T. Vaughan (Amherst: University of Massachusetts Press, 1977), 92.

19. Franklin, "Remarks," 103–4.

20. Adair, 142–43.

21. Conrad Weiser, "Journal of a Tour to the Ohio, August 11–October 2, 1748," in *Early Western Travels,* I, 41.

22. Adair, 316–17.

23. Robert Diebold, "A Critical Edition of Mrs. Mary Rowlandson's Captivity Narrative," Dissertation, Yale University, 1972, 17.

24. Diebold, 57.

25. Jonathan Dickinson, *God's Protecting Providence,* ed. E. W. Andrews and C. M. Andrews (New Haven: Yale University Press, 1945), 61.

26. John Gyles, *Memoirs of Odd Adventures, Strange Deliverances, etc.,* in ed., Richard VanDerBeets, *Held Captive by Indians Selected Narratives, 1642–1836* (Knoxville: University of Tennessee Press, 1973), 116.

27. William Byrd, *History of the Dividing Line,* in *Prose Works of William Byrd,* ed. Louis B. Wright (Cambridge: Harvard University Press, 1966), 288.

28. Adair, 439.

29. Lawson, 62.

30. Lieutenant Henry Timberlake, *Memoirs, 1756–1765,* ed. Samuel Cole Williams (Marietta, Ga: Continental, 1948), 56.

31. John Bartram, *Observations on the Inhabitants, Climate, Soil, Rivers, Productions, Animals, and Other Matters, Worthy of Notice* [in Pennsylvania] (1751; reprint, New York: Arno, 1974), 22.

32. Wroth, 756.

33. Wood, 106–7.

34. William Strachey, *The Historie of Travell into Virginia Britainia,* ed. Louis B. Wright and Virginia Freund (London: Hakluyt Society, 1953), 66.

35. Byrd, *History of the Line,* 307.

36. John Heckewelder, *History, Manners, and Customs of the Indian Nations who once inhabited Pennsylvania and the Neighboring states,* in *Memoirs of the Historical Society of Pennsylvania* (Philadelphia: Historical Society of Pennsylvania, 1876), XII, 321–22.

37. Hector St. John de Crèvecoeur, *Letters from an American Farmer* (London: J. M. Dent, 1912), 79–81.

38. Lawson, 132–33.

39. Lawson, 47.

5

Red, White, and Black: Indian Captivities, Colonial Printers, and the Early African-American Narrative

John Sekora

How black writing began in America has been a topic of growing interest for several decades. In a major example, we know that the earliest slave narrative, by Briton Hammon, was published in Boston in 1760 by Green and Russell. Years of speculation notwithstanding, we know virtually nothing else: about Hammon, his printers, circumstances of publication, or the social climate his narrative entered. Even the mere *fact* of publication is a thorny issue. For, given the views of most historians of early America, the mid-eighteenth century was a very harsh time for *all* people of color—slave, free black, or Indian.

From the early 1740s distrust between white settlers and Indians in most colonies had deteriorated beyond a tense contest for land. Even before the outbreak of open warfare in the middle of the next decade, white political figures frequently denied that there could be anything like a friendly or peaceable tribe. With the coming of actual war, such attitudes hardened into the genocidal. Toward free blacks the policy was less extermination than malevolent neglect. The tiny groups of free blacks in, say, Charleston or Boston were threatened by greater fertility of slaves in the South and by a large influx of Africans into the North. Where skilled labor had previously been found in creole and free black communities, now it was being cultivated exclusively among bound slaves. In the large towns of the North increased numbers of slaves meant that all labor was cheaper to secure, and a new young slave was

much more profitable than an old one. In such circumstances "freedom" often went to the old who had outlived their strength; "freedom"
meant having to earn one's living after one was too infirm to work.
Often driven from their previous settlements, "free" blacks were confined to woods or hovels on the outskirts, left to die out of sight.[1]

Attitudes toward slaves were likewise undergoing swift change. Results were checkered, since each region adjusted differently to a rapid
growth in the slave population. In the Carolina and Georgia low country
the increase was so great, whites said, that they were in danger of being
inundated. In *Black Majority* (1974) Peter Wood has described the white
response as a brutal, inflexible system grounded in fear, separation, and
surveillance. In the region of the Chesapeake, planters expressed a
similar but more moderate anxiety over the fact that for them slavery
was going so well. They were wary because their slaves were living well
enough and long enough to reproduce themselves. A higher birthrate
then created, for the first time in colonial history, a balance of males and
females and further chances for families and reproduction. Economic
growth was most pronounced above the Chesapeake in the northern
colonies; with that growth came the call for more bond laborers. Until
the 1740s, the North had been least interested in the direct import of
slaves and most interested in assimilating those already arrived. During
the next twenty years, however, many more large shipments of slaves
arrived than ever before, reaching a peak in the late 1750s when a
wartime blockade stopped the supply of white indentured servants from
Ireland and Germany. The new numbers halted or delayed whatever
assimilation had been going on and gave rise in its stead to novel legal
codes and increased vigilance. Writing his "Observations Concerning
the Increase of Mankind" in 1751, Benjamin Franklin probably spoke
for all regions in his concern for the future, for slavery had already
"blacken'd half America."[2] Elsewhere he had written of a curious
interplay of settlers' attitudes toward Indians and toward slaves.
Although Franklin the printer and bookseller did not pursue the point,
other booksellers eventually did. But that is to get ahead of the story. For
1760, the question is clear and stark: Why were hostile or indifferent
white printers willing to invest in an African-American subject?

Perhaps not all were indifferent. An informal, speculative consensus
holds that the work was done by some radical printer, an early Tom
Paine, with an incipient sense of egalitarianism. This notion is inspired
by the later, nineteenth-century period of the abolitionist movement, led

as it was by such printing families as the Phillips, the Lundys, and the Garrisons. The elder John Phillips was first apprentice, then partner, to a printer in Charleston. His son John was the first mayor of Boston. *His* son Wendell was the noted abolitionist and associate of Douglas and Garrison. Lundy was printer and publisher of *The Genius of Universal Emancipation*. Garrison, who had been apprentice to Lundy, said that abolition depended upon printers, who would—in his words—"scatter tracts, like raindrops, over the land, on the subject of slavery." William Wells Brown said the happiest months of his early life were spent as apprentice to Elijah Lovejoy at the *St. Louis Times*. Much earlier, Samuel Sewall, one of Boston's earliest printers, became a judge of superior court (and later, chief justice) and while on the bench published *The Selling of Joseph: A Memorial* (1700), a record of a slave sale and probably the earliest antislavery document in America. (The pamphlet, by the by, was printed by Bartholomew Green, grandfather of John Green, who in his turn printed Briton Hammon.) Indeed, printing as an occupation in all likelihood produced on both sides of the Atlantic more activists for abolition than any other calling.

The eighteenth-century situation, nonetheless, was largely different. Green and Russell were not radical printers. Boston in fact did not possess a radical or underground or opposition press in 1760—nothing like those in place at the time in London or Paris.[3] The story of Briton Hammon was published because of a peculiar set of circumstances obtaining at the beginning of the decade. These can be simplified into four: (1) the impact of the Seven Years' War, particularly upon the economy of Boston; (2) the singular appeal for the moment of the captivity form in which Hammon appears; (3) the social status of Hammon's printers; and (4) Hammon himself, considered in terms of his age, his owner, his education, and his position in a system of domestic slavery. Because the subject is large, what follows will be but part of a part—the role of the captivity narrative and its influence upon later black writing.

In retrospect it seems paradoxical that the first narrative by an American slave should be a tale of *Indian* captivity—but only in retrospect. From the eighteenth-century perspective it seems inevitable. For if the story of a black man or woman was to be told at all, that story would necessarily be shaped into a popular form. No form was more popular than the captivity, and no figure loomed larger in the colonial imagination than the Native American. Of the four narratives published between 1680 and 1720 that could legitimately be called "best-sellers," three

were captivities (the other was *Pilgrim's Progress*). Northeastern
readers between 1740 and 1760, when they sought literary and historical
fare, turned not to essays or poetry but to descriptions of actual life in the
new land: travel books, captivity narratives, and Indian treaties. A typical midcentury American bookshelf, according to Lawrence Wroth, was
loaded down with accounts of Indian negotiations and the even more
popular captivities. Compared with dry-as-dust histories, these were
expansive works, works to stretch the imagination, yet of undoubted
practical value. Pushing the imagination ever westward, they described
the large and potent nation represented by the colonies and sought to
bring accord and coherence to the whole.[4] They were of use, too, in the
ideological construction of the American myth, for booksellers used
them to convey alternating attitudes toward Native Americans. Accounts of Indian treaties showed them in noble mien; the captivities
displayed their putative savagery. The cruelty described in the one justified violating the treaties described in the other. This ambiguity on the
part of the educated would play as important a role in sustaining slavery
as in reducing the American Indian.

Historians have traced this division to the last decades of the seventeenth century, making it coterminous with the captivity narrative itself.
From its beginnings the captivity had provided a theologically powerful
as well as physically useful version of manifest destiny. The short title of
one of Cotton Mather's tracts suggests the formula at its most succinct:
Humiliations follow'd with Deliverances (1697). English settlers might
be thwarted or humbled, yet such reverses would be merely temporary,
for providence would surely deliver them to glory. The full title suggests
the mythology of the genre and its influence on later narratives: ''A Brief
Discourse on the Matter and Method of that Humiliation which would be
an Hopeful Symptom of our Deliverance from Calamity. Accompanied
and Accommodated with a Narrative of a Notable Deliverance lately
Received by some English captives, from the hands of Cruel Indians.
And some Improvements of that Narrative. Whereto is added a narrative
of Hannah Swain, containing a great many wonderful passages, relating
to her captivity and Deliverance.'' Another tract printed in Boston by
Bartholomew Green, grandfather of the printer of Briton Hammon—the
Green family indeed printed most of the writings of the Mather family—
this possesses several characteristics that endured. The captivity would
meditate upon events as much as relate them. Typographically the largest word by far on Mather's title page is *Humiliations,* and his emphasis

is on *collective* humiliation and *Collective* deliverance. The individual lives he recounts are analogical, the ground upon which the Lord works for all of New England. The Indians who must be subdued in the process are doubly foul—heathen as well as brutal. Mather, like later booksellers and clergymen, feels free to introduce and otherwise "improve" the stories that come to his hand. The talismanic legend so important later, "Written by her own Hand"—as in Mary Rowlandson's tale of 1682—would distinguish such efforts from those "improved" by booksellers. He taught several generations of readers to see God's handiwork in the narrative's blend of sensation and piety, of blood and holy water—precisely the combination that gave it its extraordinary popularity. Present from the beginning too is an enveloping hostility toward virtually all aspects of Indian life. This could be separate from or joined to repulsion against slaves. Jonathan Dickinson's *Gods Protecting Providence* (1699) presents a pointed comparison of what he considers the disgusting habits of Indians and blacks. Finally, Mather's formula of trial by captivity leading to physical and spiritual salvation would be transferred from the captivities directly to the slave narratives of the abolitionist period. Between Cotton Mather and William Lloyd Garrison readers might be taught that a man or woman need no more be degraded by slavery than by captivity.

Because of constant tension between settlers and tribes in the North and West, the captivities always possessed a timeliness. But that relevance was aggravated with each new quarrel. A new narrative or (more often) a new edition of a previous one appeared most years during the eighteenth century. The most serious quarrel of all, the Seven Years' War, as a matter of course gave birth in the 1750s and early 1760s to a new round of narratives and editions. In the early 1750s the narratives were appearing at the rate of about one every six months. When the war intensified at mid-decade and invective against both French and Indians rose sharply, they appeared nearly twice as often, or every three or four months. Put another way, with the coming of a major conflict that brought several early British defeats, the Indian and the tales in which he figured so prominently were more central than they had been at any time since the early settlement. In the practical terms of the bookseller, war fever served to heat the presses. As more persons and families claimed contact with the Indians, an apparatus was needed for verification, composition, and publication—as abolitionists discovered some eighty years later. As their tales grew more and more horrific, so grew the use of

legitimizing prefaces and afterwords that testified to the piety and re-
liability of the narrator—as, for example, in Reverend Gilbert Tennent's
preface to Robert Eastburn's *Faithful Narrative* (1758)—devices the
abolitionists also retrieved.

Documenting many of these changes is the most successful narrative
of the 1750s, Peter Williamson's *French and Indian Cruelty* (1758),
which was not printed in America but in York, England. As its success
spread—seven editions in as many years, all shipped in large numbers to
the American colonies—it became longer and fiercer. Already long for
the genre, the first edition held 103 pages; later editions expanded the
charges of atrocity, growing to 112 pages. While British publications of
course attacked the French and Indian cause, the Williamson tale held
great curiosity, for he was kidnapped near Aberdeen at age 8 by slave
traders and then sent to the colonies. Held captive for months when he is
older, he escapes, enlists as a soldier, and takes part in several battles
against the Indians, notably the battle of Oswego. The most popular
narrative printed in America during the same decade—that of William
and Elizabeth Fleming—had a similar publishing career and has the
additional interest of being printed by Green and Russell.

By 1760 when Hammon was published, Green and Russell were
probably the foremost of the approximately two dozen printers in Boston, the publishing center of the colonies. But they were not the leading
printers of captivities, for this distinction was held by the partnership of
Fowle and Draper. Bound to Green and Russell by family and business,
Fowle and Draper specialized in the short pamphlet relating either Indian captivity or military expedition or, ideally, as in the case of Peter
Williamson, both at once. During the North American phase of the war
they brought out as many of each as they could obtain, including early in
1760 the captivity tale of a young white man named Thomas Brown.
Brown has largely disappeared from the annals of America, yet he
represented a group of utmost importance at the moment, the young
soldiers who, having defeated the enemy, returned to a devastated economy in Massachusetts that cannot provide for them. To his printers his
story must have seemed perfect for the disconsolate mood of early 1760,
condemning as it did the French army and several Indian tribes with
equal virulence. Not only did it describe the horrors of Indian captivity,
but like Peter Williamson's narrative it also related the details of numerous battles, first from the British, then, after Brown's capture, from
the French point of view. It must have pleased its audience as much as its

printers, for three editions were called for by summer. It must also have
been heavily read, since examples of the first two editions have virtually
disappeared. While full of the blood and piety that mark the most successful examples of the genre, Brown's tale stretched the captivity narrative in several directions. Born in 1740, Brown is but 16 or 17 when he
is taken into the army, injured, left for dead, and finally captured—and
only 20 when he escapes. A full title page speaks of the *plain* narrative,
first of uncommon sufferings, then of remarkable deliverance; his great
loss, that he has been absent from his father's house for three years and
eight months. The maxim of miraculous deliverance, purchased by terrible pain of course, is repeated. Yet here it has been expanded to accommodate the sensational experiences of a very young man who describes
scalpings, decapitations, eviscerations, and burnings to death; who kills
his own prisoners rather than allow them to escape; and who does not so
much escape himself as negotiate coolly with his captors for his release.
In the long history of the captivity genre, this is indeed remarkable
material.

It is therefore all the more arresting to discover a finely wrought
preface explaining that Brown is too young to be able to interpret properly the significance of his own life:

> As I am but a Youth, I shall not make those Remarks on the Difficulties I
> have met with, or the kind Appearances of a good God for my Preservation,
> as one of riper Years might do; but shall leave that to the Reader as he goes
> along, and shall only beg his Prayers, that Mercies and Afflictions may be
> sanctified to me, and relate Matters of Fact as they occur to my Mind.[5]

The closing portion of the whole narrative is likewise a statement of
religious piety and humility, justifying the preceding pages by glorying
in divine providence.

> After repeated Application to General Amherst, I was dismissed, and re-
> turned in Peace to my Father's House the Beginning of *Jan.* 1760, after
> having been absent 3 Years and almost 8 Months.
> "O! that Men would praise the LORD for his Goodness, and for his
> wonderful Works to the Children of Men!"—
> "Bless the LORD, O my soul!"—[6]

At the nadir of his years among the unnamed Indians, when his pains
are greatest and hopes faintest, Brown allows himself one brief expression of despair: "I fared no better than a Slave."[7] It is at this point that
the relation between Brown and Hammon can be glimpsed and the

distinctive flavor of Briton Hammon's story for a northeastern audience can be appreciated, for he is a bondsman doubly bound—a person of color, and outsider in eighteenth-century New England, captured and violated by a people whose skin is as dark as his. (One can hear the expected, self-comforting response: "What those people won't do to one another!") While possessing all the attractions of earlier captivity narratives like Brown's, this first slave story has an additional, invaluable, polemical ingredient for a colony besieged externally by a very real enemy and internally by its own racial myths: it is as if he said, "Ah, if those terrible Indians would be so cruel to one whose skin color is so close to their own, imagine, oh fair maidens, what they would do to *you!*"

Precisely when in 1760 Hammon's *Narrative* was published is not known, but it was certainly after Brown's. It probably appeared after the third edition of Brown's narrative had been placed on sale, most likely late summer or early fall. The connections between the firm of Fowle and Draper and that of Green and Russell were as much personal as commercial. John Green (1731–87) was the last member of America's earliest printing dynasty, the oldest family of printers and booksellers in New England. Great-grandson of Samuel Green who had taken over Stephen Day's Cambridge Press in 1649, he was the son of Bartholomew Green, Jr. He was also closely tied to the Draper family, for his father was brother-in-law of John Draper. After apprenticeship with John Draper, he married Draper's daughter, Rebecca (an event that turned his aunt into his mother-in-law). Once established for himself, John Green formed a service relationship with another Draper, Samuel, who was a nephew of John Draper. This connection between the two main printing families in the printing center of the colonies allowed for the convergence of loyalist political sympathies and the sharing of indispensable government contracts. Green's partner, Joseph Russell (1734–95), had a further connection with the Fowles, for he had been apprenticed to Daniel Fowle, brother of Zechariah. For the business association to work, moreover, the two firms shared capital, type, paper, and completed volumes. And to make exchanges easier, they were located close to one another. Fowle and Draper kept a very large shop on Marlborough Street; Green and Russell were a short distance away on Queen Street. Such proximity was often required. For instance, Green and Russell were the nominal printers of Nathaniel Ames's very popular *Astronomical Diary and Almanack*. In practice, Green and Russell printed one half-sheet, Fowle and Draper another. The full edition was gathered, sold at both shops, and its profits shared. Besides such routine arrangements, the two firms shared rush jobs for the government; whenever the governor or council wished speedy completion of a large printing order, Green and Russell often divided the tasks with Fowle and Draper. The strong bond between the two firms represented a sign of the needful sharing of profits and privileges in printing at a time when there was relatively little to go around—and most of that was controlled, one way or another, by colonial government. Most firms sought such cooperation; Fowle and Draper's work with Green and Russell was simply one of the most successful efforts, especially at keeping profits and influence within the family.[8]

To the trained eye, a connection of some sort between the two firms beyond the conventions of the day could be deduced from the title pages of Thomas Brown's and Briton Hammon's narratives. Using essentially the same layout and typographical style, they give greatest emphasis to the word *Narrative* and to the name of their respective subjects. Both undergo uncommon sufferings, while Brown's deliverance is "remarkable" and Hammon's is "surprising." Brown is recorded as the one *"Who returned to his Father's House the Beginning of* Jan. 1760, *after having been absent three Years and about eight Months."* Although Hammon's delayed return is not given the accent of italics, it does receive certain prominence, for it was he "who returned to *Boston,* after having been absent almost thirteen years." Hammon, like Brown, could represent the many young men pulled from their homes who were returning in 1760. Under the heading of "CONTAINING," each title page provides a précis of events, with stress upon the sensational, especially torture and murder. At work here is apparently a common house style, since far more resemblance exists between Fowle and Draper and Green and Russell than between either and any other Boston printers.

Thus it may be to an element of formula that we owe our recognition of Briton Hammon as a black man. Both firms preferred to use some legend beneath the name of the subject of a narrative. With Brown we get "of *Charlestown,* in *New England."* For Hammon, in smaller type, it is the crucial line "A Negro Man,—Servant to . . ." Had the first half of that line been omitted, we never could have been certain of Hammon's blackness, for the text itself contains no reference. That line may be considered essential to the next, since General Winslow (who has no role in the tale other than, passively, as Hammon's master) is given nearly as much prominence of name as Briton Hammon himself. In the retrospect of two centuries, what is most arresting about this reference to blackness is how *little*—insignificance as well as size—is made of it. Although centrally located for the eye on the page, it is almost buried there—needed at identifying legend but less important than the *three* notices on the page of Hammon's subservience to Winslow. (The penchant for identifying legends is carried over to the text, where his slain comrades are identified as *"Elkanah Collymore* and *James Webb,* Strangers, and *Moses Newmock,* Mollatto."9) Winslow is named and then in the synopsis becomes "his Master" and "his *good old Master."* He is thus a formidable absence in the story, which has no obligation to feature slavery when it can emphasize stewardship. It possesses in this light a message of social value beyond the standard propaganda of captivity narratives. As Brown's tale is encased in an envelope of filial piety, so Hammon's is wrapped in a coat of social/ occupational piety, addressed in its sanctity to all servants black and white, young and old, throughout the colonies. It is a social appeal all the greater in a city where and a time when many young men are being carried off and killed by warfare, leaving the remaining servants with more work, more influence, more responsibility, and more numerical prominence.

Subordination is indeed the central issue of Hammon's brief preface. In language echoing Brown and the most carefully crafted sentence in the tale, Hammon asserts the singularity of his situation:

> As my Capacities and Condition of Life are very low, it cannot be expected that I should make those Remarks on the Sufferings I have met with, or the kind Providence of a good GOD for my Preservation, as one in a higher Station: but shall leave that to the Reader as he goes along, and so I shall only relate Matters of Fact as they occur to my mind.10

Hammon concludes with the same biblical quotation as Brown, and, like Brown, he clearly had something to teach his contemporaries about the "Matters of Fact" pertaining to those whose conditions were low. What his tale can suggest to us is that to have a genuinely unusual publishing event in the mid-eighteenth century, such as a captivity narrative with a black subject, several remarkable circumstances would have to flow together.

With the *Narrative of Briton Hammon* such coincidence did indeed occur: (1) In 1760, Boston was suffering a postwar economic and political depression.[11] (2) The governor, the council, and the ruling class generally were eager temporarily to accommodate new or unusual groups, particularly returning soldiers and their families. (3) The perennially popular captivity narrative now had an acute political significance, as it roused the populace and flayed the enemy. (4) Thomas Brown's narrative was uncommonly successful, partly because he was an uncommon subject for a captivity, partly because he was such an apt one in 1760. A relatively marginal figure in the life of the colony before the war, Brown was of much greater importance now: as a soldier, an enemy of the French and Indians, and a young man seeking stability and familiarity after the fighting. (5) Brown's printers, Fowle and Draper, were solid establishment figures, who (6) had strong business ties with Green and Russell. (7) Green and Russell, in their turn, were even closer to the needs and purposes of colonial government. (8) The subject of their captivity tale, Briton Hammon, is another marginal figure whose social consequence has increased because of the war.[12] He is of the right age and the right social history, voices the right social pieties, and represents that group of slaves who, because of the death and impoverishment of white men, are now a more prominent feature of the Boston economy. To give a quick illustration: In 1750 a fairly prosperous chandler's shop was operated by a middle-aged white couple, their son, and a single black slave. By 1760 the son had been killed in the war, the father had sickened at the news and, after two years of lingering illness, died. Both mother and slave overtaxed themselves, but he recovered and took full control of the business. (9) Finally, both Brown and Hammon tell their audience, chastened and anxious as they themselves are, that with God's grace and their cooperation life can once more return to normal—an appealing message anytime, particularly so in Boston in 1760.

In order to carry the story of the captivities into the nineteenth century, it would be possible to list at least fifty characteristics that link Hammon with Douglass or Hammon with *Clotel* and *Our Nig*. What stands out of such a welter of influences, however, are two enduring traits. As obvious as it is significant, the captivity narrative taught its readers that only barbarians would hold other human beings captive. In the hands of such writers as William Wells Brown and Harriet Jacobs that would prove a potent message indeed. In the eighteenth century, slave writing was simply conscripted into the movements and vagaries of American bookselling. In the nineteenth, however, some slave writers could themselves determine such movements. Briton Hammon's presence as a subject for a captivity for a time expands the scope of the captivity tale, but at the same time it creates the terms of possibility for the slave narrative. As a slave writing, a captivity undermines that form but strengthens alternative life stories for other slaves, so the meaning of one narrative is sometimes another one. The earlier tale of Indian captivity is easily turned to the later story of southern bondage. One escape teaches another.

One kind of mythmaking likewise teaches another. For two centuries influential white Americans used stories of Indian captivity to invent a history, a cultural history, for a people who otherwise lacked one. They took an "American" event, white settlers held by native peoples, and declared it ordained, unique, indigenous. Then it became a symbolic structure through which all reality would be passed: what happened to the captives could occur to the nation as a whole, and in the revolution of the decade after Brown and Hammon it soon would. (As the captivity narrative provided the pattern for understanding the Revolutionary War, the slave narrative did so for the Civil War. In the earlier century the American colonies were held in thrall by a distant uncaring foe; in the nineteenth, one region held back to moral and economic progress of the nation as a whole. In each instance an entire nation is in bondage.) Learning that lesson, formerly enslaved writers turned the narrative into the only moral history of American slavery that we have. Outside its pages, slavery was a wordless, nameless, timeless time. It was time without history and time without immanence, the only duration slaveholders would permit. The slave narrative changed that forever. Many writers were quite unaware that they were reshaping that forever. Many writers were quite aware that they were reshaping for their own lives the Christian story of the Crucifixion within the national crisis of human slavery, and they were not daunted. They found a symbolic structure to give a measure of fixity in a life of painful flux. In this sense, to recall one's history is to renew it.

Notes

1. This and the following paragraph draw upon Gary B. Nash, *Red, White, and Black: The Peoples of Early America* (Englewood Cliffs, N.J.: Prentice-Hall, 1982), 173–78; Winthrop D. Jordan, *White over Black: American Attitudes toward the Negro, 1550–1812*

(Chapel Hill: University of North Carolina Press, 1968), 276–78; Peter Wood, *Black Majority: Negroes in Colonial South Carolina from 1670 through the Stono Rebellion* (New York: Knopf, 1974), 130–35; and William D. Piersen, *Black Yankees: The Development of an Afro-American Subculture in Eighteenth-Century New England* (Amherst: University of Massachusetts Press, 1988).

2. Benjamin Franklin, "Observations Concerning the Increase of Mankind, Peopling of Countries, &c.," in *Benjamin Franklin: Writings* (New York: Library of America, 1987), 373.

3. Compare the situation in Paris described by Robert Darnton, *The Literary Underground of the Old Regime* (Cambridge: Harvard University Press, 1982). For London, see Robert Donald Spector, *English Literary Periodicals* (The Hague: Mouton, 1966), and James G. Basker, *Tobias Smollett, Critic and Journalist* (Newark: University of Delaware Press, 1988).

4. Lawrence C. Wroth, *An American Bookshelf, 1755* (Philadelphia: University of Pennsylvania Press, 1934), 101–8.

5. Thomas Brown, *A Plain Narrative of the Uncommon Sufferings and Remarkable Deliverance of Thomas Brown* (Boston, 1760), [3]. Title page calls this the third edition of Brown's narrative.

6. Brown, 24.

7. Brown, 19.

8. Fowle and Draper's business practices are described by their earliest apprentice, Isaiah Thomas, *A History of Printing in America, with a Biography of Printers and Account of Newspapers*, ed. Marcus A. McCorison from the 2d ed. (Barre, Mass.: Imprint Society, 1974). See also Benjamin Franklin, V., ed., *Boston Printers, Publishers and Booksellers: 1640–1800* (Boston: G. K. Hall, 1980), and William C. Kiessel, "The Green Family: A Dynasty of Printers," *New England Historical and Genealogical Register* 104 (April 1950), 81–93.

9. Briton Hammon, *A Narrative of the Uncommon Suffering and Surprising Deliverance of Briton Hammon* (Boston: Green & Russell, 1760), 6.

10. Hammon, 3. See John Sekora, "Is the Slave Narrative a Species of Autobiography?" in James Olney, ed., *Studies in Autobiography* (New York: Oxford University Press, 1988), for more on Hammon.

11. See Gary B. Nash, *The Urban Crucible: Social Change, Political Consciousness, and the Origins of the American Revolution* (Cambridge: Harvard University Press, 1979), 147–76.

12. See Piersen, chapters 8 and 9.

6

Recapturing John Marrant

Benilde Montgomery

In recognizing that John Marrant's captivity narrative "inaugurates the black tradition of English literature," Henry Louis Gates, Jr., undoes a century and a half of the narrative's neglect.[1] Although John Marrant's narrative was among the first books written by an African American and was, from its first edition in 1785, one of the most popular of the Indian captivity narratives, it has remained largely unread since its last edition in 1835 until Gates rescued it from obscurity.[2] Even its author, whom both Dorothy Porter and Arthur Schomburg identify as "undoubtedly one of the first, if not the first, Negro ministers of the gospel in North America," is ignored by those dusty and ponderous histories of early Methodism where some literary commentators suggest he belongs.[3] When the narrative has been reproduced, moreover, it is often mistaken as a slave narrative, its editors ignoring that Marrant was born a free man of some apparent means. Some reformers of the American canon, who have gone to great lengths to include figures like Equiano and Wheatley, have ignored Marrant, favoring writers more self-consciously black or African. Because Marrant identifies himself as "black" only twice in his narrative, his work apparently lacked interest for both nineteenth-century abolitionists and certainly for Protestant nativists. Up to now, he has continued to be ignored or dismissed. A new reading of Marrant's narrative, however, shows it to be a clear example of an emerging, polyethnic American identity, an identity that Werner Sollors would call a "consenting" coincidence of European, African, and Native American cultures and that Mechal Sobel would recognize as an instance of a "world they made together."[4] As a witness to a sense of the American self that has been lost, Marrant's narrative is an important document in the development of American culture as a whole.

105

To begin, Marrant's narrative defies the patterns frequently invoked to account for the evolution of seventeenth-century captivity narrative into nineteenth-century fiction. Both Roy Harvey Pearce and Richard VanDerBeets agree that the early narratives—Mary Rowlandson's is the chief example—began as typological tracts designed to justify the ways of God to man by attesting to the redemptive power of suffering.[5] By the late eighteenth century, however, most of these tracts, originally devotional, had evolved into mere bigoted indictments against the nonwhite, non-Protestant minority, particularly the Indians, the French, and the Roman Catholics. These later narratives favored sentiment and sensationalism over fact. A contrast between the opening of Mary Rowlandson's seventeenth-century narrative and Mary Kinnan's of 1791 makes this clear. Rowlandson writes, "On the tenth of February 1675 came the Indians with great numbers upon Lancaster: Their first coming was about Sun-rising; hearing the noise of some Guns, we looked out; several Houses were burning." Mary Kinnan begins, "Whilst the tear of sensibility so often flows at the unreal tale of woe, which glows under the pen of the poet and novelist, shall our hearts refuse to be melted with sorrow at the unaffected and unvarnished tale of a female, who has surmounted difficulties and dangers, which on review appear romantic, even to herself."[6]

Although published a hundred years after the Rowlandson narrative, Marrant's narrative more closely adheres to her spirit and design than it does to those of Kinnan, his contemporary. While Marrant may have lapsed more frequently from the facts than Rowlandson, he keeps, nonetheless, to a similar discourse, a discourse resembling the medieval hermeneutic tradition of initiation. Like her medieval male counterparts, Rowlandson's journey takes her from the landscape of the familiar and formed into the alien and chaotic, from which she returns enlightened and reborn. Rowlandson's "proof texts" connect her journey to Daniel in the lion's den, to Jonah in the whale, to Moses and the Hebrews in the desert. Her point is always clear: her captivity is part of a cosmic design. What Auerbach says of Dante is, at least in this regard, true of Rowlandson: she does not regard history as a mere pattern of "earthly events, but in constant connection with God's plan; so that every earthly phenomenon is at all times . . . directly connected with God's plan; so that a multiplicity of vertical links establishes an immediate relation between every earthly phenomenon and the plan of salvation conceived by Providence."[7] Rowlandson's private experience has political and ultimately cosmic significance. Her testing in the wilderness is a test of the whole New England experiment; her captivity in the wilderness is a single instance of God's test for all humanity. It reproduces and relives the testing of Christ in the desert, his descent into hell, his resurrection and apocalyptic victory.

Mary Kinnan's self-proclaimed "romantic" adventure claims no significance beyond the psychological. On the other hand, her contemporary John Marrant's remains grounded in a typological conception of history and in that regard demonstrates Mechal Sobel's observation that among the less powerful classes in the eighteenth-century South, especially Virginia, "a wide range of values, including many that were closer to the medieval Catholic world view . . . continued to develop."[8] Unlike Kinnan, Marrant does not understand himself as the victim of frivolous circumstance but rather as an active participant in the evolution of a providential design. While Marrant has for the most part freed himself from Rowlandson's dependence on "proof texts" to clarify his typology, he recalls the events of his captivity in such a way as to make their relationship to salvation history perfectly obvious. For example, he recalls George Whitfield's first summons to his salvation at a Charleston prayer meeting in typological language—"Prepare to meet thy God, O Israel"—and throughout the narrative he remembers his experience as the antitype of scriptural events. Like Rowlandson's, his deliverance from the Indians is the "delivering of the three children in the fiery furnace, and of Daniel in the lion's den." His subsequent deliverance from a school of man-eating sharks is the antitype of Jonah's, whose prayer is "the Lord did not shut me out." Furthermore, Reverend William Aldridge, Marrant's "authenticator," identifies him with David, who "without sling or stone, engages, and with the arrow of prayer, pointed with faith, wounded Goliath, and conquers the king."[9]

While Rowlandson's typology derives primarily from the Old Testament, Marrant's source, as one might expect in a post-Awakening narrative, is almost entirely the New Testament. While Mary Rowlandson only implies that she is a seventeenth-century antitype of Christ, Marrant reconstructs his experience to leave no doubt that his model is the Messiah Himself. In this regard, he resembles Jonathan Edwards, who, unlike his contemporaries who regarded themselves only as successors to John the Baptist, insisted consistently that the Christian minister was a type of Christ.[10] In the course of his narrative, however, Marrant has to discover his messianic identity by passing through a series of identifications with other preliminary New Testament types. In true hermeneutic style, the first of these is Lazarus. Laid ill after his initial encounter with Whitfield, Marrant languishes the requisite three days in the care of his sister, who cries out, "The lad will surely die." Whitfield arrives unannounced as the minister/Christ to effect the rebirth. Some weeks later, after Marrant has accepted his conversion, he comes to understand himself as the antitype of John the Baptist. He climbs "the fence . . . which divided the inhabited and cultivated parts of the country from the wilderness" and wanders for several weeks, surviving attacks by wolves, wild pigs, and bears, living in a tree, eating grass, and drinking mud and water.[11] After his capture by the Cherokee, he announces the gospel to a Herod-like king and his Salome-like daughter, but unlike his scriptural type, he keeps his head and brings about the conversion of the Herod and his daughter to whom he preaches.

The ultimate identification with Christ begins with Marrant's description of a later threat of his execution: "at the appointed hour" he is stripped, "taken out and led to the destined spot, amidst a vast number of people." He is shown the "sharp pegs" that are to be struck into him and cries out, "If it be thy will that it should be so, thy will be done."[12] This prayer might be dismissed as the prayer of any pious Christian were it not followed some pages later by a lengthy description of Marrant's return from capture, composed entirely of incidents contrived to echo John the Evangelist's account of Christ's life after the Resurrection. In his absence Marrant's family had searched for him for "three days," and finding what they supposed was his "carcas torn," they buried it. Dressed in new clothes borrowed from the Indian king, he returns to the familiar world only to be turned away by neighbors, an uncle, his brother, and finally his own mother, all of whom are gathered to mourn in their own version of an upper room. Only his youngest sister recognizes him, but, predictably, when she announces that he has returned, they all Thomas-like refuse to believe. Ultimately they are convinced, clasp him about the neck, and rejoice, Marrant adding, "Thus the dead was brought to life again."[13]

Marrant's almost exclusive dependence on a typology of rebirth and resurrection separates his text further from Rowlandson's less evangelical imagery and reflects the strong influence of Whitfield and the other preachers at whose hands Marrant experienced his conversion. Moreover, while Rowlandson's captivity brings about only a series of perceptive changes, Marrant undergoes a complete change of identity, the fullness of his rebirth signified by his assuming the wardrobe of an Indian king. Marrant's emphasis on metamorphosis places him clearly in the camp of Whitfield, whose primary contribution to the ideology of American evangelicalism is this kind of rhetoric of "New Birth." In fact, Whitfield's insistent defense of his particular doctrine of regeneration provoked constant disapproval. The 1738 publication of his most famous sermon, "The Nature and Necessity of Our New Birth," heralded his arrival in America and outlined the specific doctrine of regeneration for which he was best known and most frequently condemned. Summoned before a church board in Charleston, for example, Whitfield heard Alexander Garden, Anglican rector of St. Philip's, condemn him for defending "the belief and expectation of a certain happy moment, when, by the sole and specific work of the Holy Spirit . . . you shall at once (as 'twere by magic charm) be metamorphosed."[14] No doubt Marrant's later training at the hands of the countess of Huntingdon, for whom Whitfield served as private chaplain, and his subsequent ordination into the Methodist "connection" of which she was the almost exclusive support gave him the vehicle, rhetoric, and imagery by which to recount his own experience.

This particular "connection" and the accompanying alienation that Marrant recounts in his narrative exempt him from the charge that Houston Baker lays against other African-American writers of the same period. While Phillis Wheatley, another protègè of the esteemed countess, may indeed have "moved in harmony with the larger culture of white America," and Equiano may have embraced certain dimensions of Christianity as a "comfort against life's uncertainties," as Baker suggests, Marrant's presentation of his rebirth as an early disciple of Whitfield puts him at the center of the great "transethnic" theological debate between "piety" and "reason" violently divided America after the Awakening.[15] H. Richard Niebuhr describes it as between those who "saw the reality of the order of being other than that walled and hemmed-in existence in which a stale institutional religion and bourgeois rationalism were content to dwell" and those who did not.[16] Heimert sees the conflict as *the* great debate of the eighteenth century. Already free and already in possession of the assurances of bourgeois culture, in accepting Whitfield's call to rebirth Marrant rejected what Baker sees as the universal object of the African Americans' search, that is, "some terms of order."[17] Like other African and white Americans after the Awakening, Marrant rejects the terms already available to him in the bourgeois world in pursuit of an uncertainty. His abandonment of bourgeois rationalism in favor of evangelical piety turns his family against him and sends him in flight from the formed city to the chaos of the countryside. After his conversion, he is, like Jesus, a prophet dishonored in his own country. Marrant's sister charges him in the language of the prevailing theological debate: he is "crazy and mad," she says, and so reports "it among the neighbors, which opened the mouths of all around against [her]." His other relatives call him "every name but that which is good." Finally, like the Jesus in Matt. 12:48 who asks, "Who is my mother? and who are my brethren?" Marrant reports, "My mother turned against me also, and the neighbors joined her, and there was no friend left to assist me, or that I could speak to."[18]

Of course, Marrant is not exempt from the charge of acculturation, but the culture with which he feels most "comfort against life's uncertainties" is neither exclusively European nor African; it is also Native American. A Cherokee brave rescues him; a Cherokee chief and his daughter are his first disciples; and unaware of the debate between rationalist and pietist, the Native Americans find his beliefs neither "crazy" nor "mad" but consistent with their own sense of a divine immanence. Significantly, Marrant's life among the Indians most clearly associates his narrative with those other contemporary captivities in which, as Slotkin points out, the figure of the European captive blends into a composite that includes hunter, trader, and finally Indian scout. Out of these European accounts of the late eighteenth century, the prototype of American culture heroes like Daniel Boone and Natty Bumppo begins to emerge. Indeed, Marrant's description of himself as an African returning to a European civilization dressed as a Cherokee king is close to the images we have of Leatherstocking and Boone: "My dress was purely in the Indian style; the skins of wild beasts composed my garments, my head was set out in the savage manner, with a long pendant down my back, a sash around my middle, without breeches, and a tomahawk by my side."[19]

Within the context of Whitfield's imagery of metamorphosis, such dress suggests Marrant's rebirth as a Christian; but it also suggests the appearance of a new, more complex conception of what an American might be. The costume encourages us to read him as Marius Bewley and others have read Boone and Leatherstocking, as an early embodiment of the fundamental synthesis inside the whole of American experience;

Marrant's skin color requires that another component be added to Bewley's synthesis. Like his European counterparts, Marrant too is caught between freedom and law, between nature and civilization, between the religion of piety and rationalist theology—Balzac's ''magnificent moral hermaphrodite, [re]born between the savage and civilized states of man.'' Marrant returns to a bourgeois culture, but black and white, as, to borrow an image that the Native American and African cultures share, a mediating ''trickster'' whose profound ambiguity, whose transethnic ''otherness,'' neither the prevailing rationalism nor Mary Kinnan's sentimentality could absorb. In this regard, it may be significant that after Marrant's seminary training in Wales, the countess of Huntingdon sent him as a missionary to the Indians of Nova Scotia.

Marrant's distinction from his European counterparts is also clear from his use of language. Gates has already made Marrant's manipulation of the trope of the ''talking book'' the centerpiece of his argument that Marrant stands at the head of a uniquely African-American tradition in letters. I would add two other considerations to that discussion. Needless to say, unlike his European counterparts Marrant did not become a popular American culture hero for any racial group: white, black, or red. While Boone's exceptional and somewhat self-aggrandizing knowledge of the wilderness assured him a place in a culture that admired Poor Richard, Marrant fell into obscurity. Never abandoning his religious stance for the cool and detached humanism of Boone or Leatherstocking, Marrant gains his freedom by what John Edgar Wideman calls ''the magic of the word.''[20] Unlike the similarly religious Mary Rowlandson, whose escape is entirely ''Providential'' and who defends herself from her captors with a shield of printed texts—so annoyed do the Indians become with her incessant Bible reading that one enterprising woman ''snatched it hastily out of [her] hand, and threw it out of doors''[21]— Marrant, a trained and successful musician, adapts easily to the oral culture of the Indians and masters their spoken language. If Rowlandson appreciates written texts as a tool with which to defend the authority of a received tradition, Marrant, like Douglass and later generations of enslaved Africans after him, appreciates the capacity of language to carry him toward something new. As Baker suggests, just as Douglass's future is determined by the moment he comes to understand the ''power of the word'' and as every slave learned that the manipulation of the master's speech was the key to his own survival, Marrant, not a slave, also understands the relationship between freedom and language that characterizes so much African-American discourse.[22] Marrant uses his skill at spoken language to win freedom from his Indian masters:

> I prayed in English a considerable time, and about the middle of my prayer, the Lord impressed a strong desire upon my mind to turn into their language and pray in their tongue. I did so, and with remarkable liberty, which wonderfully affected the people. . . . I believe the executioner was savingly converted to God. . . . the first words he expressed, when he had utterance, were, "No man shall hurt thee till thou hast been to the king."[23]

Moreover, Marrant shares in a significantly African-American consciousness not only in his equation of freedom and language but also in his stylistic use of a particular kind of structural repetition. James A. Snead argues that the use of certain kinds of repetition helps distinguish African from European discourse. He notes particularly how the "cut" used in American jazz, that is, "an abrupt seemingly unmotivated break [an accidental da capo] with a series already in progress and a willed return to a prior series," has a counterpart in African-American fiction.[24] Both in music and in fiction, this "cut" sets up a series of expectations for the listener/reader only to destroy them at irregular intervals. European literature, Snead argues, suppresses repetition in order to maintain the illusion of linear progression and of clearly discernible goals. This distinction is useful when we compare Marrant's "African captivity" with Rowlandson's "European captivity." Rowlandson's account is structured around twenty logically plotted chapters she calls "removes." Each "remove" takes her farther from the familiar until at around the tenth remove, she begins a trek home. Once returned, she assesses the results of her trial: her election seems sure and, like Job, her economic future is stable. She acknowledges the superficiality of her former ways, and instead of the wilderness diet of raw horse liver and grass, she rejoices, "Now we are fed with the finest of Wheat. . . . Instead of the Husk, we have the fatted calf."[25] Marrant's narrative, however, though it shares Rowlandson's European typology, never comes to rest in financial security or gastronomic reward. In fact, there is no clear, linear progression in Marrant's narrative at all. His journey is not a single continuum but a pilgrimage interrupted by a series of fortuitous accidents or unexpected "cuts" that, on the one hand, literally and consistently return him "home" but, on the other, leave the actual outcome of his adventure open-ended and unassessed. For example, having once achieved remarkable success as a teen-aged musician in Charleston, Marrant unaccountably returns home. Admitting that he is as "unstable as water," he returns to Charleston and physically stumbles into Whitfield's revival, only to be "carried home by two men." Later, captured by Indians, he says first that "he would rather die than go home," but not so long after, he has an "invincible desire of returning home."[26] Impressed by a British frigate during the Revolution, he finds himself brought home at the siege of Charleston. On board once again, he is washed overboard only to be returned home by a providential wave. The final image of the narrative has Marrant preparing to return home from England to work once more among the Indians of North America. No doubt, as pietistic propaganda, these remarkable seizures emphasize the distance between the orthodox Puritan preparationist models and those of the revivalists, but they also help define Marrant's captivity not only as a European but also, quite specifically, as an African-American narrative. In Marrant's transethnic narrative, as in jazz, there is no illusion of progress or control. Instead, Marrant's "cuts" make room for accident and rupture in a vision that does not equate the unpredictable with a test of faith, as does Rowlandson, but rather embraces it as yet another discovery of a "divine excellency" wholly different from anything that is reducible to received categories.

Perhaps Marrant's resistance to any single set of categories has been at the root of his neglect, and Gates's study on the reception of these early African-American texts will certainly add light to the question. Not only did Marrant defy the narrow categories of his contemporaries, he too often eludes our own. If, as Sollors argues, our well-intended ethnic categories remain as reified as our ancestors' theological categories, we will resist coming to terms with the kind of transethnic culture that Marrant epitomizes. While Marrant's appreciation for the pervasive immanence of divinity made him too "red" for many of his contemporaries, including his own family, his skin made him too "black" for others, and for yet others—perhaps his Cherokee captors, perhaps some modern readers—I am sure he is too "white." Indeed, his text is neither African nor European, nor Native American, but is a kind of *coincidentia oppositorum,* a gathering of transethnic contacts that manages to retain the powerful stamp of all three. In that, I think, is its chief significance. As an icon of possibilities, it revels in the kind of shared cultural activity that seems once to have been at the center of American experience but somehow got lost along the way.

Notes

1. Henry Louis Gates, Jr., *The Signifying Monkey* (New York: Oxford University Press, 1988), 145.

2. Peter Williamson's *Adventures and Suffering* (1757) and Mary Jemison's *Captivity* (1824) were two other tales that surpassed in number of editions Marrant's account. A complete list of Marrant's editions is in Dorothy B. Porter, "Early American Negro Writings: A Bibliographical Study," *Papers of The Bibliographical Society of America* 39 (1945), 192–268.

3. Dorothy Porter, *Early Negro Writing, 1760–1837* (Boston: Beacon Press, 1971), 404.

4. Cf. Werner Sollors, *Beyond Ethnicity: Consent and Descent in American Culture* (New York: Oxford University Press, 1986), and Mechal Sobel, *The World They Made Together* (Princeton, N.J.: Princeton University Press, 1987).

5. Roy Harvey Pearce, "The Significance of the Captivity Narratives," *American Literature* 19 (1949), 1–20; Richard VanDerBeets, ed., *Held Captive by Indians: Selected Narratives, 1642–1836* (Knoxville: University of Tennessee Press, 1973), xi–xxxi.

6. Mary Rowlandson, *The Soveraignty and Goodness of God,* and Mary Kinnan, *A True Narrative of the Sufferings of Mary Kinnan,* in VanDerBeets, 42, 320.

7. Erich Auerbach, *Mimesis,* tr. Willard Trask (Princeton, N.J.: Princeton University Press, 1953), 194.

8. Sobel, 7.

9. John Marrant, *A Narrative of the Life of John Marrant* (London, 1787), 3, 12, 21, 1. Like Marrant, William Aldridge (1738–1797) was a member of the Methodist "connection" of Selina Shirley Hastings, the countess of Huntingdon (1707–1791). Although he broke with her about 1777, Aldridge presided over her funeral service. His introduction to Marrant's narrative insists, "No more alterations . . . have been made than were thought necessary."

10. Alan Heimert, *Religion and the American Mind* (Cambridge: Harvard University Press, 1966), 7.

11. Marrant, 4, 7.

12. Marrant, 12.

13. Marrant, 20.

14. Quoted in Heimert, 37.

15. Houston Baker, *The Journey Back* (Chicago: University of Chicago Press, 1980), 12, 20.

16. H. Richard Niebuhr, *The Kingdom of God in America* (New York: Harper, 1937; Reprint 1959), 110–11.

17. Baker, 1.

18. Marrant, 5, 6.

19. Marrant, 17.

20. John Edgar Wideman, "The Black Writer and the Magic of the Word," *New York Times Books Review,* January 24, 1988, 1.

21. Rowlandson, 62.

22. Baker, 34.

23. Marrant, 12–13.

24. James A. Snead, "Repetition as a Figure of Black Culture," in *Black Literature and Literary Theory* (New York: Methuen, 1984), 67.

25. Rowlandson, 89.

26. Marrant, 2, 4, 9, 17.

II

Varieties of
Ethnic Representation

7

Representation of Ethnicity Among Colonial Pennsylvania Germans

William T. Parsons

Ethnicity among the German element of Pennsylvania must be judged against a value system different from those held by other ethnic groups in the commonwealth. The fact was that no unified political Germany existed in modern Europe until 1871. So when German ethnic settlement began in Pennslyvania in 1683, it recollected a cultural and linguistic base rather than a political framework. Nonetheless, it did constitute a very real factor in the province of Pennslyvania from that date of origin until the termination of that particular migration in the year 1815. German ethnic pride of achievement, that is, folk culture and its ethnic value system, centered in the language. These people celebrated a certain ethnic pride but hardly a German national unity or pride of place. Rather, all Germans in colonial America shared customs in their common language community. Germans in the New World viewed themselves as Palatines, Swabians, Hessians, or Bavarians rather than as national Germans. They were aware of competing national groups around them, such as the Irish, Swedish, or English people in Pennsylvania. But Germans understood that their cohesion was of a different sort.[1]

Their term, "Pennsylvania German," nearly always expressed in the dialect terminology, *"Pennsylfaanisch Deitsch,"* meant "German-speaking Pennsylvanians." It included emigrants from Switzerland and French Alsace, as well as from the Rhineland-Palatinate and Swabia. They all honored Martin Luther's Standard German for formal use in church or provincial legal affairs, but the great majority of them spoke dialect variations of German in family and occupational activities. Many wrote letters or journal diaries in the dialect, and more than a few registered wills or land deeds in Pennslyvania German dialect in counties where public servants at the county seat shared the same background.[2]

Germans in Pennsylvania fought long and hard to maintain the use of their distinctive German language form, which they considered to be superior to any other language. Fortunate they were that William Penn and later Penn proprietors were indulgent, that they included freedom of language use in the Quaker Province. Cultural and religious differences were abundant here. William Penn's concept of religious freedom most specifically permitted religious services to be conducted in the language of the settlers, whatever that was. So Swedish, German, Welsh, or French was used with no attempt to designate a preferred language. In legal action and court proceedings under English law in Pennsylvania, documents in German were just as valid as those in English.

Many specific illustrations of that belief in the superiority of the German language (and from time to time, of Germans) are to be found in book and almanac writings of Pennsylvania German authors. In particular, German values are stressed by Christopher Sauer the Elder in his newspaper, *Der Hochdeutsch Pensylvanische Geschicht-Schreiber,* or in translation, "The High-German Pennsylvania History Writer," but which could also mean "The German Language Pennsylvania Story Teller" (or by extension, the teller of tall tales). Over the years, the title did change several times, especially when Sauer became painfully aware of errors of fact in early accounts he published. His newspaper was later quite well known as *Pensylvanische Berichte,* or "Pennsylvania Reports."[3]

In 1677, when William Penn toured the Rhine Valley from Rotterdam and Amsterdam to Cologne, Mainz, and over to Mannheim, he saw diligent, industrious German farmers working lands that had been staked out by noble German landlords generations before. It seemed to Penn that they were a basic agricultural population, just as good and worthy citizens as in any other farming area, especially if they had an opportunity to obtain farm tracts of their own. On that trip he converted some German intellectuals and a few craftsmen to the Society of Friends. He was a young Quaker, so he wrote most extensively about spiritual encounters and conversions in his *Journal.* In his active mind, Penn tucked away the recollection of those diligent workers whose production of food and fiber products would add value to any settlement.[4]

More important to the development of a future Pennsylvania, he remembered them when that territorial dream became reality in 1681. His vision of Pennsylvania as an ideal state foresaw "magistrates honourable for their just administration . . . and a people free by their just obedience . . . for liberty without obedience is confusion, and obedience without liberty is slavery."[5] That was the Holy Experiment he advertised in two pamphlets he circulated to attract settlers. Some of them he trusted would be Quakers, but others "Freemen and Adventurers." The second of those tracts, *Some Account of the Province of Pennsylvania,* he had translated into Holland Dutch and German languages and circulated there to assure that his ideas were thoroughly understood by potential settlers from the German Rhineland.[6]

The initial settlement in 1683 under Francis Daniel Pastorius was composed of both German and Holland Dutch Rhinelanders, organized at Krefeld on the German side of the border. Very few of the settlers who followed were *Hollandisch,* even though they were all called "Dutch." The same F. D. Pastorius, friend of the proprietors and land agent for them, acted simultaneously as spiritual adviser and consultant for the Germans he had led to their new home in Pennslyvania. He acknowledged his leadership status among the German element while at the same time mingling easily with the Logans, Lloyds, Norrises, and governmental officials in the Pennsylvania experiment.[7]

An indication of the wide-ranging aspects of Pastorius's spiritual leadership among Germans in the Germantown settlement was the Petition of 1688, which objected to the institution of Negro servitude which he saw in the Delaware Valley region nearby. He voiced the almost unanimous sentiment of the German community there:

> These are the reasons why we are against the traffick of men-body, as followeth: Is there any that would be done or handled at this manner. Now tho' they are Black, we cannot conceive there is more liberty to have them as slaves, as it is to have white ones. There is a saying, that we shall doe to all men like we will be done ourselves; making no difference of what generation, descent or colour they are. And those who steal or rob men, and those who purchase them, are they not all alike?[8]

In most aspects of the government of Pennsylvania, this so-called German Quaker credited the wisdom of William Penn, who applied these laws to the province. Pastorius was one German who found that the application of English law in a benevolent fashion by Penn produced a stronger, healthier, more stable commonwealth than in any other governments he had ever seen.

With his fellow Germans, he respected (almost revered) the German language, yet he advised all the Germans who had come to the Quaker province that they urgently needed to learn English. As an example to them, he served as a justice of the peace, using either English or the German language in the cases he handled in that office for his clients. By his own actions, he demonstrated that Germans in Pennsylvania must surely react and intermingle with their English neighbors. Like many contemporaries in Pennslyvania, Pastorius failed to be consistent. He often reiterated his viewpoint that Germans ought to Anglify their activities in Pennsylvania. When he changed his German name of Schaeffer, however, he did not use the English equivalent name, Shepherd, but Latinized it to Pastorius instead.[9]

The Provincial Council of Pennsylvania made a clear representation against these ethnic Germans following the arrival of three full shiploads of Germans in September 1717. In what was surely an ethnic representation against such arrivals, Governor William Keith sent a letter to the council on September 17, 1717:[10]

> Observed to the Council, that great numbers of foreigners from Germany, strangers to our language and Constitution, having lately been imported into this Province, daily dispersed themselves immediately after Landing, without producing any Certificates from whence they came or what they were; . . . That as this Practice might be of very dangerous Consequences, since by the same method, any number of foreigners from any nation whatever, as well Enemys as friends might throw themselves upon us; . . . all masters of vessels who have lately imported any of these foreigners, [shall] be summoned to appear at this Board, to render an Account of the Number and character of their Passengers . . . be Required . . . to Repair . . . to some Magistrates . . . to take such Oaths appointed by Law (or any Equivalent assurances in their own way and manner) as are Necessary to give assurances of their being well affected to his Majesty and his government. . . . The Master shall first give an exact list of all their passengers imported by them.[11]

That 1717 regulation was ignored for a decade by most of the ship captains and the men who provided for the maintenance of port and province. German-speaking migrants into Pennsylvania continued to arrive at an astonishing rate. Governor Patrick Gordon and the Board of Trade for the Colonies adopted decrees for their management that required German-speaking immigrants who arrived in 1727 or later to take an oath of allegiance to the English monarch and to the province of Pennsylvania.[12] Their order read in part:

> As these people . . . come under the Protection of his Majesty, It's requisite that in the first Place they should take the Oath of Allegiance, or some equivalent to it to his Majesty, and promise Fidelity to the Proprietor & obedience to our Established Constitution. . . . 'Tis ORDERED that the Masters of Vessells importing them shall be examined whether they have any Leave . . . for the Importation of these Foreigners, and that a List shall be taken of the Names of all these People [and] a Writing be drawn up for them to sign declaring their Allegiance & Subjection to the King of Great Britain & Fidelity to the Proprietary of this Province.[13]

That law made some German immigrants uncomfortable, but the majority signed nonetheless. Some of the Germans hesitated to swear such a binding oath, but when a prerequisite to landholding, most managed. Others gave an affirmation of loyalty, like the Quakers.[14]

Pennsylvania Germans knew that they were good farmers, hardworking and frugal. Wherever possible, they took advantage of opportunities to buy land or just work as a hired hand or tenant on farmland located in Pennslyvania. In the German Rhineland, they had not had any opportunity to own land of their own, for, after centuries of bitter struggle, warfare, and peasant revolution, the land had all been staked out by the feudal lords: the families of wealth and power. All the simple farmer had was a chance to work the land, and so long as he and his family did not get out of line, a small payment in the new generation might yield a feudal extension of the right to continue working the same parcels of land that his father or family predecessor had tilled. That whole process tended to underscore his ethnic values as German farmer, though he emphasized both parts of that equation.[15]

The Pennsylvania Germans had to learn that not all English in the province were as gracious or concerned as was William Penn. Many of British origin whom they encountered considered the German neighbor to be a lumpish lout who couldn't even speak proper English. To that patronizing kind of Briton, these were really "dumb Dutch."

Whether true or false, the German farmer and tradesman in Pennsylvania was convinced that he was a better steward of land and opportunity than were any representative workers from the British Isles, whether British, Scotch, Welsh, or Irish. Dr. Benjamin Rush agreed with that stated German position, and Rush was anything but German. Indeed, the Scotch-Irish doctor commended the German farmers in several instances. According to Rush, the "manners of the German farmers" were calculated to achieve a maximum production.[16] They often built the barn before the house. "Barn and stables were generally under one roof," so built as to utilize farm space most effectively.[17] They grew grass and red clover especially to provide fodder for the animals. "They feed their horses and cows . . . in such a manner that the [horses] perform twice the labour of those horses [owned by non-Germans], and the latter yield twice the milk of those cows that are less plentifully fed. There is great oeconomy in this practice, in a country where so much of the labour of a farmer is necessary to support his domestic animals."[18]

They kept their house gardens that provided fresh vegetables just as they had in Germany, which in many ways, such as their quartered shape and raised growing beds, were unlike any neighboring patches, clearly stated the German ethnic variation. Although they grew farm crops similar to those of other ethnic groups around them, they consumed the less salable crops like rye, buckwheat, and Indian corn and sold their wheat, barley, and oats on the market as cash crops.[19]

In Pennslyvania the supposedly stodgy German farmer demonstrated a remarkable social agility. In the Germanys, farmers had gathered in rural towns whose population clustered about a sizable *Hof,* or courtyard manor, while working fields in a circumference about the town; these same persons became different farmer types in Pennsylvania, where they lived on their own acreage. The house stood solitary, perhaps with one or two outbuildings nearby. No other person had houses on his land. He was surrounded by farm fields. Most surprising, that change in the style of living, from village to individual farm, was made in two generations, and few regretted losing the Germanic town unit. In that isolated posture, some of these Germans suffered human casualties or property loss in hit-and-run frontier Indian raids. But that changeover very seldom required more than two generations.

That individual residence on the farmer's solitary farm also drew the ire of at least one German Reformed preacher who insisted that they really should have maintained the German farm village in America. The Reverend William Stoy wrote in September 1757 that such solitary settlement cost lives.[20] "The colonists here neither inhabit homes connected with one another, nor do they live in villages. They settle down and live wherever they find a spring, a river or a grove which suits them. Hence the incursions of the Indians are so easily made."[21] It is true that a few Pennslyvania German farm settlers were captured or did die on the northern frontier of the state, but many more escaped attack while they enjoyed an almost euphoric sense of independence on that same frontier. West of the Susquehanna, the frontier farm element did generally consist of a Scotch-Irish element, but in fact, Pennsylvania German frontier farmers worked from Harris's Ferry on the Susquehanna to Stroudsburg on the Delaware.[22]

Benjamin Rush recommended that farming techniques of the German farmers might well be closely observed by their English farm neighbors, who should not hesitate to imitate the German farm workers.[23] On the other hand, the German farmer in Pennsylvania learned from Native Americans to use fish entrails and bones for fertilizer when growing maize (Indian corn) in the farm fields. Similarly, his English Quaker neighbors taught him to rotate his crops, to plant nitrogen-rich clover and other field-renewal products, and to use a three-field system of planting. Those same English Quaker neighbors were also occasionally masters of this German immigrant indentured servant. The worker was oftentimes required to plant orchards and to build rail fences or plant shrub fences as a contractual action when he rented a farm or served as day laborer or hired hand.[24]

Since field labor represented one of the perpetual shortages on the farms of eastern Pennsylvania, men, women, and children all joined in to do the drudging field work during long work days of farm seasons. Women workers, wives and sisters, posed very few objections to the fact they were expected to work, and many of them simply figured this their share in helping to keep the family farm solvent. Be that as it may, some ethnic farm neighbors, German and Scotch-Irish, chided each other over work practices. Scotch-Irish farm folk complained that only Germans would force their wives to toil long hours at field work, whereupon Germans objected that the Scotch-Irish worked their women just as hard, but they did it inside the house where no one could observe.[25]

The fact was that farm work was so seasonal that the number of laborers needed from one week or one month to the next varied so greatly that a farmer had much difficulty keeping his work force at the fluctuating level that was required from one season to the next. Special cases often posed particular problems. Witness the experience of Conrad and Katie Steiger on an Isaac Norris II farm plantation just north of Philadelphia from 1752 to 1764. Katie's passage had been paid upon departure from Rotterdam, but Conrad had to serve his five-year passage

indenture for Isaac Norris, his master in the Northern Liberties of Philadelphia. However, as noted above, Conrad and Katie worked together in
the fields, especially at harvest time when laborers were quite scarce.
Since Norris kept meticulous farm records, he noted that while Conrad
simply worked off his required days of service for his master before he
could spend time on his own crops, Katie worked for a cash wage of one
penny per day, sunup to sunset.[26] The money she earned, those pennies,
made it possible for him to complete his service indenture almost six
months early. The understanding of Isaac Norris as master may also
have helped to make that happy result possible. Norris had stated much
earlier that he preferred to employ German workers on his farms
whenever that proved possible. He had written to Lawrence Williams,
fellow Quaker in Lancaster County, in 1739 that the German farmers
preferred not to remain in debt for very long. "What remains unpaid, I
believe, will not remain long, because the Dutch are uneasy while they
pay interest."[27]

In 1750 Quaker assemblymen had vigorously objected to bills proposing that harsh taxes be levied upon German immigrants, thus reducing
the number who came. It was Benjamin Franklin, no Quaker, who made
the greatest endeavor to limit those Germans. One result was a Quaker-
German coalition in provincial politics. Christopher Schultz, a leader in
the Schwenkfelder community of plain Germans, put it this way: "The
Quakers are qualified men to be your Representatives; they will protect
your beloved freedoms."[28]

So, in Pennsylvania politics, Germans often deferred to English
Quaker neighbors. For example, in Lancaster County in those days,
fewer than a hundred Quaker families lived among the two thousand
Pennsylvania Germans there. Yet the two regularly elected assemblymen were generally English. Isaac Norris, a Philadelphia Friend who
was one of the main allies of the German element, had this to say: "It is
remarkable that the Frontier County of Lancaster, composed of all sorts
of Germans and some Church of England Electors, have chosen their
Representatives out of ye Quakers, to' there are scarcely one hundred of
that Profession in the whole county."[29] But the assembly ordinarily
conducted business in English. German voters in Lancaster were well
aware of their deficiencies in that language, foreign to them. Moreover,
the English Quakers were caring and trustworthy.

In 1752, the same Schwenkfelder Christopher Schultz conducted a
letter-writing campaign to assure that friendly members of the assembly

be reelected. "Restore them to *their* place, lest we lose *our* place"[30] was his rallying call. The Pennsylvania Germans were indeed reluctant to hold public office and be required to speak English there, but they never hesitated to sign their name on petitions asking for an action or road or appointment to be made. They eagerly went on record by their signature in a way that would have invited an official's retaliation back in the old country.

The value of an ethnic solidarity and the corresponding dangers of careless intermingling with other ethnic people were underscored by Christopher Sauer I in Volume One, Number One of *Der Hoch-Deutsch Geschicht-Schreiber,* on August 20, 1739. There he recounted the tale of a German housewife in Pennsylvania, who, in a show of ordinary hospitality on a sometimes sparsely populated frontier, engaged in conversational small talk with a traveler who appeared in her backyard. He was "en Eirischer" (an Irishman who was a vagabond). She even invited him into the house for something to eat. But, added Sauer, the only thanks she got for her efforts was to be beaten by the Irishman: "uffem Kopf geklotzt" (knocked in the head), as Christopher Sauer put it.[31] He followed that story with a moral lesson, as he often did: Be careful in your dealings with non-Germans who may turn out to be aggressive.

German Americans in Pennsylvania found themselves faced by another ethnic group who posed a threat that varied according to German proximity to the frontier: the American Indian, the Native American. As in so many other cases, different groups of Pennsylvania Germans held varying opinions of the Indian. To the Moravians in Bethlehem, Nazareth, and Lititz, missionary in outlook, Indians (like blacks) simply represented other potential converts.[32] Unlike some other Europeans in the province, who baptized Indians into a kind of halfway Christianity but would not receive them by communion into full membership, Moravians had no such limitation. In the *Gottesacker* ("God's acre," or cemetery) of the chief settlement of Moravians in eastern Pennslyvania, Indians, blacks, and German Moravians lie buried side by side in the ultimate equality of death.[33] Those Moravians continued to maintain faith in that belief, even though some white Moravians were killed at the Gnadenhutten Massacre in 1755 by an Indian attack.[34] They simply recalled all their missionaries back to Bethlehem.

Other Germans on that northern frontier from Stroudsburg to Harrisburg, Lutheran and German Reformed in particular, suffered, fought, and died defending their new homestead against the Indian. Virtually the entire Gilbert family, German-speaking Alsatians, were wiped out by another such massacre near Broadheadsville in Northampton (now Monroe) County, as were the Hoeths near Kresgeville in 1755.[35]

In the same year Indians raided the farm where Nicholas Silfies lived and in 1758, the farm of John Jacob Beyer (Boyer) on Aquashicola Creek, just north of the Lehigh Gap in the Blue Mountain. Both John Jacob and his wife were shot and scalped, massacred by the Indians. The children Frederick and his sister were then walked up to the Indian settlement in Ontario. Frederick and Nicholas did menial jobs under the Indians, whereas the Boyer girl was married to a sort of subchief in the Indian camp. When they were again turned over to the British, their residence was reported to be "Plow Park," which made no sense. What they really said was *"Blo' Barick,"* which was dialect for "Blaue Berg" or "Blue Mountain" in Standard German. All three were repatriated to Northampton County in 1762, where the men resumed farming. The girl, known as "Esther, the Indian Queen" or "Esther, the White Indian," retained fond memories of the kindly treatment at Indian hands. She would not stay in Pennsylvania but returned to the Indian village.[36] She rests there in the burial grounds of the white frame Indian chapel.

In consequence of numerous similar happenings, ordinary Germans on that northern frontier retained quite hostile feelings toward Indians. Typical was the report of Reverend William Stoy in 1757:

> With regard to the Horrors of war . . . our Indians, more savage than wild beasts, have either dragged away innumerable inhabitants . . . as captives, or have slain them. They scalp the living, and what is more, even the dead. I myself have seen them slay them and mutilate their bodies with tomahawks. . . . They have devastated our land far and wide. We have lost some of our congregations either entirely or in part. The largest part of the people at Tulpehocken, among whom I lived, have either fled, or were led into captivity, or killed by Indians.[37]

In the French and Indian War of 1754–63, quite a number of Pennsylvania Germans served, virtually all of them as enlisted men. This highlighted the differences within the German ranks: Plain Folk, or the Anabaptists, had religious scruples against bearing arms and against killing. Virtually none of them served in British North American units on behalf of Great Britain, a kind of absentee landlord. On the other hand, the Church Germans, composed of German Reformed (or German Calvinists) and the Evangelical Lutherans, had no compunctions against military service and did serve by the thousands. For these German Americans, now landowners in their own right at last, they fought in defense of that land. They attacked the French who tried to take it from them.

The emigrants from the German states represented the variation in style and values that one would expect and that the German area of the old Holy Roman Empire already contained in Europe. Inhabitants of the Palatinate enjoyed a reputation as easygoing, fun-loving innovators, while the Bavarians and Prussians had already earned theirs as strict and humorless disciplinarians.[38]

But most distinctive of the provinical types were the Swabians. They were generally regarded as slow, thick, dim-witted country bumpkins who learned very slowly, even when shown how things should be done. They were the mountaineers in the German homeland. Their status was quite comparable to the Normans in France, quite a nonsophisticated frontier type also. The Swabians have also been compared to a late Kentucky hillbilly caricature, although never entirely the same.

Swabians were distinguished by both style and customs. Originally they had inhabited the old German kingdom of Swabia. These people helped to create their own definition, which then helped define their own unusual category. In standard German they were called *schwäbisch,* but in their own Swabian or South German dialect they were *schwowisch.* One Swabian was, in his own words, a Schwob, which was often rendered into English as "a Swope." That was definitely not a compliment. Early on, in the old country, these Swabians had earned the unenviable reputation as muddled thinkers and slow learners.

In Pennsylvania, as in the German area, other regional Germans made fun of the "slow Swabians." In the ethnic category of oral stories, "die Sieben Schwaben" or "Die Sivve Schwowe" were elaborate jokes told at the expense of ethnic Swabian Germans. Note that variation on the ethnic theme: Germans recounted ethnic jokes at the expense of other Germans much more often than at the expense of French or English.

One or two examples of Seven Swabians jokes, told in South Germany and in Pennsylvania, will suffice to indicate theme and style: These seven wanderers, always led by the brightest of the lot, Herr Schultz, bore Swabian nicknames such as Vitele, Michele, and Hans. In trying to determine just how many they were, Herr Schultz counted off those he could see and never reached the count of seven. Like a flash of light it came to Herr Schultz that if they all pressed their noses into the mud at the end of the bridge, then counted the noseprints, he might succeed. And lo and behold, it did total seven.[39]

That was the European German version, but the Pennsylvania version was much like it. Herr Schultz was still the leader, but Jakey, Mikey, and Felty were followers. These *Schwowe* also had trouble with the count, but their solution was to press their noseprints into a cow flop, then count up in the same way. Sure enough, their total also came to seven. Another time, as they walked along a dirt road of eastern Pennsylvania, they came over a rise and spied a flax field in bloom. When they saw this waving blue surface, all disrobed and jumped in for a swim; disappointed, they then realized the blue color was flax flowers.[40]

In the city of Ulm, not far from the northern boundary of Switzerland, there stands a statue to the Ulmer Spatz (the sparrow of Ulm), in honor of its example, which enabled homeland Swabians to complete their cathedral. It seems the builders had begun this mighty structure, forgetting that they needed a ridgepole the length of the church building. Fearful that they might have to tear down the entire structure in order to place that long ridgepole along the crest of the roof so as to start building anew, they rested in its shadow. A sparrow in the process of building its nest in the wall flew up. It carried a straw crosswise in its bill and tried to enter the hole in the wall. It tried without success, for the hole in the wall was merely three inches wide and the straw measured twelve. Then the sparrow cocked its head and held the straw upright. Still not successful, the sparrow turned and tried to back in. No luck again. The workers continued to watch sympathetically, for their problem was much like that of the sparrow.

With that, the sparrow hopped to the end of the straw, picked it up lengthwise, and then entered the nest hole just as slick as a whistle. When the cathedral builders imitated the sparrow, they managed to hold the ridgepole in such a way that they maneuvered the pole endwise through a window aperture and then set it at the peak of the roof. The workers cheered and vowed to erect a statue to that ingenious sparrow. The monument they promised stands in the town square of Ulm to this very day.[41]

The Swabian effort to build a log church in Pennsylvania brought a slightly different result. They figured to build their church in a meadow at the foot of a wooded slope, cutting trees for building logs and stacking them on the hillside to roll them down to the building site one by one. But as they pried the first log out to roll it down the hill, the entire stack of logs came loose and all rolled down to the bottom. "Aha!!!," said the foreman, "that is a better way to send the logs down!" So they carried all the logs back up to the top, stacked them there, and finally kicked out the critical log at the bottom of the heap, and the whole pile came rolling down pell-mell. The congregation stood elated at the bottom and sang the praises of this ingenious foreman.[42]

One of the architectural structures that represented a marked ethnic difference from the other Pennsylvania buildings was the Pennsylvania barn (Pennsylvania German barn) or *Schweitzer Scheier,* often called "Dutch barns." Large and spacious, it was distinguished by a uniform floor plan. These buildings were intended to fit into the sloping hillsides of the Swiss mountains in a split-level design. Thus a ground floor on the downhill side provided stalls and feedways for horses, cows, and sheep with a fenced *Scheierhof,* or barnyard, outside those lower entry doors.

The upper level, with a ramped entrance to the threshing floor, had one large sliding door or two large hinged doors. The threshing floor was flanked by hay mow and straw mow that accounted for the rafter construction and typical high roof. "Bottom barns," from the dialect word *Buddem* (ground), were built flat on the ground and used outside pulleys to raise grain, hay, and straw to the upper level.

In an example of reverse cultural baggage, six or seven Pennsylvania barns did appear in the north of England. That misled some careless researchers to state that the *Schweitzer Scheier* (Swiss barn) came originally from England, not from the Continent. In fact, the value of a ramped, overshot forebay barn commended itself in some areas that were really not hilly, so that a bridge ramp had to be artificially constructed. On the other hand, that barn style was transported by German internal migration to Ohio, Wisconsin, Nebraska, and Ontario, Canada.[43] One cultural geographer who found ramped, overshot barns in Texas in the very early nineteenth century was about to call them "Pennsylvania Barns" in his title when he found that the Swiss emigrants who built them in Texas had never been to Pennsylvania but came directly from their Swiss mountain cantons to Texas.[44]

A similar contradiction of ethnic cultural style was the union church throughout Pennsylvania and in neighboring areas of Maryland and Ohio. In such operations, two small congregations, usually one Lutheran, the other German Reformed, pooled their resources to build a single church building and then worship alternately in a pattern they agreed to establish. The chief surprise in this arrangement was that the two congregations differed in polity as well as denomination: Lutherans were episcopal, while the German Reformed were presbyterian. While the members often insisted that the difference was in the initial wording of the Lord's Prayer (Lutherans said *Vater unser,* while the Reformed said *Unser Vater*), it was obviously more than that.[45]

Not all eighteenth-century Reformed and Lutheran churches began as union churches; some enjoyed large enough congregational support of their own that they were financially independent from the start. In 1771, Johan Heinrich Helffrich brought a German Protestant book by Erasmus S. Hohfner to Pennsylvania with him. It was entitled *Lutheraner and Calvinisten, das ist, Der Evangelischen Kyrchen Einigkeit zum Uhralten Glauben* (Lutheran and Calvinist, that is, Unity of the Evangelical Church by Age-old Beliefs), which demonstrated in print that Reformed and Lutheran units enjoyed common precepts and beliefs and so naturally belonged together.[46] Such books were even used in denominational seminaries. Thus, it was more than coincidence that had brought Lutherans and Reformed congregations together. Another similar solution was the rural charge, in which one minister would handle from three to eight local churches of his denomination, working out a schedule of services to accommodate all those congregations, many of them in union church situations as well.

In the union churches many intermarriages occurred. Each person usually kept his or her own denomination, but among the children, boys went to the denomination of the father, while girls followed the mother's. Occasionally members switched to the other side because of disputes or to follow a popular minister. The union church made it possible for many very small congregations to survive.[47]

Food items and products also served as a means to identify ethnic groups in Pennsylvania. Of course, those products reflected agricultural patterns and crops raised. Just as British in Pennsylvania brought their sheep and cattle with them, they also retained the food dishes of cold mutton and roast beef. The Germans, if they chose to raise beef and sheep, generally sold them and derivative foods to market, but they also raised more hogs and fowl and ate pork and chicken dishes at home. Like most American farmers of any generation who grew hogs, they simply allowed the hogs to run wild, acting as natural garbage disposal units. Individual hogs were captured in the woods in fall at harvest time and were slaughtered as a seasonal crop.

Another distinctly German activity was to produce cooked meat (or ground meat) combinations in the butchering process to use up component parts of the animal. Thus scrapple, liverwurst, souse, and sausage included those lesser meat products such as liver, kidney, rib meat, brain, and tough meat that could be ground up. In my lifetime I have observed as farmers' wives concocted those meat products. They also used stomach and intestines as casing in which they packed liverwurst and sausage for cooking and winter storage in cellars or cool cellars. Just as all parts of the slaughtered animal were effectively utilized, all available workers were employed in the processing. Thus both men and women joined in the work; children of almost all ages likewise sliced hog fat to produce lard for home cooking all winter long, carried wood to stoke fires, ran errands, and stirred boiling kettles.[48]

While some other proximate ethnic groups adopted a few of these local products, most were not sufficiently appetizing to them to encourage such use. For example, Pennsylvania Germans made *Seimaag* (pig stomach stuffed with sausage and seasonings) as a New Year's festive dish or other holiday treat,[49] but they would not touch Scottish haggis. The Pennsylvania Germans did eat Indian corn, squash, pole beans, and succotash, all adapted from American Indian dishes. Europeans continued to consider those dishes fit only for animals to eat.

Just as the mixed and ground meat products reflected the tendency to use all that animal's meat, the Pennsylvania German practice of wild fruit pies effectively used the resources of nature and of the blessings of God. Cherry, apple, blueberry, and blackberry were probably their favorite domestic fruits, supplemented by wild cherry, grape, huckleberry, ground cherry, and hog-huckleberry (whortleberries) for pies and tarts. Raisin pie was usually served at funerals; in fact, it was often called funeral pie. After all, dried raisins were available at all times and seasons when other pie filling was not.

Many *Deitsch* housewives served potatoes and pie at every meal, including breakfast, for the men needed energy to work in the fields. That also produced what these Pennsylvania Germans called *es zehn Uhr Schtick* (the ten o'clock morning snack in the field). *Pennsylvannisch Deitsch* ate sumptuous meals and enjoyed eating all the while food was available. *Schoffe am beschte wan ma gut gesse hen!*—"You work best (hardest) when you have eaten well!" That was a favorite saying.

Germans in Pennsylvania observed church and political holidays and held huge celebrations of those events. Unlike the Pilgrim fathers in New England, German Americans celebrated Christmas, New Year's

Day, Easter, and Whitsuntide with special foods. To eat roast goose for
Christmas may sound English, but Pennsylvania Germans did that, too.
Baked ham for Easter, Harvest Home, and Thanksgiving may sound like
monotonous fare, but many Germans never tired of ham on the table.
Chicken was the ordinary meal whenever the preacher came. Christmas
cookies shaped like animals or holiday symbols were common.[50]

Pennsylvania Germans learned many nature cures from the Indians:
mint, sassafras, pennyroyal tea, and jack-in-the-pulpit root were some.
Mixing them with plant cures brought from the German states, they also
adapted old English formulas. They planted by the signs of the moon
and were almanac oriented in farm activities and food product use.

While Germans have traditionally been known to drink schnapps or
beer, many of them in Pennsylvania made their own wine or brewed
their own hard cider. They used one of those in place of water, which
was often tainted. Whenever pure water was easily available, they
tended to drink it at every meal. As a result of their hearty fare, some of
them grew obese as they grew older. Many of them literally worked so
hard that they became tough rather than fat.

At the end of the successful Seven Years' War, in which numerous
Pennsylvania Germans took part, inflation had markedly increased. In
addition, money was needed to pay British troops who remained even in
peacetime; more tax revenue was needed. Taxes were not increased
much but were more efficiently collected. That appeared to the German
element in Pennsylvania both threat and burden.

The levy of the Stamp Tax was unpopular with nearly all colonial
Americans, but especially with the Germans. They complained about
this new tax, which had never been levied before and which contained
provisions directed specifically at them. For example, penny newspapers were rated a half-penny tax for all purchasers. But for Germans,
there was more:[51]

> For every skin or piece of vellum or parchment, or sheet or piece of paper,
> on which an instrument, proceeding, or other matter or thing aforesaid,
> shall be engrossed, written, or printed, within the said colonies and planta-
> tions in any other than the English language, a stamp duty of double the
> amount of the respective duties before charged thereon.[52]

Which foreign language, other than that of the Pennsylvania Germans,
was in use? None! This tax on documents and papers in "other than the

English language'' was clearly aimed at this Pennsylvania German minority. For a small penny newspaper in German, a 100 percent tax was levied; for every large-size single-sheet penny newspaper, a 200 percent tax; and for every folding newspaper of four pages costing twopence, a tax of eight pence. Every advertisement in German cost four shillings per insertion. An agreement for apprentice service normally taxed at sixpence per pound value became a shilling tax on twenty shillings value if in German. Tax indeed! It seemed confiscation.[53]

Henrich Miller refused to publish *Der Philadelphische Staatsbote* again until the tax was repealed. In a province where one out of five newspapers was a German-language paper, far fewer papers were issued.

The number of Pennsylvania Germans who served in the state militia or in the Continental forces during the American Revolution was quite high, despite the fact that many of these Germans were Plain Folk with religious scruples against military service.

Many German pastors here became chaplains in militia and regular army units. Reverend Abraham Blumer had been a chaplain in the Swiss Regiment Meyer in Sardinia Piedmont for nearly a decade before he came to Philadelphia in 1771. Just above five years after his arrival, he became chaplain in the First Northampton County Militia and served the rest of the war.[54]

Many Germans felt they owed that service to their new homeland. On the other hand, Lieutenant Andreas Wiederholt, a captured Hessian, gave a different estimate: ''They want to imitate the hospitality and candor of the others but they remain raw and unrefined German peasants. They are steeped in the American idea of Liberty, but know nothing of what liberty really is, and are therefore worse than all the rest.''[55]

When Joh. Friederich Hilligass, the immigrant, landed at Philadelphia in 1727 from the ship *William & Sarah,* William Hill, Master, as a member of George Michael Weiss' German Reformed colony, his family was listed as four and a half persons. With Weiss and the others, they eventually wound up in the Goshenhoppen congregation in the rural end of Philadelphia County, but they first lived in Philadelphia city.[56] Frederick Hilligas, as he was most familiarly known, established family business enterprises in sugar refining and as an iron manufacturer. Michael Hillegas, born in Philadelphia in 1729, took over the family businesses in 1750, at the age of 21. In 1759, he opened a music store there, which he continued to operate through 1779. Music, including sheet music, was commonly used by Sir William Johnson at Johnson Hall in the 1760s.

In time, the family acquired land at the far northwestern end of Philadelphia County. Young Michael continued to be active as a member of the German Reformed church and as a businessman in Philadelphia and the adjacent area. Some letters from the start of his music store enterprise have long resided at the Historical Society of Pennsylvania but were not published until October 1989.[57]

Michael Hillegas was first elected to the Pennsylvania Assembly in 1765, when just 35 years of age. He also served in the last Provincial Assembly under the Pennsylvania Charter of 1701, which met in 1775–76. He was named to the Committee on Supplies and Rations for the State Troops and to the Pennsylvania committee of Public Safety. Fellow officials chose him treasurer of Pennsylvania as war began.

His service there was so satisfactory that in October 1776 he was concurrently appointed treasurer of the Continental Congress. After two short months of service as joint state and national treasurer, he was ordered away from Philadelphia to join the displaced Congress at York, Pennsylvania. From there he ran lottery arrangements to help finance the war.

Peter Roads (originally Roth), a storekeeper in Allentown, became an officer in the Pennsylvania militia, justice of the peace in civil government, and, when Lehigh County was erected, the first resident judge there. He commanded a company of local troops on the Pennsylvania frontier in 1778. Bernhard Klein, a local farmer, served under him as a private; Klein soon rose to the rank of second lieutenant. They did their service in the German language.[58]

Henry Melchior Muhlenberg was a leader of the Lutheran church in Pennsylvania. His three sons served in public life. Peter Muhlenberg raised a regiment of German soldiers for the Patriot Army in Virginia during the Revolution, who served throughout the war. Frederick Augustus Conrad Muhlenberg, Peter's brother, was elected to the first House of Representatives of the United States, where the members elected him to be the first Speaker of the House in 1789. Pastor Henry M. Muhlenberg tried to remain equally faithful to Britain and to Pennsylvania.

Most of their fellow Germans lacked the language facility that both Peter and Frederick Muhlenberg had gained. As the fighting expanded,

Pennsylvania sent even more soldiers. Pastor Henry M. Muhlenberg, in Trappe, Pennsylvania, recorded his reaction as soldiers passed. He was quite ambivalent about this war. He did not contradict his sons but remembered his sworn allegiance to both king and province. He watched

> a company of men from Reading, a hundred strong, on the march to the province of Jersey. Most of them were settlers and young men born in this country and recently enlisted with others to form an army of observation in Jersey. Those soldiers camped nearby . . . , a few billeted at two inns in the village of Trappe. [Another company of riflemen passed through a short time later.] Most of them [were] native youngsters from in and around Reading who learned bush fighting like that of the Indians.[59]

When the soldiers prayed for land and home, they prayed *"fer Pennsylvaanie, unser Heemet"* (for Pennsylvania, our home). But they talked very little about it. Simply, when action was needed, they acted and did not say much at all. Continually berated as poor soldiers, more Pennsylvania Germans served as Revolutionary soldiers in Pennsylvania than any other nationality. Some of them fought reluctantly and sang their camp songs in German. But they listened to the boasts of other soldiers in silence.

Just before the British occupied Philadelphia in September 1777, an action, both pragmatic and symbolic, took place. The State House bell with its inscription, "Proclaim Liberty throughout the Land, Unto all the Inhabitants thereof," stood to be melted down for British war use if captured. Happily it was not.[60] In a well-kept secret, the bell was removed from the bell tower and loaded on a Pennsylvania German farm wagon. As the Continental Congress left Philadelphia for York, the Liberty Bell was hauled north to Allentown,[61] where it was hidden in Reverend Abraham Blumer's Zion Reformed Church while British were in Philadelphia. Even frugal German Calvinists willingly tore up floorboards and dug a pit under the sanctuary in which to hide the sentimentally valuable bell.[62]

At the termination of their military service, these Germans were happy to accept bounty land for the time and effort they had expended. Their service was generally forgotten or ignored once again by their fellow citizens.

After the war ended, they resumed a life of quiet farming, content to live on what they had wrested from the land and confirmed with the government. They honestly believed that they had earned their way and that they continued to contribute to the economic good of the locality, state, and country. They seconded the belief of Thomas Jefferson that this was a nation of small farmers. Many of them were Jeffersonian Republicans, but many others were Federalists.

Those Pennsylvania German Federalists were heartily embarrassed by the subsequent actions of Yankee Federalist John Adams in 1798. So as to be able to pay the costs of an upcoming war against France, the Federal Congress passed a tax bill based on real estate and on slaves, to be taxed at fifty cents a head. Each of the states would decide how to raise the money to pay its proportionate share on real estate.

Pennsylvania had very few slaves. To make up the major share of taxes due, the Pennsylvanis state legislature decided that the real estate tax would be determined by the number of windows in houses on a given property. That assumed wealthy people had more windows and could better afford to pay the tax. It was not that easy.[63]

The window tax reminded the Pennsylvania Germans of a hated hearth tax in the Rhineland, which was assessed by the number of fireplaces. In Pennsylvania, many of the country Dutch folk had used cheaper small-sized glass for windowpanes and mounted them six over six or six over nine. They believed that each pane would be taxed separately so they would have to pay disproportionately high amounts of tax. English, Irish, and Scotch-Irish were blamed for the political fiasco.

When the federal assessors came around to examine properties and count windows, a veteran of the Revolution named Jacob Fries organized a resistance to the tax. He told housewives to stand at second-floor windows and pour boiling water on the assessors.[64] No tax could be levied then. Meanwhile, Reverend John Jacob Eyermann spoke against the tax from the pulpit in his German Reformed church, though he said he was just advising the people of his congregation.[65]

Federal marshals were sent out to arrest Eyermann and bring him to jail in Bethlehem. Reverend Eyermann was arrested while preaching a Saturday morning funeral sermon. Fries then got out his Revolutionary War rifle and sword and marched on the jail at the Sun Tavern. There he held the federal marshal at gunpoint and freed the preacher, who made a major error when he ran away to New York. Later Jacob Fries was apprehended when given away by his dog, Whiskey; both were held in Bethlehem for trial, Fries on the federal charge of treason and Eyermann for prison break, opposing the direct tax law, and advising an unlawful conspiracy. Because of the yellow fever in Philadelphia, the trials were held at Norristown. Federal court officers and government lawyers were so strident that no lawyer wanted to defend Jacob Fries, although Alexander James Dallas finally did. Eyermann never had a lawyer and was tried without one. The trial was conducted in English, and there is no evidence that Eyermann really understood why he had been charged.

"Did I not pray for the government, President and Vice-President?" said Eyermann in his own defense. John Serfass, an assessor, who was a government witness, responded, "Yes, you did when in the pulpit, but when you were out, you prayed the other way."[66]

Fries was convicted of treason and sentenced "to be hanged by the neck until dead."[67] Evidence that a juryman had declared in public that Fries ought undoubtedly to be hanged resulted in a new trial for him. He was convicted again but received a presidential pardon. Eyermann was convicted and sentenced to one year of imprisonment and a fifty-dollar fine, which was more than his annual pay.[68] His reputation as a pastor was ruined, and he never got his pulpit back.

The Pennsylvania Germans, with their Swabian background thrown in were as fine storytellers as any immigrants in Pennsylvania. They liked to work, they liked to eat, and they liked to laugh. This German element was clannish to protect its community and to control the land it had finally acquired. As an ethnic group, it participated in provincial and church affairs and sent leaders onto the regional stage. Since their language was so important, the Pennsylvania Germans held it high. Not until the twentieth century did they begin to apologize for shortcomings in English and the funny way they sounded when they spoke.

Notes

1. William T. Parsons, *Pennsylvania Germans: A Persistent Minority,* new ed. (Collegeville, Pa.: Chestnut Books/Keschte Bicher, 1985), 17, 37, 53.

2. Scott F. Brenner, *Pennsylvania Dutch: The Plain and the Fancy* (Harrisburg, Pa.: Stackpole Co., 1957), 6–7.

3. Stephen L. Longenecker, *The Christopher Sauers* (Elgin, Ill.: Brethren Press, 1981), 73, 101; Parsons, *Pennsylvania Germans,* 39–40.

4. William Penn, *Journal of William Penn While Visiting Holland and Germany in 1677* (Philadelphia: Friends Book Store, 1878), vii, 13–14; Longenecker, 58–59.

5. William Penn, "Certain Conditions or Concessions Agreed upon by William Penn . . . and those who are the Adventurers and Purchasers in the Same Province, 11 July 1681," *Minutes of the Provincial Council of Pennsylvania* (henceforth, *Colonial*

Records) (Harrisburg, Pa.: T. Fenn, 1838), I, xxiii; William T. Parsons, "Francis Daniel Pastorius, Public Servant and Private Citizen," *Pennsylvania Folklife* 33:2 (1983–84), 79.

6. William Penn, "A General Description of the Province of Pennsylvania; its Air, Water, Seasons and Produce . . . and the Good Increase Thereof," in *A Collection of the Works of William Penn* (London: J. Sowle, 1726), II, 699–704.

7. Parsons, "Francis Daniel Pastorius," 77–79, 81–82.

8. Francis Daniel Pastorius, Gerrit Hendericks, Derek Op den Graeff, and Abraham Op den Graeff, "Petition [of] 18 April 1688," Samuel W. Pennypacker, "Settlement of Germantown and Causes which led to it," *Pennsylvania Magazine of History and Biography* 4 (1880), 28–30.

9. Parsons, "Francis Daniel Pastorius," 79–81.

10. Ralph Beaver Strassburger and William J. Hinke, *Pennsylvania German Pioneers* (Norristown, Pa.: Pennsylvania German Society, 1934), I, xvii.

11. *Colonial Records, III*, 29.

12. *Strassburger and Hinke*, I, xx–xxi.

13. *Colonial Records*, III, 280–83.

14. Strassburger and Hinke, I, 2–4.

15. Parsons, *Pennsylvania Germans*, 26–28.

16. Benjamin Rush, *An Account of the Manners of the German Inhabitants of Pennsylvania* (with a new Introduction by William T. Parsons) (Collegeville, Pa.: Chestnut Books/Keschte Bicher, 1974), iii–vi.

17. Rush, 4.

18. Rush, 5.

19. Parsons, *Pennsylvania Germans*, 84, 87.

20. William T. Parsons, *Another Rung up the Ladder: German Reformed People in American Struggles, 1754–1783* (Collegeville, Pa.: Chestnut Books/Keschte Bicher, 1976), 6.

21. Reverend William Stoy to the Most Reverend Sirs, 30 September 1757, *Minutes and Letters of the Coetus of the German Reformed Congregations in Pennsylvania, 1747–1792* (Philadelphia: Reformed Church Publication Board, 1903), 163–64.

22. Parsons, *Another Rung*, 4–5.

23. Rush, 23–24.

24. William T. Parsons, "Isaac Norris the Councillor, Master of Norriton Manor," *Bulletin of the Historical Society of Montgomery County* 19:1 (1973), 22–23.

25. Parsons, *Pennsylvania Germans*, 222–23.

26. Workers and Tenants Accounts, Norris Account Book #6, pp. 59–64, 68, Norris Papers, Library Company of Philadelphia in Historical Society of Pennsylvania. The Steigers harvested grain and hay for Norris, who in turn paid Conrad Steiger's provincial tax.

27. Isaac Norris to Lawrence Williams, 6 April, 4 August, and 30 November 1739, Norris MS Letters, Norris Papers, Historical Society of Pennsylvania.

28. Christopher Schultz to [————?] 28 September 1752, Schwenkfelder Library, Pennsburg, Pa.; Christopher Sauer II, *Anmerckungen über ein noch nie erhört and gesehen Wunder hier in Pennsylvanien* (Germantown: C. Sauer, 1764), 3, 7, 13–14.

29. Isaac Norris II to Robert Charles, 29 April 1755, Norris MS Letters 1719–1756, 70, Historical Society of Pennsylvania.

30. Christopher Schultz to [————?] 28 September 1752; William T. Parsons, "Pal-

atines . . . and Other German-Americans on the Colonial Frontier," in Karl Scherer, *Pfälzer-Palatines* (Kaiserslautern: Selbstverlag Heimatstelle Pfalz, 1981), 122.

31. Christopher Sauer I, *Der Hoch-Deutsch Pennsylvanische Geschicht-Schreiber* (Germantown). I, 1 (20 August 1739).

32. Parsons, *Pennsylvania Germans,* 68–69.

33. *Gottesacker* (Cemetery) of Central Moravian Church, Bethlehem, Pa.

34. Frederic Klees, *The Pennsylvania Dutch* (New York: Macmillan, 1950), 156.

35. Perry L. Smith, *The Story of Kunkletown* (Kunkletown, Pa.: Kunkletown Bicentennial Commission, 1976), 36.

36. "Return of English Children delivered up by the Indians and Canadians, that were taken in the Province of Pennsylvania . . .", A. F. C. Wallace Collection, Papers relative to William Parsons, American Philosophical Society, Philadelphia.

37. William Stoy to the Most Reverend Sirs, 30 September 1757, *Minutes,* 163–64.

38. Parsons, *Pennsylvania Germans,* 102. Many Pennsylvania soldiers among British forces in the French and Indian War were German speaking. Major William Parsons reported in 1756: "[Captain Nicholaus Wetterholdt] has put the 2nd and 6th Articles of War and the Oath and Certificate all into Dutch, that his Men may better understand them." William Hunter, "German Settlers and Indian Warriors," *Der Reggeboge* 3 (1969), 5–6.

39. Ralph S. Funk, "Die Siwwe Schwowe," in Earl C. Haag, *A Pennsylvania German Anthology* (Selinsgrove, Pa.: Susquehanna University Press, 1988), 59–60.

40. Interview with Thomas A. Greene, Palmerton, Pa., 15 June 1962. He told me several Swabian stories and jokes he had heard from his father (my grandfather), Charles W. Greene, who descended from Tobias Grünzweig of Neidlingen in the Swabian Alb and who was schoolmaster in Neidlingen, Württemberg, from 1738 to 1744.

41. John Birmelin, "Der Ulmer Spatz," in Preston A. Barba, *The Later Poems of John Birmelin* (Allentown, Pa.: Schlechters, 1957). It is also Volume 16 of the publication of the Pennsylvania German Folklore Society.

42. Interview with Thomas A. Greene, 15 June 1962.

43. Alfred L. Schoemaker, *The Pennsylvania Barn* (Lancaster, Pa.: Pennsylvania Dutch Folklore Center, 1955), 4–11, 22–27; Robert F. Ensminger, "A Search for the Origin of the Pennsylvania Barn," *Pennsylvania Folklife* 30:2 (1980–81), 50–55.

44. Terry G. Jordan, "A Forebay Bank Barn in Texas," *Pennsylvania Folklife,* 30:2 (1980–81), 72–75.

45. Brenner, 33–35; Parsons, *Pennsylvania Germans,* 68.

46. Erasmus S. Hofner, *Lutheraner and Calvinisten, das ist, Der Evangelischen Kyrchen Einigkeit zum Uhralten Glauben* (Cassel: Wilhelm Wessel, 1607). Johan Heinrich Helfferich's copy is in the Myrin Library of Ursinus College, Collegeville, Pa.

47. Interview with Florence Parsons, Palmerton, Pa., 15 July 1976.

48. Hog slaughter and butchering at the farm of Charles W. Greene, Towamensing Township, Carbon County, Pa., each November from 1932 to 1939.

49. Interview with Arlene Moyer, Alburtis, Pa., 5 December 1973. Mrs. Moyer had her own recipe for stomach filling. I enjoyed Palatine *Saumaag* on New Year's Eve of 1975–76. There is little difference between Rhineland and Perkiomen Valley style.

50. Alfred L. Shoemaker, *Christmas in Pennsylvania: A Folk-Cultural Study* (Kutztown, Pa.: Pennsylvania Folklife Society, 1959), 40–43, 92–96.

51. Parsons, *Pennsylvania Germans,* 109–10, 116.

52. "The Stamp Act, 22 March 1765," in Edmund S. Morgan, *Prologue to Revolution: Sources and Documents on the Stamp Act Crisis, 1764–1766* (Chapel Hill: University of North Carolina Press, 1959), 41.

53. Parsons, *Another Rung,* 7.

54. William T. Parsons, "Der Glarner: Abraham Blumer of Zion Reformed Church, Allentown," *Swiss-American Historical Society Newsletter* 18:2 (1977), 8, 13–15, 20.

55. Quoted in Ernst Kipping, *The Hessian View of America, 1776–1783* (Monmouth Beach, N.J.: Philip Freneau Press, 1971), 24, 29–33.

56. Strassburger and Hinke, I, 7, 9.

57. JoAnn Taricana, "Musical Commerce in Eighteenth-Century Philadelphia: The Letters of Michael Hillegas," *Pennsylvania Magazine of History and Biography* 113 (1939), 609–13.

58. Parsons, *Another Rung,* 13.

59. Theodore Tappert and John Doberstein, eds., *Notebook of a Colonial Clergyman,* (Philadelphia: Lutheran Publication Board, 1959), 162.

60. William T. Parsons, "Isaac Norris, Provincial Affairs and the Liberty Bell," *Bulletin of the Historical Society of Montgomery County* 21:4 (1979), frontis., 300–304.

61. Robert K. Mentzell, *The Liberty Bell's Interlude in Allentown* (Sellersville, Pa.: Historical and Achievement Authority, 1974), 2, 4–8.

62. Parsons, "Der Glarner: Abraham Blumer," 13.

63. Parsons, *Pennsylvania Germans,* 184–86.

64. Thomas Carpenter, *The Two Trials of John Fries on an Indictment for Treason; Together with a Brief Report of the Trials of Several Other Persons, for Treason and Insurrection In the Counties of Bucks, Northampton and Montgomery in the Circuit Court of the United States* (Philadelphia: William W. Woodward, 1800), 221–24.

65. Reverend John Jacob Eyermann, MS Protocol of St. John's German Reformed Church, Towamensing, Pa., 1798.

66. Carpenter, 223.

67. Carpenter, 204.

68. Carpenter, 226.

8

Cosmopolitanism and the Anglo-Jewish Elite in British America

David S. Shields

During the eighteenth century, cosmopolitanism contributed to the attenuation of ethnicity as a ground of self-understanding. My concern here is to determine how literary neoclassicism assisted in the cosmopolite project of overcoming indigenous identity. I will also illustrate some effective limits of cosmopolitanism by examining the self-expression of members of the Levy-Franks family, British America's wealthiest and most articulate Jewish clan. In particular, I will show how cosmopolitanism enabled the Jewish elite to participate in the conversation and commerce of the public sphere but provoked a crisis of identity when it enabled the intermarriage of Jew and gentile, threatening the traditionalism of the Jewish family.

The Levys and the Franks were mercantile families which intermarried early in the eighteenth century.[1] Based in New York City, they established an effective transmaritime trading network during the 1710s that lasted to the end of the century. Their participation in the world of trade is a matter of importance, since one of the concerns of this study is to recall to scholarship an ignored constituency of cosmopolitanism, the merchant elite. Merchants were, in the words of Rousseau, "those cosmopolites who break down the imaginary barriers which separate peoples, and who, by their examples, serve a state which embraces all mankind."[2]

The Political Context of Jewish Cosmopolitanism

Histories of cosmopolitanism generally feature the efforts of European philosophes to promote a broadly defined "human interest"—an interest untrammeled by the chauvinism of church of state.[3] They attempted in the name of a "citizenry of the world" to transcend the constraints of birth and custom that troubled society and to evade the passions of party and creed that disturbed national life. The cosmopolitanism of the philosophes owed much to a nostalgia for the Latinate, pan-European culture of an earlier era. Yet it also refracted contemporary ambitions to recreate politics on a global level. That cosmopolitanism reemerged in European life at precisely that time when Spain, France, Holland, and England were projecting world empires is a historical *factum brutum* that cannot be ignored. Nor can we forget that cosmopolitanism came into being in antiquity as an imperial ideology, justifying Alexander the Great's *oikouméne,* the world civilization created by the synthesis of elements of all indigenous cultures.[4] The European imperialists do not allow us to forget it, since they justified their own ambitions for global dominion by invoking classical apologia.

The modern empires wore their classical dress with varying degrees of fitness. The Spanish, who believed the church's divine commission mandated the forced conversion of native populations to the cross, could never bleach from their imperial discourse the stain of *la leyenda negra.* The French, too, found their imperial civilization repeatedly attacked for its "perfidious" program of territorial aggrandizement. Only the Dutch and English succeeded in promulgating an imperial ethic that possessed the philosophical potency of the ancient *oikouméne.* They did this by downgrading the acquisition of land as the goal of empire, by legislating an "enlarged" notion of imperial citizenship, and by instituting commercial exchange as the principal medium of imperial communication. Both the Dutch and the English championed the ideal of the "empire of the seas," the *imperium pelagi,* a global transmaritime mercantile hegemony over world trade.[5] Both asserted the morality of their enterprises on the grounds of trade, for "God hath by his providence so ordered, that no one Country hath all Commoditys within it self, but what it wants, another shall supply, that so there may be a mutuall Commerce through the world."[6] The global interdependence of nations was mandated by the economy of providence. Empires that formed their polities to serve the need of "mutuall Commerce" of the world benefited mankind in general.

In theory the *imperium pelagi* would preserve the autonomy of the various nations with whom the imperial metropolis would trade. In practice, the Dutch and English commercial empires never operated completely free of the territorial colonialism that their rhetoric disavowed. Nevertheless, the Anglo-Dutch wars of the seventeenth century were not exercises in land grabbing, nor were they dynastic struggles. They were commercial contests fought with arms rather than products. The distinctive character of the Anglo-Dutch wars is best conveyed by the means of their resolution—merger of the contesting parties rather than conquest or compromise. The Glorious Revolution in 1688 consolidated an Anglo-Dutch commercial interest that would succeed in creating a global material culture (silk, tea, coffee, potatoes, tobacco, sugar, indigo, chocolate, and medicinal plants transforming the metropolis; cloth and manufactories from the metropolis transforming the nations of the world). The Anglo-Dutch commercial nexus also encouraged the expansion of a mercantile class imbued with a sensibility sufficiently liberal to service a global trading network. The experience of parlaying with foreign peoples encouraged a pragmatic cosmopolitanism, which found expression in the metropolis as well as in the provinces and trading outposts. This class took pains to redraw the circle of peoples with whom they declared common cause. In private society—in the world of clubs, coffee house corporations, and Freemasonry—the merchant instituted table fellowship with Turks, Jews, and Europeans of all nationalities.[7] In society at large, the merchants championed against long-standing public prejudice an expanded citizenship, extending the privileges of the metropolis to many who had been deprived of them.[8]

The Jews were beneficiaries of the tendency to cosmopolitanize imperial civic identity. Holland had granted refuge to Sephardic Jews fleeing Spain during the latter decades of the sixteenth century. The Dutch shared with these Jews an animosity toward Spain and an interest in banking and trade. A spirit of religious toleration contributed to making Amsterdam the capital of European Jewry in the seventeenth century. In England an interest in the Jews developed during the years of Cromwell's Protectorate, in part because of Fifth Monarchist beliefs that their conversion must be accomplished before the imminent outbreak of the final things, in part because Cromwell saw the Jews as useful vehicles for his imperial ambitions. The Stuarts did not disavow the program of employing Jews in setting up England's colonial scheme. When the Glorious Revolution merged the political fates of England and Holland, the Sephardic Jews took advantage of the arrangement by circulating through the network of Dutch and English colonies in search of advantageous locales for trades. After 1702 the Ashkenazim began to appear in the New World in some numbers, many choosing the center of Anglo-Dutch culture, New York, as their principal place of settlement.[9] Both Moses Levy and Jacob Franks consolidated their businesses and social positions in New York during the commerical boom occasioned by Queen Anne's War (1702–13). The period saw a wave of Jewish settlement in America's most active depot for arms and victuals. The marriage of Levy's daughter, Abigail, to Jacob Franks in 1712 amalgamated the two families into the most formidable commercial combine in British America. Their commercial power won them social recognition among New York's heteroglot gentry. The Levy-Franks family made use of their social cachet by educating their children at the elite school run by Alexander Malcolm.[10]

Cosmopolitan Style and the Problem of Jewish Tradition

How can we locate the ethnicity of New World Jews in an area that understood *ethnos* to be a function of the genius loci of a people? Instead of a land, the Jews had a book. The language of that book, Hebrew, was not the language of the hearth or street. The Sephardim spoke Ladino; the Ashkenazim spoke Yiddish. Residence in British America compelled Jews to employ English over either. The clash of customs between Spanish and eastern European Jews troubled worship in the New World synagogues.[11] In October 1739 Abigail Levy Franks wrote a letter to her son Naphtali, a young merchant in London, which included the following confession:

> Pray Give my humble Service to Mr. Pecheco and thank him for the Prest of the book he Sent me its Very entertaining to me for I confess it to be agreeable to my Sentiments in regard to our Religeon Whoever wrote it I am sure was no Jew for he thought too reasonable You will Say Perhaps I pay a Compliment in that Expression to myself but I Must Own I cant help Condemning the Many Superstitions wee are Clog'd with & heartly wish a Calvin or Luther would rise amongst Us I Answer for my Self, I would be the first of there followers for I don't think religeon Consist of Idle

Cerimonies & works of Superoregations Wich if they send people to
heaven wee & the papist have the Greatest title too.[12]

What book spurred Abigail Franks's confession? Her remarks suggest
the answer: the first part of William Warburton's *The Divine Legation of
Moses demonstrated on the principles of a Religious Deist* was published in London in 1738. This famous work expounded the Mosaic
books of legislation not as Jehovah's incomprehensible dicta but as a
scheme of comprehensible and reasonable regulation for human affairs.
Abigail Franks's judgment that "the book" could not have been written
by a Jew because of its rationality is an attestation of the irrational
grounds of Jewish hermeneutics. Her characterization of the Jewish
religion as superstitious, ceremonious, and supererogatory—her liken-
ing of the Jewish religion to a Catholic church in need of a Luther—
shows the grounds of her judgment to have been a religious reformism
that conflated rationalism with the doctrine of *sola scriptura*.[13] In her
thought the Jews have misconstrued the book that imbues them with
their identity. The grounds of their identity should be appropriation to
the divine reason of the law. But their current condition is typified by
their irrationality, their displacement from the law, and their misunder-
standing of the book. Only by embracing philosophical rationality could
the Jew reform self-understanding.

What were the works of supererogation that Franks found so worthy
of rebuke? An answer is suggested in the news contained in the letter of
October 1739. "I should be Glad to know what Mr. Pecheco Says to his
Nephews intended Marriage . . . the Portugeuze here in a great fer-
ment about it." The "Portugeuze" were the Sephardic element of the
Jewish community in New York. The possibility of a Sephardic boy
marrying an Ashkenazic girl had instigated the ferment. (The fact that
Abigail Franks, an Ashkenazim, engaged in intellectual commerce with
Mr. Pacheco, a Sephardim, illustrates her own transcendence of traditional differences.) To the charge of quarrelsomeness, Abigail Franks
adds that of dullness in a letter dated December 20, 1741. "I don't often
See . . . any of our Ladys but at Synagogue for they are a Stupid Set
of people. but Mum for that." The "people of the book" were, it
seems, too unfamiliar with books for Mrs. Franks.

The books that mattered to Abigail Franks can be adduced by reviewing the letters for titles and hunting down allusions: Addison's *Maxims,
Observations, and Reflections, Moral, Political, and Divine;* Cowley's

Several Discourses by way of Essays on Verse and Prose; the works of Raspin; Dryden's *Fables Ancient and Modern;* Montesquieu's *Persian Letters;* Pope's letters; Chesterfield's letters; Massauet's *Histoire des Rois de Pologne et des Révolutions arrivées dans ce royaume;* Arbuckle's *Hibernicus Letters or a Philosophical Miscellany;* Forrester's *Polite Philosopher: An Essay on That Art Which Makes Man Happy in Himself and Agreeable to Others;* de Boyer's *Letters Juives, ou Correspondance philosophique, historique, et critique entre un Juif Voyageur a Paris et ses correspondans en divers endroits;* and Smollet's *Adventures of Roderick Random.* Two genres predominate: the philosophical letter and neoclassical belles lettres. Particularly noteworthy is the preponderance of "philosophical observator" writing—a favorite cosmopolite genre in which a foreigner (Persian, Jew, Hibernian, Chinaman, etc.) takes up residence in a European metropolis and comments on the mores of his host nation in a series of letters addressed to a reasonable friend.[14] The effect was to dramatize how arbitrary the customs of a nation are when viewed through the eyes of a "reasonable other." The philosophical bemusement of the letter for which the reader becomes a substitute recipient establishes a *sensus communis* in opposition to the customs and humors of the host nation. Thus the letter establishes a worldly common sense in which the reader participates. Neoclassical belles lettres, the other favored genre of Abigail Franks's reading, also acted as a solvent of national traits and figurations, for it afforded a uniformitarianism of style and a universality of scope available to every literate person in the West.[15] In certain works found in Franks's library—Pope's correspondence, Chesterfield's letters—the "observator" genre and neoclassical belletrism coalesced into a form quintessentially ecumenical.

Abigail Franks's epistles to Naphtali share something of the spirit of Chesterfield's letters. The attempt to combine the urbanity of learning and taste with the friendly intimacy of a family correspondence; the concern with instructing youth in the ways of the world by using maxims that distill the common sense of the ages; the impartiality and occasional irony with which she represents the broils of provincial party politics— all bespeak common concerns. Yet the differences in circumstance give rise to distinctions in matter: Abigail Franks evinced a maternal distaste for the tavern, that cosmopolitan institution whose sociability has a distinctively masculine cast. She addressed a son already entered into the world of business, in need of practical advice rather than Chesterfieldian instruction. Consider her admonition concerning the public expression of religious belief:

> I must recom[men]d to you not to be Soe free in y[ou]r Discourse on religeon and be more Circumspect in the Observence of some things Especialy y[ou]r morning Dev[otio]ns for tho' a Person may think freely and Judge for themselves they Ought not to be to free of Speach nor to make a Jest of what ye multitude in a Society think is of the Last Consequence. (Letter July 9, 1733)

In this advice we discover the central tenent informing cosmopolitan style: suppress that element of yourself that will provoke the antagonisms of the society with which you deal. Circumspection, politeness, and deference were the qualities that constituted the cosmopolitan style. These were the qualities that characterized the conversation of the merchants in the exchange, where Naphtali pursued his trade. *The Spectator* observed of the Royal Exchange, "Sometimes I am justled among a Body of Americans; sometimes I am lost in a Crowd of Jews, and sometimes in a Group of Dutchmen. I am a Dane, a Swede, or Frenchman at different times, or rather fancy myself like the old Philosopher, who upon being asked what countryman he was, replied that he was a Citizen of the World."[16] The imaginative polyethnicity of *The Spectator* was enabled by the polite attenuation of distinctions by Americans, Jews, Dutchmen, Danes, Swedes, or Frenchmen. It was easier to become a Dane if that Dane did not seem to differ from one greatly.

In *The Spectator*'s account, a visit to the exchange becomes an aesthetic experience, an experience of play that teaches us "to place next to our life another life, next to our world another world." This "detachment from the roles and situations" of ordinary affairs is, according to Hans Robert Jauss, the theoretician of *Rezeptionäesthetik,* the primary structural property of aesthetic experience. Strolling through the bourse was an act of spectation, akin to fantasizing about the scenes in a bazaar.[17] There was more to the aesthetic experience of the Royal Exchange than the aesthesis of the curious gaze. Trade made use of the imaginative projection into another situation, because it entailed an understanding of the demands of the other. International trade entailed of a trader a work of cultural translation to agree with the foreigner upon a scheme of common value enabling exchange. It was the transformative experience of the "dialogue of the trade" that made the merchants, in the eyes of the philosophes, "those cosmopolites who break down the imaginary barriers which separate people."

Were the barriers imaginary that separate people? Were the ethnic peculiarities that distinguished peoples merely phantasms to be exorcised by an act of anamnesis, eclipsed by a more powerful vision of humankind as a homologous entity? Both the philosophes and the merchant families demonstrated their belief in a human ecumenicity by associating in private societies that pointedly ignored the differences of race, religion, and rank. The polity of the clubs was the practical fulfillment of the cosmopolitan program. Though certain clubs projected "reformation of manners" and "improvements" from private society to society at large, the accomplishment of cosmopolitanism remained effectively limited to the club world.

Moses and Richa Franks in the Club World

The spirit of sociability governed the club world. We should understand sociability in all its ramifications. Sociability based community upon friendship rather than love or kinship. As a historical phenomenon, its rise has often been correlated with the urbanization of culture.[18] In place of the old ties of family, church, and neighborhood, sociability offered an affiliation of shared taste, feeling, or circumstance. Shaftesbury distinguished the sociability of private society from the "publick spirit" by observing that the *sensus communis* of the club enjoyed a spirit of permission encouraged by the shared laughter at wit.[19] The liberty of conversation that Shaftesbury understood to be the spirit of sociability presented dangers. Certain matters of conversation risked destroying the voluntary fellow feeling of circles. To guard against the dissolution of friendship, circles often imposed *leges conviviales*. The Tuesday Club of Annapolis, for instance, required any contentious remark about politics, religion, or commerce to be drowned immediately in laughter by the assembly.[20] Newport's "Society for Promoting Virtue and Knowledge, by a Free Conversation," constrained liberty of discussion by legislating that "nothing shall ever be proposed or debated which is a distinguishing religious tenet of any one member."[21] Newport's Jewish Gentlemen's Club prohibited "conversation relating to Synagogue affairs, on the forfeit of the value of four bottles good wine."[22] Private societies that were grounded upon a common "devotion to the muses" frequently dispensed with *leges conviviales,* substituting a literary code in its stead. The permissions and prohibitions of discourse in these circles operated with great subtlety.

Moses and Richa Franks, the children of Abigail Franks, belonged to a literary circle gathered around Archibald Home, a Scottish resident of New York City and Trenton.[23] The life of this circle was captured in the posthumous collection "Poems on Several Occasions By Archibald Home. Esqr. late Secretary, and One of His Majesty's Council for the province of New Jersey: North America" (Laing Manuscripts III, 452, University of Edinburgh Library).[24] Besides Home's verse—much of which he addressed to Richa Franks—the collection included the poetry by Moses Franks, Joseph Warrell (attorney general of New Jersey), Abigail Streete Coxe (the woman Benjamin Rush deemed the most learned of any in the middle colonies), David Martin (sheriff of Trenton), and Louis Row (minister of the French church in New York). Though Archibald Home presided as the archpoet of the circle, a spirit of collaboration prevailed among the membership. Mutual aid was freely tendered and accepted by the writers with the end of perfecting poems. Indeed, the notion of the perfected work, manifesting correct numbers, appropriate language, cogent argument, and precise imagery, seems the superintending ideal of club activity. Home's corrections to his own works were preserved in the posthumous collection, illustrating his subordination to the canons of neoclassicism. His emendations to work by his friends were designated by quotation marks, to show the corporate enterprise of improvement in art toward the ideal. The sociability of literary clubs was enabled by a shared subservience to the ideal of an objective, "impersonal" standard of artistry, identified with "the classical." The process of working toward this ideal entailed a twofold eradication of self-expression: that entailed in the willing acceptance of a collaborator's assistance; that constituted in the effort to eradicate "the peculiar" in the work of art in favor of "the correct."[25]

Moses Franks composed a verse testimony "To the Lady [Abigail Coxe] who made Severall Beautifull Amendments on my Poem Sacred to the Memory of Archibald Home Esqr." It recalled how "Emelia saw" that Moses Franks under the influence of grief had blurted forth his tribute "wanting all of Elegance and Art," and with friendly commiseration,

> . . . taught the Lines to prove
> Worthy thy [Home's] Name, thy Honour, and the Love
> Bid the harsh sounds in softer notes to flow
> And Spread the fairest Mantle o'er my Woe.[26]

The testimony presumed that "harsh" or "strongly urg'd" expression should be subordinated to the "grace" and "just proportion" of art's "rich design." Yet "soul-felt" feeling was not eradicated by art's design, merely softened. Neoclassicism attenuated expressions of self but did not annihilate them.

When we turn to Moses Franks's elegy, "To the Memory of Archibald Home Esqr.," we can see why neoclassicism was a mode of communication proved so serviceable to the cosmopolitan project of mitigating ethnic identity. It could at one and the same time obscure yet manifest the selfhood of the speaker. It was not, as romantic poetry would be, a means of showing forth the genius of a people in the proclamation of a speaker. Consider Franks's treatment of the trope of immortality conventional to elegy.

> Or say if we cou'd rob the Arms of death
> Snatch Thee to Earth restore they Precious Breath
> And for some Moments, to beguile our Pain,
> Drag Thee unwillingly to Life again!
> Oh no! let no rude Hand thy Peace molest,
> Or shake the Calm which now o'er spreads thy Breast.

Franks's disinclination to resurrect Home in his person or in his work could be understood in terms of a Jewish demurral at the Christian figuration of "life after death"; yet it is couched in terms of that classical picture of immortalization wherein the only life after death available is the return from the place of shades to life in the world. This reprieve from the grave is refused. Franks's rejection of the consolation offered by classical "life after death" could be endorsed by his Christian comrades in the club. Neoclassical imagery here occasioned a community of disapprobation. Classical imagery also provided analogies to Jewish and Christian figurations of the life of the soul sufficiently broad to blur distinctions. When at the end of the poem Franks promises "My Muse shall hail Thee to Thy Native Skies," Home's celestial nativity suggests more the gnostic scheme of immortality than the Christian heaven. Gnostic imagery provides a common ground precisely because gnosticism was the syncretic combination of Hellenic, Jewish, and Christian religions.[27] Classicism provided a rich variety of symbolism instrumental to the work of cultural amalgamation undertaken by eighteenth-century cosmopolitans.

In the communication of the club, the participation of a variety of voices was encouraged by a tolerance condoned by the spirit of friendship governing the circle. Moses Franks characterized his poetry as "friendly Verse." While historians stress friendship's role as the "glue of sociability," it may be more insightful to notice the distance between persons that friendship permits. Friendship preserves individual autonomy, the right to say "no," the ability to criticize in its amiability. The pleasure of participating in a club depended upon the degree to which a playful distance was maintained between the members. In Home's circle the adoption of classical personae (Florio = Home; Emilia = Abigail Coxe; Flavia = Richa Franks, etc.) was one means of maintaining that displacement from ordinary affairs necessary to the experience of aesthetic pleasure. I would argue that the conversation of Home's club instanced the working of art and that belletristic clubs generally understood themselves to be aesthetic entities, set apart from the necessities of affairs.[28] The friendly play of the club was a means of disowning "the bus'ness of the noisy town," as George Webb reminds us.[29] Yet it also operated as an alternative to the thralldoms and compulsions of that other sort of human interaction—love.

Clubs that had male and female members risked the disruption of friendship with love; indeed, the prohibition of opposite sex membership in private societies during the eighteenth century took place because of the fear of this disruption. In Home's circle the danger arose from Home's love for Richa Franks. This love provoked a crisis in the Franks family as well as threatening the amity of the literary fellowship. For Abigail Franks the prospect of the marriage of her daughter to a gentile raised the most fundamental anxiety about Jewish identity. When friendship passed into love, the cosmopolitanism of the Franks family found its practical limit in the covenant tradition of the household, and ethnicity reasserted itself.

The Choice

The permission to live regardless of the constraint of parents, tradition, or circumstance issued from literature. The "choice poem," an extremely popular neoclassical genre, promulgated the doctrine that happiness was a product of individual will and that love was truest when it fulfilled humane wishes.[30] Moses Franks portrayed the beloved of his hopes in ''The Wish.''

> Give me a Nymph (if such the Fates design
> If such their Pleasure dictate to be mine,)
> Fair as when Venus from the Ocean sprung
> Like her resistless, blooming Gay and Young
> By no false Passion studying to conceal;
> What she would with more willingness reveal,
> Slave to no Custom, and to Nature true,
> Well knowing what she would, or would no do;
> Quite unaffected all compos'd of ease,
> And not when pleasing, lab'ring to displease;
> Untinctur'd by Coquet, unstain'd by Prude
> Unmov'd by Folly, and by worth subdu'd
> Oh! Let her be all Excellence and Love;
> Gentle and Mild as Angels are above
> Gay as my wishes, warm as my desires
> Loose as the Transports which young Love inspires;
> All undeceiv'd sole mistress of her will
> When right—if wrong to be Corrected still,
> Nor frail, nor rigid, but well bred and free
> And such a woman to attract must be.

Moses Franks's ''nymph'' can in no way be construed as that female ideal of the Jewish tradition, the praiseworthy wife of virtue and industry described in Proverbs, chapter 31. Being a ''Slave to no Custom'' freed the woman of Franks's wishes from a connection to customary exempla. It did not free her from traditional canons of beauty, for the nymph recalls the fairness of Venus. The poet's recourse to the classical analogy is notable, for the Shulamite of ''The Song of Songs'' provided an image of delectability as expressive. Yet the Shulamite's beauty cannot be divorced from her exemplary actions in love, actions that do not harmonize with the qualities of freedom and naturalness that Franks advanced as his behavioral ideals. The Shulamite could in no way be construed as the ''sole mistress of her will''; indeed, the rapt absorption of the Shulamite in the beloved (and the beloved's love for the Shulamite) has as its point the transcendence of human autonomy in a divinely sanctioned mutual belonging. Nature, too, has only subordinate value in ''The Song of Songs,'' as a medium revealing divine intentions.

In sum, the realm of Moses Franks's wishes is not the realm of wisdom that was his Jewish heritage; it was a place where will prevailed over custom and nature over virtue.

The practical consequences of the decision to choose one's mate freely confronted the Franks family in the spring of 1743 when Phila Franks revealed that she had been secretly married to Oliver DeLancey, an aristocratic young gentile, for six months. Abigail Franks reacted strongly to the revelation:

> Good God Wath a Shock it was when they Acquainted me She had left the House and Had bin Married Six months I can hardly hold my Pen whilst I am writting it Its wath I never could have Imagined especially Affter what I heard her Soe often Say that noe Consideration in Life should Ever Induce her to Disoblige such good parents. . . . My Spirits Was for Some time Soe Depresst that it was a pain to me to Speak or See Any one I have Over come it Soe far as not to make My Concern Soe Conspicuous but I Shall Never have that Serenity nor Peace within I have Soe happyly had hittherto My house has bin my prisson. (Letter 31, June 7, 1743)

Abigail Franks's spiritual despondency arose from something more than Phila's disobligation of parental desire. Phila's abandonment of familial expectation entailed a flight from Jewish identity. The divine promise that circumscribed that identity—the Abrahamic covenant— made genealogy the medium by which God's favor was transmitted to His chosen people. Abraham's posterity would know that the Lord was with them by the land, prosperity, and offspring He bestowed. The family, particularly after the Roman annihilation of the Jewish polity in A.D. 135, became the primary institution wherein the Jewish heritage was preserved.[31] Phila's departure from her heritage to enter the house of a gentile foreclosed the ownmost promise defining the Jews as a separate and chosen people. When Abigail Franks communicated her disquiet, her imagery of the "house" becoming a "prisson" well conveyed the closing off of the Jewish solace of posterity. It also identified the effective limit to Abigail Franks's cosmopolitanism. Cosmopolitanism governed self-understanding in the public sphere. Within the ambit of the household the covenant was heeded. The two spheres came into critical conflict only when the issue of marriage arose.

After Phila's elopement, the issue of marriage became complicated for the other Franks children. David Franks married Margaret Evans, a gentile, within the year. Richa, Phila's sister, was being courted by

Archibald Home. Home's poems addressed to "Flavia" (Richa) attempted to create a discursive space resistant to the issues of deracination that threatened the romance. Neoclassicism provided a temporary refuge. Consider the reassuring message of Home's epigram "Wrote, on a Fan With the Story of Perseus and Andromeda":

> Chain'd to a Rock expos'd a Monsters Prey:
> See Gallant Perseus wings the Dauntless Way
> To Succour Suffering Beauty, and to prove
> Monsters and Chains how weak, oppos'd to Love.

The mythological dress of this brief attestation to the perseverance of love abstracts the message sufficiently to prevent a literal application to present circumstance. If Richa wished to read the poem as an assurance of relief from monstrous parental restriction, she could. Or she could simply read it as a timeless testimony to the heroism of love in the face of obstacles.

The reader of the neoclassical epigrams addressed to "Flavia" apprehends the problem of the relationship in the repeated reimagining of situations in which the author is in physical contact with her. In each instance a distance or prohibition is figured in the scene. "On Flavias Fan" has the author refuse the gift of a fan because "What you receive from *Flavia's Hands / But serves to Fan the Fire.*" In another epigram the poet petitions Jove to metamorphose the poet into an earring:

> Give me this *Happy Pendant's* shape to wear,
> To dangle in my charming *Flavia's* Ear
> There whispering in tender plaints my Flame,
> Help to adorn the bright the matchless Dame
> O'er paid my Suffrings, if the Fair bestows
> One pitying Sigh on her Adorer's Woes.

Warrant to imagine "that I, / Might my Lov'd Flavia's Zone untye" is only provided when the wish is presented as being the echo of a Roman poet's words in "Ode: From the Latin."

Imitation of the classics ultimately failed to supply images and language that could bridge the disjunctions of custom and circumstance that separated Archibald Home from Richa Franks. We witness its failure in the one epigram in which Home broke the protocols of classical imposture and revealed Richa Franks to have been the woman to whom the poems to "Flavia" were addressed, "To Miss R F With the Following Address to Flavia."[32]

Blest Heav'ns Example follow, nor refuse
This humble offspring of an Artless Muse
More skill'd my Fingers, tunefuller my Tongue
Alone to thee still should be Lyre be Strung

To Flavia

In Eden such the first made Beauty show'd
Fresh from his hands, the Master-Work of God:
Oh! had her Breast been form'd like thine within,
The Devil in vain had tempted her to sin;
Eternal joys the happy Pair had prov'd
And Envying Angels wonder'd how they lov'd

The argument of this compliment audaciously imagined the eradication of the distinction between Jew and Christian. If Eve had possessed Richa's heart, then the fall would not have occurred. If the fall had not occurred, then there would have been no sin, and no need for the redemption of sin. In Eden man and woman would have known a love manifesting eternal joy. Only Flavia/Richa, an Eve greater than Eve, can suggest the possibility of a re-creation of Eden and the restoration of a paradisiacal love. In effect, a poety inspired by Richa might supplant the scripture in which the divisions of Christian and Jew are inscribed.

One of the wittiest of Home's poems provides a scabrous assessment of the scriptural judgments cast on the relation of the sexes. Taking its name from a traditional Scots fiddle tune, Home called his verse the "Black Joke: A Song":

The various ills that have happen'd to man
Have taken their rise, Since this World began
   From a black Joke &c.
What I have asserted the Bible shall prove
And demonstrate our miseries Sprung from the Love
   of a coal black Joke &ca
Our Paradice Dad ne'er had eaten the Fruit
If that Sly Devil Eve had not tempted him to't
   With her black Joke &ca
He tasted the Pippen, he mounted his Bride
He damn'd his whole race, and drove on till he dy'd
   At her coal black Joke &ca

The "black Joke" was that the Creator would make a creature whose sexual allure would kill Adam and damn humankind in perpetuity.

(God's creation, Eve, is the "Sly Devil.") The Bible proves that such grim consequences follow upon those who surrender to the impulse to untie the "Zone" of a "Flavia." Home's witty exercise in the hermeneutics of suspicion indicates that a poetry that served as a solvent for the narrative of the fall was his artistic remedy for the disjunction with the wished-for. He died in 1744 before the obstacles to his love for Richa could be entirely cleared. The poem his friends selected as the coda for his posthumous collection distilled his perplexity. It is an epigram upon his execution of a bookworm that violated a Bible by eating through Genesis. In the poem the speaker cast himself in the role of Jahweh, cursing and killing the transgressor:

> *Vermine accurst,* how couldst thou thus abuse
> This Precious product of the Noblest Muse?
> I gave thee Ample range o'er ev'ry Shelf,
> This Sacred Fruit reserving for my self;
> Eve thus in Eden broke tho's Gods betrest,
> And Damn'd Mankind to gratify her Taste,
> Nor dos't thou perish, tho thy Blood is Spilt,
> While thus the Muse perpetuates thy Guilt
> Like his thy Crime, like his thy Thirst of Fame,
> Who burnt a Temple, to preserve a Name.

Divine judgment was deflated by analogizing it to the resentment of a book lover crushing an insect. The promise of immortality, too, was parodied in the poet's fiat endowing the worm with everlasting life in a writing that perpetuated the creature's guilt. Writing, therefore, operated as the medium of a negative immortality in which being is preserved by "the Muse" in its perversity. The epigram also suggested that the immortality granted Eve by the Scriptures was that of the everlasting curse. The poem's concluding couplet alluded to the classical legend of Herostratus, the Athenian who set fire to the temple of Diana at Ephesus so that his name might be remembered. It supplied an ironic commentary on the nature of appetite—that faculty that led to Eve's and the worm's condemnation. What precisely was the hunger that made Eve break "Gods betrest"? The gratification of taste? The desire to be like God? The comparison to Herostratus proved the absurd answer, the yearning for the immortality of a bad reputation.

Home's attempt to dissolve Genesis did not preserve his name. He failed to obtain the Old Testament immortality of having his name perpetuated in his posterity, for he did not marry Richa Franks. He also failed to achieve that immortality granted by writing that was the solace of the cultivated pagans who were his literary models. Clubs were evanescent institutions and manuscripts precarious vehicles for preserving a reputation over time.

Richa Franks died without marrying. In a curious historical irony, she last appears in the written record in a pastiche of biblical history entitled "The Chapters of Isaac the Scribe,"[33] published in several issues of the *New York Journal or General Advertiser* beginning September 10, 1772. The anonymous author narrated her abandonment of America for London in 1769 upon the death of her parents. We learn that,

> 6. And Ri hie worshipped the God of her fathers, even of Abraham, of Isaac, and of Jacob, according to all the commandments wherewith he commanded his servant Moses.
>
> 7. She went not after other Gods, neither professed she in Jesus, the son of Mary, albeit the precepts of his law practiced she continually, doing unto all men as she would they should do unto her; yea doing justly, loving mercy and walking humbly before her God,—the same is the law, the prophets, and the gospel.

While "Isaac the Scribe" might conflate the law and the gospel and assert the moral equivalence of Jew and Christian, one cannot help viewing that Richa's gratification of her parents' wishes in the maintenance of her tradition entailed great personal cost. Her heritage made her "a barren vine," the immortality of posterity being forestalled. Her character as preserved in writing is refracted into an intangible classical phantasm or a pious Jewish daughter seeking the retirement of a brother's house after the death of her parents. We lack any unmediated testimony of her own self-understanding.

Cosmopolitanism, while it may have liberated the Jewish elite's conversation in the public realm, risked the annihilation of Jewish heritage and custom when that enlarged dialogue enabled love between Jews and Gentiles. Then the family/household where ethnic identity was most insistently manifested was threatened by assimilation to another tradition. The conflict between the public and familial spheres proved particularly troublesome for the mercantile elite, whose prosperity depended upon a broad commerce with persons of other cultures. Abigail Franks's distress at the intermarriage of her children would prove justified over the course of time. Every one of her grandchildren would eventually be baptized as a Christian. Even Moses, who despite his professions in favor of classical nymphs married his cousin Hila to keep with the faith, saw his daughter marry a gentile and avow Christianity. By the end of the eighteenth century both cosmopolitanism and its literary host, neo-classicism, became the subjects of intense critique within a Jewish tradition intent upon preserving itself. Thereafter, cosmopolitanism would be a critical threat as well as a liberating opportunity.

Notes

1. For the genealogy of the Levy-Franks clan, see Malcolm H. Stern, *Americans of Jewish Descent: A Compendium of Genealogy* (New York: Ktav Publishing House, 1971), 55–61. Also, Samuel Oppenheim, "Genealogical Notes on Jacob Franks," *Publications of the American Jewish Historical Society* 25 (1917), 75–80.

2. "ne réside plus que dans quelques grandes ames cosmopolites, qui franchissent les barrieres imaginaires qui séparent les peuples, et qui, à l'example de l'Etres souverain qui les a crèèes, embrassent tout le genre humain dans leur bienveillance." J. J. Rousseau, "Discours su l'origine et les fondemens de l'inégalité parmi les hommes," in *Oeuvres Completes De J. J. Rousseau,* 57 vols. (Paris, 1790), VII, 147.

3. For instance, Charles H. Lockett, *The Relations of French and English Society, 1763–1793* (London: Longmans, 1920). Ernst Cassirer, *The Philosophy of the Enlightenment,* trans. F. C. A. Koelln and J. P. Pettegrove (Princeton, N.J.: Princeton University Press, 1954). Peter Gay, *Enlightenment, an Interpretation* (New York: Knopf, 1967).

4. Hugh Harris, "Greek Origins of the Idea of Cosmopolitanism," *International Journal of Ethics* 38:1 (1927), 1–10. See also Thomas J. Schlereth, *The Cosmopolitan Ideal in Enlightenment Thought* (South Bend: University of Notre Dame Press, 1977), xvii–xix.

5. David S. Shields, "The Literary Topology of Mercantilism," in *Oracles of Empire: Poetry, Politics, and Commerce in British America, 1690–1750* (Chicago: University of Chicago Press, 1990).

6. The maxim appears as the last of Anne Bradstreet's "Meditations Divine and morall," in *The Works of Anne Bradstreet in Prose and Verse,* ed. John Havard Ellis (Gloucester, Mass.: Peter Smith, 1962), 73. It is a commonplace of the period.

7. Margaret Jacob, *The Radical Enlightenment: Pantheists, Freemasons and Republicans* (London: George Allen & Unwin, 1981).

8. Thomas Perry, *Public Opinion, Progaganda and Politics in Eighteenth-Century England: A Study of the Jew Bill of 1753* (Cambridge: Harvard University Press, 1962).

9. Jacob R. Marcus, *The Colonial American Jew, 1492–1776,* 3 vols. (Detroit: Wayne State University Press, 1970), I, 308–9.

10. An Aberdeen-educated schoolmaster, Alexander Malcolm taught "Latin, Mathematicks, Geometry, Allgebra, Geography, Navigation, and Merchant Book Keeping after the Most Perfect Manner." The members of the New York gentry sent their sons to his school for instruction.

11. Doris Groshen Daniels, "Colonial Jewry: Religion, Domestic and Social Relations," *American Jewish Historical Quarterly* (1947), 375–400.

12. Leo Hershkowitz and Isidore S. Meyer, eds., *The Lee Max Friedman Collection of Jewish Colonial Correspondence: Letters of the Franks Family, 1733–1748* (Waltham, Mass.: American Jewish Historical Society, 1968), 66–67. This collection of correspondence, mostly by Abigail Franks in New York to Naphtali Franks in London, contains a wealth of information on the circumstances of New World Jews. It is the primary literary document of American Jewry of the provincial era. All quotations from Abigail Franks's letters will be drawn from this text.

13. Abigail Franks here is rejecting the Jewish "oral law" and embracing a scriptural literalism akin to Reformed Protestant hermeneutics.

14. See Marie Rose de Labriolle, "Le Journal étranger dans l'histoire du cosmopolitisme littéraire," *Studies on Voltaire and the Eighteenth Century* 56 (1967), 783–97.

15. J. W. Horsely, *The Formation of English Neo-Classical Thought* (Princeton, N.J.: Princeton University Press, 1950).

16. Joseph Addison and Richard Steele, *The Spectator* (May 19, 1711).

17. Hans Robert Jauss, *Aesthetic Experience and Literary Hermeneutics,* trans. Michael Shaw (Minneapolis: University of Minnesota Press, 1982), 30–34.

18. Peter Clark, "Clubs and Sociability in Britain and the American Colonies in the 18th Century," Paper delivered to the Institute of Early American History and Culture, Williamsburg, Va., 1987. P. H. J. H. Gosden, *The Friendly Societies in England: 1815–1875* (Manchester: Manchester University Press, 1961).

19. Anthony Ashley Cooper, third earl of Shaftesbury, "Sensus Communis," in *Characteristicks of Men, Manners, Opinions, Times,* 2d ed. (London, 1714). See Lawrence E. Klein, "The Third Earl of Shaftesbury and the Progress of Politeness," *Eighteenth-Century Studies* 18 (Winter 1984–85), 186–214.

20. Elaine Breslaw, *Records of the Tuesday Club of Annapolis, 1745–1756* (Urbana and Chicago: University of Illinois Press, 1988), 86.

21. "Articles of the Society for Promoting Virtue and Knowledge, by a Free-Conversation," *Newport Historical Society Magazine* (1882), 67–71.

22. "A Club formed by the Jews, 1761," *Newport Historical Society Magazine* (1883), 58–60.

23. Archibald Home (1705?–1744), the third son of Sir John Home, baronet of Berwick, was the great poet of provincial New Jersey. Educated in Scotland, he emigrated to the colonies in 1733 in search of a place in the imperial bureaucracy. While residing in New York City, he attracted the notice of Lewis Morris, the deposed chief justice of New York, then engaged in a propaganda war against Governor William Cosby. When Morris ascended to the governorship of New Jersey in 1737, he appointed Home deputy secretary of the province, then secretary of the provincial council, then a member of His Majesty's Council. Residing in Trenton, the provincial capital, Home gathered around him a literary circle.

24. One of several copies of the poetry collection prepared after Home's death in 1744, Laing III, 452, was probably the manuscript carried by Archibald's brother, James, from Charleston to Scotland, when James became baronet of Berwick in 1746. Another copy was destroyed in the great fire of Paterson, N.J., in 1902.

25. The subordination of self to art in the labor of this working toward perfection may be viewed as antithetical to the cult of literary celebrity that booksellers were constructing around Alexander Pope during this period, for the cult elevated the author above the work, commodifying the creator's name.

26. Moses Franks may have known Home as early as 1733, the year of Home's arrival in New York City. Franks was then enrolled as a student in the school conducted by Andrew and Quenten Malcolm. Quenten Malcolm and Home were members of the Scots club that feasted on St. Andrews Day. The schoolmaster may have introduced his pupil to Home in order to inaugurate the young man's education in poetry, a subject not taught in the classroom.

27. Hans Jonas, *The Gnostic Religion: The Message of the Alien God and the Beginnings of Christianity* (Boston: Beacon Press, 1963), 31–34.

28. Of British American clubs the Tuesday Club in Annapolis most elaborated their self-understanding as an aesthetic entity. The conduct of club affairs became a playful parody of civil life in the British Empire. They devised a club mythology, history, politics, and rite. These are captured in Alexander Hamilton's *History of the Tuesday Club,* 3 vols., ed. Robert Micklus (Chapel Hill: University of North Carolina Press, Institute of Early American History and Culture, 1990).

29. George Webb, *Bachelors Hall* (Philadelphia: Franklin, 1730).

30. Popularized by publication of John Pomfret's *The Choice* (London, 1700), the genre produced countless personal programs of preference. For direct analogues to Moses Franks's poem see Philander, "The Choice," *Boston Gazette* (5 March 1751); Unnamed Poem, *New York Gazette* (5 July 1764); Royall Tyler, "Choice of a Wife," *New Hampshire and Vermont Journal* (6 December 1796).

31. This is not to diminish the immense importance of synagogues and rabbinical academies in the survival of the tradition. During those periods of European history when public worship was forbidden by the state, however, the family proved to be the essential binding force of the religion.

32. That R F was a Jewess is indicated in Home's explanatory note to the poem: "The Jewish Law (a Law dictated by God himself) allow'd the poor to make oblations proportion'd to their Abilities; He who could not attain to a bullock, A Ram, a Lamb &ca might attone for a trespass, or express his Gratitude to the great Author and Preserver of his Being by a Turtle Dove, or a Young Pidgeon." Richa Franks was the only Jewish R F known to have been in the circle of Home's acquaintance.

33. Samuel Oppenheim, "The Chapters of Isaac the Scribe," *American Jewish Historical Society* (1914), 40–51.

9

Ethnic Humor in Early American Jest Books

Robert Secor

There are few better indicators of the cultural anxieties and tensions behind ethnic attitudes than the jokes people tell. As Keith Thomas says, "When we laugh we betray our innermost assumptions."[1] One of the best sources for understanding ethnic attitudes in early America is the overlooked jest books that flourished in the eighteenth and early nineteenth centuries. The first jest book published in America was probably the pamphlet-sized *Collection of Funny, Moral, and Entertaining Stories and Bon Mots,* issued by Daniel Bowen of New Haven in 1787. Two years later, in the year of Washington's first inauguration, John Wyeth published for Mathew Carey of Philadelphia America's first extensive jest book, and its most popular: *The American Jest Book,* with its attached second part, *The Merry Fellow's Companion*. About 200 pages long, it would see at least eight different editions by the end of the century. Jest books continued to proliferate into the 1830s (the last edition of *The American Jest Book* was 1833), when they faded before the advent of the comic almanacs. In all, the following discussion of ethnic humor results from a review of twenty-three jest books published in the eighteenth and early nineteenth centuries, with the focus on the ethnic attitudes revealed in those published between 1787 and 1811.

When different cultures come into contact with each other, we can expect ethnic humor. As the colonists were forming attitudes toward the two groups they would most exploit in building their country—the one that they found native to the land and whom they would eventually displace, and the one that they brought here in order to enslave—they began shaping stories and telling jokes involving Native Americans and transplanted Africans. At the same time, the English settlers brought with them their prejudices and their stereotypes of other ethnic groups, such as the Irish and Scottish, the French and the German, the Dutch and the Jews, and a large percentage of entries in these jest books can be traced to English sources or settings. Since these ethnic groups entered an American pot which did not always melt, we should not be surprised that in the new republic these groups remained targets of ethnic humor, as old ethnic jokes were retold or reconstructed and new ones invented.

While recognizing that ethnic humor predates the eighteenth century, Christie Davies has recently argued that the enormous popularity of ethnic humor in England in that century can be ascribed to its emergence as an industrial society.[2] As the first industrial nation, Britain was also the first to feel the need for ethnic humor to counter the impersonality of a large-scale capitalist society. The sense of collective identity came to be defined by ethnicity and otherness attributed to those outside ethnic boundaries, instead of simply boundaries of place. Thus in eighteenth-century England jokes mocking ethnic traits replaced those that ridiculed the characteristics of inhabitants from Nottingham or Lancashire. The British who became Americans—clearing the wilderness with a biblical sense of mission as God's chosen people doing His work, building their city on the hill while searching for a national identity—might have found particular satisfaction in ethnic humor. Such humor is, after all, based on an ethnocentric view of the world, whereby everything is referenced to one's own group as the center of value, nourishing the group's own pride and vanity. From that vantage point, humor is a device of control, serving to keep the social value system intact. Theories of humor have also described it as a device of conflict, whereby contempt of outsiders is expressed in order to support the sense of moral superiority and the social and political status of the group telling the jokes. Studies in the sociology of humor show how humor functions to police a group's or a nation's boundaries, whether social, geographical, or moral. The values of the dominant group are reinforced by ascribing to the outsider those values it rejects, mocking them as ludicrous through laughter. James Sulley called laughter "a prophylactic against contamination from outside peoples."[3]

No kind of humor serves this function better than ethnic humor, as Charles Schutz implies in summing up the historic American attitude toward ethnic immigrants:

Historically, America accepted all foreigners (who were deemed assimil-
able!), but they were to become "Americans"; that is, they were to conform to the dominant customs and values of the white, Protestant, English-
speaking, Northern European ethnic stock. The possible political penalty
for remaining outside the mainstream was to be charged with a uniquely
American political sin, "un-Americanism." A much less drastic social
penalty was to be ridiculed with ethnic jokes.[4]

In this respect, ethnic humor is related to gender humor, whereby sexual
social dominance is revealed and determined by who tells the jokes. For
example, one of the jest books reports a rape case, in which the defendant says he told the plaintiff that if he caught her stealing his faggots
again he would have his way with her. When he did catch her again, in
jest he demanded personal restitution, at which point, he claims, she
willingly submitted. In dismissing the case, the judge advises the man
not to threaten the ladies that way again, unless he wants to be left
"without a stick in your hedge."[5] The jest supports a system that gives
power to the men who sit behind the bench and who own the land, not to
the poor peasant woman whose need drives her to steal wood for her fire.
At the same time, it reinforces the phallocentric belief that the rape
victim has gotten what she has been seeking all along.

What is clear is that ethnic and gender humor can be used aggressively
for political purposes in the desire to protect the social hierarchy. Noting
that Freud saw jokes as a social process, since they require a social
context in which they are shared, Werner Sollors observes that "the
community of laughter itself is an ethnicizing phenomenon, as we develop a sense of we-ness in laughing with others."[6] Perhaps no text
illustrates this function of laughter better than Hawthorne's "My Kins-
man, Major Molineux." Robin's sense of isolation from the early rum-
blings of Revolutionary America is signaled by various kinds of laughter, indicating the beginnings of a bonded society from which, until he
himself joins the laughter, he is excluded. One way of laughing at ethnic
groups who are outside a bonded society is to make fun of their way of
talking. Dialect is thus used in ethnic humor to define borders, to mock
groups for their most recognizable differences from the dominant culture, and to laugh at their inability to assimilate into it. As linguists have
pointed out, only a few stereotypic sounds will suffice to caricature the
language of an ethnic group.[7] Stories about Germans, for example,
almost always depend on such caricaturing of their pronunciation of

English, as we see in the ethnicization of the following jest from America's first jest book: "A Bill was once brought in, in the assembly of a neighbouring State, for the purpose of organizing the Militia. A venerable old man arose and opposed the Bill, for, says he, our Militia have good Drum's and Fifes, and therefore I think it needless these hard times to be at the expence of purchasing them Organs."[8] Forty years later, the jest is ethnicized as follows: "During the Embargo, a debate was had in the General Assembly of Pennsylvania, upon the expediency of a new organization of the Militia; during which, a member from one of the German shires, exclaimed, 'Mr. Speaker, me tink de Militia mit do mit de drums and fifes, mitout de organs.'"[9] The jest is thus transformed from one that pokes mild fun at a venerable old man into an ethnocentric joke about Germans. Americans defend themselves by bonding together in their militia, so in the ethnic version of this jest the difficulties the German has in understanding the dominant language as well as the accent with which he speaks it identifies him as the outsider who has not assimilated and earned the right to be considered wholly American. The ethnic outsider thus becomes what John Lowe calls "a kind of societal 'clown' who distorts the idea of the 'normal' WASP American."[10] As we will see, the use of dialect in ethnic humor differs according to the attitudes held toward the various groups being targeted.

Native Americans

In the American imagination there are, as in Cooper, good Indians and bad Indians. Howard Mumford Jones, in *O Strange World* (1952), traced some of the shifts in the western imagination from the "Image" of the heroic noble savage to the "Anti-Image" of the demonic Indian. However, ethnic images of Native Americans in the jest books of the eighteenth and early nineteenth centuries are almost wholly favorable. Theories of conflict and control thus do not seem to apply. The ethnocentric principle, by which each group assumes its own superiority but treats with contempt the customs and codes of outsiders when they differ from their own, does not seem to operate. The best theoretical explanation we have for this phenomenon is that tentatively offered by William Martineau, who speculates that in the unlikely occurrence of humor esteeming an outgroup, the latter has probably been adopted as a reference group.[11]

That early American jest books did not treat Native Americans' speech in comic dialect or give them stereotypical ethnic names (although they would sometimes be given such panegyrical epithets as "the copper-coloured warrior") signals the difference in approach between stories involving this group and those concerning other ethnic groups. In fact, the language of Native Americans in these jest books is almost always heightened, informed by eloquent rhetorical tropes: "An Indian chief of the Creek nation, being once appointed to negotiate a treaty of peace with the people of South Carolina, was desired by the governor and council to speak his mind freely, and not to be afraid, for he was among friends. 'I will speak freely, for I will not be afraid,' said he, 'for why should I be afraid among my friends, who never was afraid among my enemies.'"[12] Thomas Jefferson tried to explain why, in his opinion, Native American oratory rivaled that of the great Roman orators. His theory depended on a romantic view of unconstrained Native American societies. The reference at the end of the following passage from *Notes on the State of Virginia* is to the eloquent and moving speech of the defeated Tachnechdorus, known to the colonists as John Logan, whose family was massacred by a party of whites in 1774:

> The principles of their society forbidding all compulsion, they are to be led to duty and to enterprize by personal influence and persuasion. Hence eloquence in council, bravery and address in war, become the foundations of all consequence with them. To these acquirements all their faculties are directed. Of their bravery and address in war we have multiplied proofs, because we have been the subjects on which they were exercised. Of their eminence in oratory we have fewer examples, because it is displayed chiefly in their own councils. Some, however, we have of very superior lustre. I may challenge the whole orations of Demosthenes and Cicero, and of any more eminent orator, if Europe has furnished more eminent, to produce a single passage, superior to the speech of Logan.[13]

Tachnechdorus's speech was given wide circulation, first in the *Virginia Gazette* and then in a number of other colonial and European newspapers; in the early nineteenth century it was reprinted in Irving's *Sketch-Book* and in *McGuffey's Reader*. It thus must have played a large part in the mythic view of the Native American, whose oratorical abilities were seen as an appropriate expression of his natural nobility.

The Native American, Jefferson also said, "meets death with more deliberation, and endures tortures with a firmness unknown almost to religious enthusiasm with us."[14] Supporting this romantic image of the

Native American was the popular genre of Indian death songs, which depicted heroic Indians facing death with unyielding spirit and courage. During the approximate period of these jest books, from the 1780s to the early 1820s, Thomas Tanselle has found twenty-six versions of one of these, the "Song of Alknomook."[15] In Royall Tyler's *The Contrast* (1787), it is sung by Maria, who says afterward, "There is something in this song which ever calls forth my affections. The manly virtue of courage, that fortitude which steels the heart against the keenest misfortunes, which interweaves the laurel of glory amidst the instruments of torture and death, displays something so noble, so exalted, that in spite of the prejudices of education I cannot but admire it, even in a savage."[16] This image of the noble savage is evoked not only by Tyler but also in a number of American plays from the mid-eighteenth to the mid-nineteenth century.

Understandably, then, anecdotes concerning the bravery of Native Americans, particularly before torture and death, are staples of these jest books. When one was taken by his enemies, he "told them, with a bold voice, that he was a very noted warrior, and gained most of his martial preferment at the expence of their nation, and was desirous of shewing them in the act of dying, that he was still as much superior to them as when he headed his gallant countrymen against them."[17] So brave (and innocent) is the Native American warrior that the only explanation that can satisfy him when he sees General Forbes (in the 1758 western expedition) being carried in a litter is that conceived by Colonel Weiser: "This man is so terrible in war, that we are obliged to confine him, and let him write his orders; for if he was let loose on the world, he would deluge it with blood."[18]

The Native American is mythicized not only for his courage and gallantry before his enemies but also for his extraordinary powers of observation, which at their best made him a kind of Sherlock Holmes of the forest:

> An Indian upon his return home to his hut one day, discovered his venison, which had been hung up to dry, had been stolen. After taking his observations upon the spot, he set off in pursuit of the thief, whom he traced through the woods. After going some distance he met some persons of whom he enquired if they had not seen a little old white man, with a short gun, and accompanied by a small dog, with a bob tail. They replied in the affirmative, and upon the Indian assuring them that the man thus described had stolen his venison they desired to be informed how he was able to give

such a minute description of a person, whom it appeared he had not seen. The Indian answered thus: "The thief I know is a little man, by his having made a pile of stones to stand upon, in order to reach the venison from the height I hung it, standing on the ground; that he is an old man, I know by his short steps, which I have traced over the dead leaves in the woods; and that he is a white man, I know by his turning out his toes when he walks, which an Indian never does. His gun I know to be short, by the mark which the muzzle made by rubbing the bark of the tree against which it had leaned; that his dog is small, I know by his tracks; and that he has a bob tail, I discovered by the mark it made in the dust where he was sitting, at the time his master was taking down the meat." [19]

The frontier thesis first formulated by Frederick Jackson Turner may help suggest why earlier Americans constructed romantic anecdotes rather than abusive ethnic stories about Native Americans. According to Turner, the wilderness stripped the colonist of his European garments of civilization and dressed him in moccasins and a hunting shirt; it ejected him from his railroad car and landed him in a birch canoe. [20] In an essay preceding his classic formulation of "the American Adam," R. W. B. Lewis reflected on the "uniquely American idea . . . of a new, unspoiled area in which a genuine radical moral freedom could once again be exercised—as once, long ago, it had been, in the garden of Eden." [21] Lewis's "uniquely American idea" informed the various hero narratives, beginning in 1786 with John Filson's *Adventures of Daniel Boone,* which depicted the American at home in the wilderness; although the Native American is the enemy, nevertheless the qualities of the new American hero are frequently those he shares and even has learned from him. As usual, D. H. Lawrence was on to something when he wrote of Fenimore Cooper's "lovely wish fulfillments." While one part of Cooper loved his European place and sense of himself as the American writer abroad, another part belonged to the "tomahawking continent of America," in which he imagined himself as the Deerslayer. [22] In the case of the Native American, white settlers chose to blur rather than to protect their boundaries, which explains why the resulting ethnic anecdotes are very different from those depicting other ethnic groups. As Richard Slotkin has observed, "The savage trusted his natural passions, innocent of the consequences of his individualism and self-indulgence; the colonist had learned to use his intellect and conscience to conceive the American experience as a blending of Indian and European characteristics." [23] Now we can see the relevance of Martineau's speculation that when the in-group tells stories that esteem the out-group, it is because it has adopted the latter as a reference group.

Eighteenth-century jest books occasionally do evoke the stereotype of the Indian who has had too much to drink, but even here the emphasis of the anecdotes is very different from that of the later nineteenth-century stories collected by Dawson. Dawson's drunken Indians talk like Tonto, but the Native Americans whom Jefferson praised for their rhetorical heights wax eloquent as they lament the transforming power of liquor. "It seem to me," says the copper-colored warrior, "to be a juice extracted from the tongues of women and the hearts of lions; for after drinking freely of it, I was as loquacious as a woman and felt as bold as a lion." [24] There may be implicit in these anecdotes some self-accusation on the part of the white civilizers for having introduced firewater to these noble savages. This appears to be the meaning of the following reproof: "'I am glad,' said the Rev. Dr. Y——s to the chief of the Little Ottawas, 'that you do not drink whiskey, but it grieves me to find that your people use so much of it.' 'Ah yes!' replied the chief, and he fixed an impressive eye upon the doctor, which communicated the reproof before he uttered it, 'we Indians use a great deal of whiskey, but we do not make it.'" [25]

What other evidence is there that the dominant culture sensed the guilt of their position, as they honored the reference group through its images while exploiting it in actuality? At least one jest seems to hint at the guile white Americans used to wrest the Native American's land from him. In it, an Indian chief tells the superintendent of Indian affairs, Sir William Johnson, that he dreamed Sir William had given him one of his suits. Sir William takes the hint and makes him a gift of one—at a price, though, for at their next meeting Sir William says that he dreamed that the chief had given him a present of 5,000 acres of particularly valuable land. The chief presents him with the land immediately, "but not without making the shrewd remark: 'Now, Sir William, I will never dream with you again, you dream too hard for me.'" [26] The tale indicates that the Native American played by the rules, even if it meant he would thereby lose the game—at the same time as it reminds us that indeed he did.

There is also implicit judgment of how the Native American was being demeaned in the adaptation of a couplet Pope devised for the Prince of Wales's dog: "I am his highness' dog at Kew / Pray tell me, Sir, whose dog are you!" The sentiment reappears transformed in the jest books as follows: "A white man meeting an Indian, asked him, 'whose Indian are you?' To which, the copperfaced genius replied, 'I am God Almighty's Indian, whose Indian are you?'" This Indian is nobody's dog. He belongs to a noble race, and to God Almighty. By implication, the white man who would own him must answer to that God—and wonder to whom he himself belongs.[27]

Guilt could be denied by castigating the Spaniards as enslavers, as the following jest book entry suggests: "The horrible atrocities practiced by the Spanish ecclesiastics against the amiable and simple inhabitants of the new world, shortly after its discovery by Columbus, are familiar to every one. 'Are there any Spaniards in the Heaven which you promise us as the reward of our becoming Christians?' exlaimed a native of Cuba, to a fanatic priest. 'If there are, we desire not to follow them.'"[28] However, as the nineteenth century moved on, it became more difficult to avoid the realities of how the United States was treating Native Americans, and that treatment could not coincide with a romantic conception of them as a people of natural nobility. To rationalize and justify the country's harsh policies toward Native Americans, a different stereotype was needed. This is the stereotype we see in the stories Dawson collected, a catalog of pratfalls taken by drunken Indians who, having fallen far from Jefferson's classical orators, speak a demeaning dialect of Pidgin English. As Sollors claims, by the middle of the nineteenth century "the noble Indian became a ridiculous figure."[29] In a characteristic story from Dawson, Indian John induces Squire Hills to supply him with liquor for the funeral ceremony of his friend, Sam. However, the squire finds Sam in a drunken stupor and confronts John with his lie. "Me not lie," insists John. "Me think him dead; he say so himself."[30] Ethnic humor has often served the purposes of political aggression, even genocide, as Sollors points out in referring to anti-Armenian jokes in Turkey and anti-Jewish jokes in Nazi Germany.[31] Thus as Americans destroyed the Native Americans they had idealized, confining survivors to boundaried reservations, they found ways of shifting the stereotypes of them in their humor to satisfy their own psychic and political needs.

African Americans

The first settlement of Africans in North America was in 1619, the year before the Mayflower landed in Plymouth, when English colonists at

Jamestown bought twenty black Africans from a Dutch frigate. Most of the slaves who subsequently arrived in the colonies came between 1741 and 1810 (the legal slave trade ended in 1807), so it is not surprising that we see a number of entries treating blacks in eighteenth-century jest books.

Attitudes toward blacks in these jests were very different from those toward Native Americans from the start. The colonists fantasized that they shared characteristics with Native Americans; they believed themselves morally superior to the Spaniards who enslaved them while denying their own role as exploiters. They could not deny their own enslavement of Africans, however, and so while they romanticized Native Americans, they cast African Americans as inferior beings, in some ways perhaps less than human. In one self-justifying entry from an 1830 jest book, the enslavement of the African is explained as a humanistic impulse that was necessary to save Native Americans from the despicable Spaniards:

> The slave trade originated in a feeling of humanity: Barthelemi de las Casas, Bishop of Chiapa in Peru, witnessing the dreadful cruelties of the Spaniards to the Indians, exerted his eloquence to prevent it. He returned to Spain, pleaded the cause of the Indians before the Emperor Charles V. in person, and suggested that their place as labourers might be supplied by negroes from Africa, who were then considered as descendants of Cain, under the proscription of their Maker, and fit only for beasts of burden. The Emperor accordingly, made regulations in favor of the Indians; and consented to the slavery of the African negroes, by which the American Indians were freed from the cruelty of the Spaniards.[32]

As with the Native American, we can find in the natural consciousness two contrary images of the African American: the simpleton Sambo and the threatening savage; and as with Native Americans, these different stereotypes have been evoked according to shifting cultural needs. At times, as in the use of Willie Horton in the 1988 presidential campaign, the image of the savage has served the white American's purposes, political or otherwise. For the most part, however, as Joseph Boskin suggests, white Americans have repressed the image of the threatening savage, preferring instead to emphasize Sambo.[33] The Sambo image assuaged white guilt by conveying the notion that blacks were by nature inferior creatures, lazy and shiftless but simplemindedly happy even in their enslavement, so that their subordination was in the natural order of things. Jefferson first raised the question of racial differences in intelligence between blacks and whites, speculating that blacks "are inferior to the whites in the endowments both of body and mind,"[34] and in the late nineteenth century, social Darwinists argued that black oppression was justified because blacks were on an evolutionary track different from whites, and the rule of "survival of the fittest" had to be obeyed.

The earliest appearances of the simpleminded Sambo stereotype can be found in these eighteenth-century jest books. There he is usually called Sambo or given some comic name—Cuff, Cato, Quath, Mongo, or Caesar. Since dialect is a device used by oppressors to mark ethnic differences and suggest the stupidity of the oppressed, the jest books' black always speaks in dialect. In this dialect "th" becomes "d" or "t," "st" becomes "ss," and words may begin with a "t" where no consonant is called for; thus we have, "No, massa, dem toder tree fly away." Consonants or whole syllables can also be left off the beginning of words, so that "steal" becomes "teal" and "suppose" becomes "spose." A double "e" is frequently added to verbs so that "work" becomes "workee." Idioms are mangled, and articles and auxiliaries are frequently left out. "Me" is always used instead of "I," and "be" when grammar calls for "am" or "are." Dialect is then used in support of the stereotype of simpleton Sambo. Caesar shakes himself off after stumbling in the dark: " 'I wonder' says Caesar, rising, and rubbing the mud, &c. from off his holiday suit, 'why de debil de sun no shine in deese dark nights, Cato, and not always keep shining in de day time, when dere's no need of him.' "[35] A tradesman tells his lazy black servant that he must get up at sunrise, " 'At sun rise, massa?' replies the African. 'But suppose, massa, the sun rise before day-light—What I do den, sir?' "[36] The Sambo stereotype remains the same in the jest books of the nineteenth century. In one, a slow learner is confounded by the rules of etiquette as well as by the latest European fashion, a double-breasted coat, since he has been told to hand the plate on the buttonhole side of his guests: "He looked first at one side of the gentleman's coat, then at the other, and finally, quite confounded by the outlandish make of the stranger's garment, he cast a despairing look at his master, and exclaiming in a loud voice, 'Buttonholes at both sides, massa,' handed the plate right over the gentleman's head."[37]

Sambo is also at times depicted as a petty thief, but he is so simpleminded that he is easy to catch. When a West Indian gentleman finds some money stolen, he gathers the blacks at his sugar works and tells them that a great serpent had appeared to him during the night and told him that whoever stole his money would have a parrot's feather growing at the point of his nose. The thief, of course, immediately touches his nose, and so the plantation owner recovers his money.[38] The inclusion of dishonesty as part of the stereotype of Sambo resulted in the ethnicizing of the following jest: "Two very honest gentlemen, who dealt in brooms, meeting one day in the street, one asked the other, How the devil he could afford to undersell him every where as he did, when he stole the stuff, and made the brooms himself? Why, you silly dog, answered the other, I steal them ready made."[39] In the 1811 *Chaplet of Comus,* the jest reappears as follows: "Two negroes who dealt in brooms, meeting one day in the street, Sam asked, 'how de debil, Cato, you afford to sell cheaper than me when I teal de tuff?' 'Ah, you fool (says the other), I teal them ready made.'"[40]

Occasionally, these jests allow that the world is not as black and white as slaveholders would like to believe: "A negro servant being asked what colour he believed the devil was? Why, replied the African, the white men paint him black, we say he is white; but from his great age, and being called Old Nick, I should suppose him grey."[41] When an old gentleman tells Cato that he has arranged to have him buried in the family vault, Cato declines the honor: "Massa, suppose we be buried togeder, and de devil come looking for massa in de dark, he might take away poor negar man in mistake."[42] Here the jest teller shows at least a hint of awareness that, if anyone belongs to the devil, it is the white man. At times Sambo is allowed to express his sense of unfairness in the different roles he and his master play. An African who is not overly fond of work complains about the injustice in the fact "dat de poor negar man must worke so hard, and massa do nothing." The master tells Quath that, to the contrary, he has "head-work, and yours is mere bodily exercise." The next day Quath announces that he himself has spent the day doing head-work, but he is of course too ignorant to have succeeded: "'Well, let me hear what your head has done.'—'Suppose, massa, dere be five pigeons on dis tree, and you take a gun and soot two of dem, how many dere be left?'—'Why, three, you old sinner.'—'No, massa, dem toder tree fly away.'"[43]

The conclusion may be that head work is not for such as Quath, or the point may be that the black slave lives in the real world where birds do fly away, or it might be that, unable to do the arithmetic in which he was not trained, Quath uses mother wit to solve the problem in real terms.

Our very uncertainty reveals how ethnic humor exposes ambivalent attitudes toward the oppressed, as feelings of self-justification wrestle with repressed guilt. At the same time as white masters kept their slaves illiterate, they found their inability to read and write or to add and subtract comic characteristics, for such humor assuaged their guilt and enforced the stereotype of the black as stupid and ignorant. Some stories, including perhaps the one we have just recounted, depended on the ways Sambo got around his ignorance or the uses to which he put it. The following jest shows the pretentious scholar, also a frequent target of these jest books, bested by Sambo, because the latter is or pretends to be unable to grasp the basic principles behind mathematical questions:

> A young man, who had attended considerably to arithmetic, and formed pretty towering ideas of his skill in that science, the other day addressed himself to an African in the following manner: "Boston, I can take a pen and ink and in three minutes can cypher out and tell you how many minutes you have to live"—"Can na you massa, you must be a very good cypher indeed. I aske you a question, Which can see best, a mare stone blind or a horse without eyes?" Pho, that's no question at all. "I aske you another, 'pose he be ten rods to Nichols's, how far you call him away out yonder?" That I can't tell neither, replied he. "Well, I aske one more, 'pose fifty rail make one load, how many he take to make a da——d great pile?" So many unanswerable questions quite confounded our young conceited arithmetician. He began to think he did not know every thing, and retreated from the lists of his African antagonist, with shame and confusion.[44]

As we have seen, even while working with the stereotype of Sambo, some of these jests give hints of sympathy for his position and allow him lines that impart a sense of injustice. Only one of the jest books surveyed, however, *The American Magazine of Wit,* printed in New York by H. C. Southwick in 1808, seems seriously concerned with changing attitudes toward blacks. One jest, set during the Revolutionary War, targets the hypocrisy of the colonist fighting for his freedom while at the same time he was enslaving Africans. The master, a Connecticut clergyman, is confronted by his slave, Jack:

> To contend for liberty with one hand, and inslave the poor African with the other, was, to Jack's understanding, a palpable inconsistency:—who, under the impression of this, and sighing for that freedom which is the natural right of man, Jack, one day came to his master, and addressed him in the following manner: "I observe, sir, you keep always preaching about liberty, and praying for liberty, and I love to hear you, sir; for liberty be a

good ting: you preach well, and you pray well: but one ting, massa, you must remember; poor Jack be no free yet.''

The clergyman is struck by the propriety of Jack's plea and sets him free, ultimately to "become a man of some interest and respectability."[45]

In another entry in the same jest book, a slave defends himself before a justice of the peace in Philadelphia against the charge of possessing stolen property: " 'If de black rascal be whipt for buying tolen goods, me hope de white rascal be whipt too for the same ting, when we catch him, as well as Caesar.' 'To be sure,' rejoined his worship. 'Well den,' says Caesar, 'here be Tom's massa—hold him fast, constable, he buy Tom, as I buy the piccaninny knife, and de piccaninny cork-screw. He knew very well poor Tom be tolen from this old fadder and mudder, de knife and de cork-screw have neder.' "[46] Another jest from the same source points to the heroism of black soldiers during the Revolutionary War, particularly one who bore with the stoic dignity the painful amputation of both an arm and a leg: "Neber mind, massa, take um off—tank God, I got noder leg and noder arm left for um yet." The anecdote ends with the comment, "Had he been a freeman instead of an African, how would he have been celebrated."[47]

There is also an entry in this jest book that makes an emotional case against the horrors of slavery. It claims to be an extract from a Georgia gentleman to a friend in Newark:

> While on this subject (the importation of negroes), I will relate an affecting anecdote that came to my knowledge yesterday. My neighbour, Mr. B. had purchased twenty of that unfortunate race, a few weeks ago, in Charleston; among whom was a woman about twenty years of age. On the way home, they stopped to pass the night at a house on the road, just as the negroes belonging to the owner of the place were returning from their labour in the field. One of them proved to be the husband of the woman. They had been torn asunder two years before in Africa. They met in this distant clime, and with such emotions of joy, mixed with bitterness and grief, on the recollection of their past and present condition, as may be more easily conceived than described. They flew to each other—asked an hundred eager questions—and looking at the spectators, who sympathised in their feelings, declared they would never be parted. Mr. B., who is a man of humanity, was present at the affecting scene. He immediately offered the owner of the husband to sell the wife, or purchase the husband—but in vain! He then offered two negroes for the man—but the wretch would do

neither. The momentary pleasure the poor creatures experienced when Mr. B. was endeavouring to prevent their being separated, was converted into frantic agony when they saw nothing would avail. All who were present, black and white, united in entreaties; and every eye but the miscreant owner of the husband was in tears. Nothing would soften his obdurate heart—and the unhappy victims of his cruelty were a second time literally torn asunder.

The entry ends with a cry for humanity: "O man, man! what a devil thou art, when thou forgetest thy nature."[48]

In these jests, *The American Magazine of Wit* strikes at the very hypocrisy and immorality of the institution of slavery, underscoring its inhumanity, reminding the reader of black sacrifices and heroism in the Revolutionary War, and evoking the unnatural horrors perpetrated on the slaves and their families. Sympathetic images of slaves and their frequently cruel masters would be given fuller reality later in the century by Harriet Beecher Stowe and others for whom the plight of the black in America was no joke at all.

Irishman and Scotchman

Along with blacks and Native Americans, the Irish were the most frequent targets of ethnic humor. However, whereas the other two groups were objects of ethnic humor largely because the new Americans who told the jests were structuring their attitudes toward them in the New World, the Irish were butts of ethnic jests largely because the American settlers brought their stereotypes with them. "The Irish are a fair people," Dr. Jonson observed. "They never speak well of one another."[49] Since the colonists did not leave their prejudices or their jests behind them, we should not be surprised that the stereotype of the stage Irishman crossed the waters as well. At the same time, however, the Irish themselves also crossed the waters, so contact between the groups remained, and Irish jokes continued to serve the usual purposes of ethnic humor in preserving the cultural boundaries of the dominant group.

The Irish were the largest group of non-English immigrants in colonial America, and during the first half of the nineteenth century, particularly after the potato blight of 1845, they constituted the first great mass migration to the United States. "It's the very place for an Irishman to live in," a jest book Irishman writes from Philadelphia, "whiskey's only a hapenny a glass, and there hasn't been a man hung in this county for twenty years."[50] With so many religious and economic reasons to leave Ireland during the seventeenth and eighteenth centuries, Irish immigration to the New World can be traced to the earliest days of colonization, and it is esimated that there were about 400,000 immigrants of Irish descent in the new republic in 1790. Moreover, in the seventeenth century many involuntary Catholic emigrants were sold into indentured servitude and sent to the West Indies; as a result, by the 1660s there were more than 12,000 Irish Catholics in the West Indies, and many of these eventually found their way to the mainland colonies. The early Irish presence in the West Indies explains the following entry in a nineteenth-century jest book:

> It is but little known in the United States, that in the island of St. Thomas the Irish language is a good deal spoken, even amongst blacks. A passenger vessel having arrived at New-York, at a time when the weather was excessively hot, happened to moor next to a schooner from that island; and one day, when a sturdy Hibernian was landing with his family, he was not a little surprised to hear his native Gaelic spoken fluently by some man standing on the wharf, whose complexion was none of the fairest, and whose hands were rather more lanigerous than he had been accustomed to see in the Emerald Isle—"Arrah," says Paddy, to the man next him, "how long are you in the country, friend?" (supposing him to be from the land of potatoes, like himself)—"Only three days," replied the negro; "we reached this port on Monday last"—"Holy virgin!" exlaimed the affrightened emigrant, looking pitifully at his wife and children—"Only three days in the country, Judy, and turned as black as my hat! Och! that we were safe in oulde Ireland again!"[51]

The eighteenth century saw a variation of the indenture system, where a number of Irish immigrants came as what were called "redemptions." Unable to afford the full fare, they emigrated by paying only a part of their passage. After their arrival they would either find a "redeemer" (usually a friend or relative) to pay the balance, or they would be sold for a period of time as indentured servants. An 1833 jest captures this period of "about fifty years ago" when a ship arrived at Philadelphia from Londonderry with a cargo of redemptions, one of whom, Michael M'Sherry, is purchased as an indentured servant from the captain, "a full-fed, round-shouldered Dutch agriculturist, named Simon Stover." Simon is too fond of "a leetle sweet vine" and "goot branty-ale," which proves to be his downfall:

Mr. Stover was well pleased with the appearance of his Irisher, and, having equipped him in a decent new suit of habilments, took his departure one afternoon, in a gig, and after repeated libations, they both arrived safe at the little town of Darby, where they slept. Next morning, after some egg-nog and bitters, they started again, and M'Sherry, being by this time pretty well acquainted with the peculiarities of his German companion, thought it would be no difficult matter, and no sin, not only to obtain his liberty in this land of freedom, but also to put a little money into his pocket, to help him along the road. When Mr. Stover had slaked his thirst so frequently as to render him completely insensible to what was passing around him, his man Mike drove off the high road into a lane, and, having encased himself in the Dutchman's broad-brimmed hat, coat, and boots, replaced his own shoes, coat, and hat, in exchange, and then metamorphosed, they arrived at one of the inns at Chester, a little after dark. M'Sherry passing himself as the master, and the Dutch farmer as the man. It was no easy matter to get Mr. Stover carried up stairs, to bed; however, there he was at length deposited; M'Sherry all the while cursing his ill-luck, in having laid out his money upon such a drunken hog of a Dutch Redemptioner, and offering to dispose of him to any person who would be bothered with him, for half his cost. He was not long without a purchaser. A bargain was shortly struck; one hundred dollars was paid down for him, by the landlord himself.[52]

The story has a happy ending, however, as Stover eventually establishes his real identity as a wealthy landowner of Frederick County, Maryland, while M'Sherry ends up in western Pennsylvania, where he leads a successful life and leaves a considerable estate to his wife and children. In discussing settlement patterns of the Irish, *The Harvard Encyclopedia of American Ethnic Groups* says, "The majority of Irish immigrants remained in the Northeast, but a significant proportion, generally after 'spending some time in eastern cities, continued inland."[53] Thus the jest about Simon Stover and Michael M'Sherry not only captures the period of redemptioning, but it also conveys the immigration patterns of the poorer Irish, who sought their fortune by moving westward, since the wealthy Germans and Dutch had already settled on the best farmland in the East.

English jests frequently depict the Irish as outsiders, who when they come to London are as out of their element as any country rube. Even when they live in England, they are never seen as true Englishmen. In one jest an Irishman is asked how he can call himself an Englishman when he was born in Ireland: "'My lord,' replied the man, 'sposen I was born in a stable, that's no razen I should be a horse.'"[54] As we might expect, a number of jests extend the stereotype by similarly depicting the Irishman as an outsider in America, frequently mocking his attempts to boastful insistence on the superiority of Ireland over America. One Irishman newly arrived in America, who "made it his constant practice to run out against every thing that was the production of this country," mocks the puny size of American bees, boasting that in England they are as large as sheep. Asked how they manage to get in and out of their hives, the Hibernian shrugs his shoulders, saying that is the bees' problem.[55] Another Irishman, seeing a beautiful painting on the wall of an American building, exclaims: "'By J——s, it is a fine painting—but it was never done in America.' 'Oh sir,' says his friend, 'don't you see it is on solid wall, and therefore must have been done in this country?' 'Ah,' replies he, 'by J——s, I see that plain enough, but I only meant that the man who did it, was never in America.'"[56]

The Irishman is rendered most commonly as Paddy, but also as Pat, Mike, or Teague. Occasionally there are some identifying marks of dialect—"Arrah! by my shoul" is a repeated phrase, and "please" and "reason" might be rendered as "plaze" and "razen," or "devil" as "divel"—but these marks are surprisingly light. Perhaps Americans just do not find Irish dialect as funny as German. (Compare, for example, the use of dialect in two of our earliest comic strips, "The Katzenjammer Kids," which depended so heavily for its humor on the German accents of all of its characters, and "Bringing Up Father," in which the lower-class bricklayer and his wife (who have hit it rich in the Irish Sweepstakes), Maggie and Jiggs, do not speak in dialect.) even more surprising is how consistent the Irish stereotype has been over the years. If there were shifting stereotypes of Native Americans and black Americans over the centuries, the stereotype of the dumb Irishman adopted from England has not changed at all (although in America it might now be replaced by the Polish stereotype). Seth Kravitz, in a 1974 study of ethnic humor in England, collected more than three hundred currently told ethnic jests. He concluded that the greatest number were told about the Irish and that the dominant trait in the Irish stereotype "can be summed up in one word—*thick.* . . . the Irishman in some way does not follow normal logic or normal procedures."[57] This is just as true of the Irish presence in the eighteenth- and early nineteenth-centuries jest books. An Irish lad is sent back to the store by his fellow servants to replace a rancid piece of cheese. When he is told that the piece he has returned with is just as bad, he says he cannot understand how that could be, since he was given a new piece, the other half of the original.[58] Another Irishman on board a man-of-war is asked by his messmates to fetch a can of beer from the cellar, but he is up to their tricks: "Arrah! by my shoul, said he, and so while I am gone into the cellar to fetch beer, the ship will sail and leave me behind."[59] Two Irishmen walking to London are told they have ten miles yet to walk: "By my shoul, cries one of them, it is but five miles apiece, let's e'en walk on."[60] When an Irishman being tried on a criminal charge in a Boston court is greeted by the clerk, "guilty or not guilty," he replies testily, "Do you think I will tell you that which you have to try?"[61]

Readers of Mark Twain might recognize the following jest concerning a dumb Irishman:

> Two sailors, one Irish the other English, agreed reciprocally to take care of each other, in case of either being wounded in an action then about to commence. It was not long before the Englishman's leg was shot off by a cannon-ball; and on his calling Paddy to carry him to the doctor, according to their agreement, the other very readily complied; but he had scarcely got his wounded companion on his back, when a second ball struck off the poor fellow's head. Paddy, who, through the noise and disturbance, had not perceived his friend's last misfortune, continued to make the best of his way to the surgeon, an officer observing him with a headless trunk upon his shoulders, asked him where he was going? "To the doctor," says Paddy. "The doctor! says the officer, "why you blockhead, the man has lost his head." On hearing this he flung the body from his shoulders, and looking at it very attentively, "by my soul, says he, he told me it was his leg."[62]

Versions of this jest, which can be traced back to an English jest book of 1765 (*The Complete Jester*), survived well into the nineteenth century, where John Whitcomb Riley heard it from a circus clown. In "How to Tell a Story," Twain recalls how Riley told it on stage, from the point of view of a dull-witted farmer who has difficulty remembering the point of the joke. The soldiers are no longer English and Irish and can be taken for native-born participants in the Civil War. The transformation of the jest and the way it is told indicate how material that first entered the American jest books from England became naturalized over the years, as well as how jests can become deethnicized just as they can become ethnicized according to the needs of the storyteller and the national consciousness of the moment.[63]

There are many examples in these jest books of a particular kind of illogical statement attributed to the Irish, known as the Irish "bull."

Actually, the term well predates the Irish and may originate as far back as Chaucer, who used the word "bole" in the 1300s to describe a ludicrous error in language. With the Irish immigration into England in the 1700s, however, the term became associated with them, for it served the purpose of marking them as outsiders whose naiveté before English town life led the insider group in England to laugh at any blunders they made with language. Thus Captain Francis Grose's 1811 *Dictionary of the Vulgar Tongue* defined the bull as "a blunder made by an Irishman." The *Oxford English Dictionary* gives a more precise definition, calling a bull "a self-contradictory proposition; an expression containing a manifest contradiction unperceived by the speaker." An example of an Irish bull would be Paddy's consoling himself after his father died, saying "it does not signify grieving for it's what we must all come to, if we live long enough."[64] In another entry, we are told, "Never did an Irishman utter a better bull, than did an honest John; who being asked by a friend, 'Has your sister got a son or a daughter?' answered, 'Upon my soul, I do not know whether I am an uncle or an aunt.'"[65] One jest book entry attempts to turn the association between the bull sayer and the Irish to the Irishman's favor, while suggesting that travel is the best cure for prejudicial stereotyping: "I used to have my prejudices, but now, since I've been in France, I know that the French are not all lean men, and Ireland has convinced me that an Irishman can speak for some time without making a bull. If they make more bulls than the English, it is owning to the quickness of their thoughts, or wit. An Irishman frequently discharges his answer, before the question, and another is ready to follow, which accounts for his always being before-hand with you."[66]

The association of bulls with the Irish simply confirms the stereotype of the stupid Irishman. Davies suggests that there is particular need of creating stereotypes of stupid ethnic groups in industrial countries, pointing out that in eastern Europe it is usually members of the political elite, apparatchiks, and official heroes or the militia who are targeted as stupid for purposes of humor:

> To be stupid is to fail utterly in the face of demands of the modern economic world, that a person should be able, rational, calculating and competent, without gaining any compensating reward from the world of pleasure. . . . [S]tupidity is a despised and humiliating path to economic failure. We reassure ourselves that it is a path we will not follow by telling jokes that reserve that fate for other people, people living on the periphery of our

own group. Any anxieties that people have regarding their liability to failure through incompetence are released and dissolved by laughter at the crass stupidity of ethnic outsiders.[67]

Several jests do indeed suggest that Franklinian America might want to exclude from its boundaries Irishmen who were so dumb that they had no more chance to get ahead then Rip Van Winkle. One tells of the Irishman who tried to grab the main chance when a rich physician offered a large sum of money for the hand of each of his daughters. The Irishman offers to take two of them.[68] Another Irish gentleman offers a reward for the return of a new pair of black silk stockings. His friend comments that the reward is too small, but the enterprising Irishman has already thought of that: "Pho, (said the Irishman) I ordered the crier to say they were worsted."[69]

There are many fewer entries concerning the Scottish, where again the American jest books reiterated the English stereotype. As one entry reminds us, Dr. Johnson had no love of the highlanders: "A gentleman asking Doctor Johnson, why he hated the scotch: 'I do not hate them Sir, neither do I hate frogs, but I do not like to have them hopping about my chamber.' "[70] Some jests concerning the Scottish duplicate the stereotype of the Irish. They, too, for example, are capable of telling bulls, even if they are not named as such: "A Scottish clergyman, in what he facetiously terms, 'a faithful translation of Sonniman's travels into Egypt,' informs his readers that at Malta, 'the ridges of the houses are all flat terraces,' and that, 'at Rossetta the inhabitants cut the throats of their ducks, and in that situation keep them alive, with their wings broken,' and lastly, that 'the Orientals never take a walk but on horseback.' "[71]

And like the Irishman, the Scotchman boasts about the glories of his native country: "A paddy and a sawney were disputing one day with great warmth, upon the excellence of their respective nations; paddy, in proof that his surpassed all others, said, all the heroes, sages, and philosophers, came out of his country, that is so true, replied the sawney, that there is not one left in it."[72] The stereotyped dumb Irishman again gets the worst of it in his joint appearance with a Scotchman when the following jest from *The American Jest Book* is ethnicized: "A scholar, a bald man, and a barber, travelling together, agreed each to watch four hours at night, in turn, for the sake of security. The barber's lot came first, who shaved the scholar's head when asleep, thus waked him when his turn came. The scholar scratching his head, and feeling it bald, exclaimed, 'You wretch of a barber, you have waked the bald man instead of me!' '' In *The American Magazine of Wit* version of this jest, the bald man becomes a Scotchman, and the original target of the jest, the scholar, becomes a dumb Irishman who is left confused, scratching his head.[73]

Several jests deflate the Scotchman for his swagger. In one a Scottish major who had earned a reputation in duels confronts a Yankee: "The Scotchman looked down upon him with as much contempt as Goliath did upon David, and immediately asked, Are you a man to meet me?" The Yankee proves to be a worthy David as he bests his Goliath through some trickery. As a result, "The glory of our bragadocia was so sullied, and his feelings so mortally wounded by this indignity, that he sold his commission and left the place."[74] Another jest similarly punctures the Scotchman's arrogant self-image. It is set in 1777 and tells the story of Johnny Anderson, "a loyal Scotchman, and a lineal descendant of the celebrated, 'John Anderson my Jo.' '' In Burns's poem, the speaker recalls young John: "When we were first acquent / Your locks were like the raven / your bonny brow was brent.'' The jest book parody relates how Johnny Anderson joined the loyalist forces under the English general Burgoyne. With a captain's commission and dress to match, Johnny appears before his Janet all full of himself.

> JANET. "What now Johnny? What's this? I a'ways thought you a mickle bonny mon; but now ye look more like a gentleman than Lord Lovat himself. O Johnny, how mickle ye look like a gentleman, Johnny!"
>
> JOHN. "Hoot awa, woman! Call me na mair Johnny Anderson: I's Captain Anderson now; I've got his majesty's commission in my pocket."
>
> JANET. "An' what's that bra' thing hanging across ye'er woem, Johnny—Captain Anderson, I mean?"
>
> JOHN. "That's my braid saird, Jenny, that the general has given me to cut off the heed o' the reebels."
>
> JANET. "Ah! Johnny Anderson, (Captain Anderson, I beg ye'er pardon) I wish it may come to ony good, and that the reebels may not cut off ye'r heed; and, then, what will become o'me and the bairns, Johnny?"
>
> JOHN. "Never fear me, Jenny; I's warrant you, Captain Anderson is not such a chiel but he knows very weel how to tak' care o' himsel."

Johnny's mode of warfare, we are told, "consisted principally of manoeuvring. He fired, and then dodged the fire of the enemy by cowering with a quick jerk, that brought his legs and body into a zig-zag form, in which the seat of honour nearly touched the ground." Moreover, he had some very unromantic problems with his "seat of honor," for he has some difficulty controlling his bowels, which he mistakes as the result of a bullet wound and the oozing of his life's blood:

> "I've got my death," said John Anderson, as he sunk to the earth; "carry me home."
>
> His home was at no great distance. He entered it a woeful figure, from actual fatigue, from imaginary danger, and having his hand upon the spot where he supposed he had been wounded.
>
> "What's the matter, Captain Anderson?" exclaimed Janet, in a fit of surprize.
>
> "John. O Jenny! ca'me na mair Captain Anderson; I'se only Johnny Anderson now; and I shall soon be a deed mon, Jenny, for a' the bluid i' my body is rinning into my breeks!"

When Janet dressed his wound, she learns the truth, and Johnny's deflation is complete. "There is na wound, Johnny; and na bluid, Johnny; and thank God you are a safe mon, Johnny Anderson," Janet tells him: "but you shall never mair leave your own house to ga a'sogering, though your regimentals become you, and you look mair of a gentleman than Lord Lovatt."[75]

In some jests, both the Irishman and the Scotchman seem to get back their own. In one, "the great general Ponsonby" cuts off the nose of an ill-bred squire whom he overhears saying that he smells of potatoes.[76] In another, an Irish gentleman who danced the jig with great spirit confronts a "macaroni" imitating him at a dance. When the macaroni insists he was only dancing his natural way, the Irishman forces him to prove it by making him dance his exaggerated imitation for the rest of the evening.[77] Similarly, when General Lee tells an old Scottish officer with whom he is drinking at Albany that he would have to excuse a fault he has of abusing Scotland and Scots men when drunk, the officer tells him he understands, but that the general will in his turn excuse a little fault he has, of caning soundly anyone who abuses the Scottish.[78] A young fellow "sitting at a table over against the learned John Scot, asked him, what difference there was between 'Scot' and 'Sot'? 'Just the breadth of the table,' answered the other."[79] In all of these jests, however, the offender's error is that he has mistaken his target, for generals, gentlemen, officers, and learned men are not to be tarnished by the same stereotype as the peasant Irishman or poor Johnny Anderson. Sometimes class distinctions count more than ethnicity.

Frenchmen, Germans, Dutchmen, and Jews

When the French are targets, it is usually because of the difficulties they have with English. One, often reprinted, satiric jest attributed to Franklin caricatures the Frenchman's dialect. When the English ministry said it would repeal the Stamp Act if the colonists in their turn would pay for the destruction of the stamped paper, Franklin remarked that it reminded him of the Frenchman

> who having heated a poker red hot, ran into the street, and addressing an Englishman he met there, "ha, monsieur, voulez-vous give me de plaisir et de satisfaction,—and lete me runi dis poker only one foote up your backside." "D——n your soule," replies the Englishman. "Welle, den, only so far," says the Frenchman, pointing to about six inches of the poker.—"No, no," replies the Englishman—"d——n your soule, what do you mean?" "Welle, den," says the Frenchman, "will you have de justice to paye me for the trouble and expence of heatin de poker?"—"d——n me, if I do," answered the Englishman, and walked off.[80]

French problems with the English language are a recurring source of humor in these jests. In one, a Frenchman who seizes the hand of a beautiful young lady is advised to "be easy," which he mistakes for the word "baissez," and so begins kissing her at once.[81] Another Frenchman hears the word "press" used to imply "persuade," as in "press him to stay tonight," and so one evening instructs the company to "*squeeze* that lady to sing."[82]

However, such problems with accent and usage do not always suit the storyteller's purpose. When after the start of the American Revolution the English ambassador tells the French ambassador that in helping the colonists the French were guilty of a dishonorable act, "no less than that of debauching our daughter," the Frenchman replies: "I am sorry . . . that your excellency should put such a severe construction, upon the matter: She made the first advances, and absolutely threw herself into our arms; but, rather than forfeit your friendship, if matrimony will make any atonement, we are ready to act honourably, and marry her."[83] The Franklin story has the ethnic content of dialect because the Frenchman is being cast as ludicrous in his request, even though the true butt of the story is the Englishman who had behaved in a similar way toward the colonists. The French ambassador, however, is the hero of this last story, and so his eloquent and clever bon mot is delivered in perfect

English without accent. Unlike the jests making fun of the Frenchman's English, anecdotes depicting the suave, cosmopolitan Frenchman who is always ready with a witty reply instead admire his ability to turn a phrase.

On the other hand, as we have seem almost all stories involving Germans caricature their pronunciation of English: "Many Germans, it is well known by all who are conversant with their pronunciation, substitute the sound of d for that of TH. A gentleman from Leipsic being asked how old he was, replied, he was dirty (30)—and when asked the age of his wife, he answered that she was dirty two (32)."[84] For some reason, as humorists for Mark Twain to Sid Caesar have known, Americans have always found the German accent hilarious.[85] One jest book entry in comic German dialect is "Mine Atverdishment" for a missing horse: "Whoever will pring him pack, shall pay five tollars reward, and if he prings pack de tief vat stol em, he shall pay pesides twenty tollars, and ax no questions."[86] Another tells of a German cobbler near Philadelphia, who has become the butt of the pranks of neighborhood boys. One morning, the cobbler loads his wheelbarrow with stones that the boys had thrown at his front door and dumps them in the office of the justice of the peace: "Dere, mishter Shquiore, ail dem stones de tampt poys trow'd at my door lasht nite; dis is de way dey consult me, and I desist on satisfaction." The justice explains "that unless he brought before him the 'tampt poys' instead of the stones," he could not possibly give him the satisfaction he required.[87] The jest, which depends for its humor both on comic German dialect and on the concept of mischievous boys getting the best of their comic elder, anticipates Rudolph Dirks's "The Katzenjammer Kids" (and its spin-off, "The Captain and the Kids"), which began in the nineteenth century and lasted into the 1970s. The comic German who is the object of practical jokes recurs in these jest books, as we saw when Simon Stover (too fond of "a leetle sweet vine") was victimized by his indentured servant, Michael M'Sherry.

Actually, Stover is described both as M'Sherry's "German Companion" and as "a drunken hog of a dutch Redemptioner." The two ethnic groups were often not distinguished in these jests, and of course at times they were not terribly distinguishable. (The Dutch language is a linguistic form of Low German, and the word "Dutch" is the same philologically as "Deutsch," so that the Pennsylvania "Dutch" are really Pennsylvania "Deutsch.") Dutch immigration to North America began in the early seventeenth century and has been continuous ever since.

Unlike other immigrant groups, however, the Dutch were not poor peasants seeking opportunity or religious freedom. The first Dutch who colonized the New Netherlands on behalf of the Dutch West India Company were, like Simon Stover, financially secure. When jests do focus on the Dutch as distinct from the Germans, the stereotype is thus very different from that of the peasant Irishman. Christie Davies has argued that insofar as ethnic jests set boundaries, they are likely to pair opposite characteristics of ethnic groups as markers of unacceptability in different directions.[88] Perhaps if the peasant Irishman who smells of potatoes sets one boundary, the other is set by the stereotype of the overfastidious Dutchman: "The Hollanders keep their apartments religiously clean, and to prevent their being dirtied by the consequences of smoking, sit around the room in a circle, and he who has reason to spits into his neighbor's mouth, who passes it on to a third; until it gets into the mouth of the man who sits next the door, who passes it out of the room."[89]

There are only a few entries concerning Jews, understandably perhaps given the fact that there were not many Jews in the early years: in 1700 there were about 250 in the English colonies, and only about 2,000 by the Revolution. Jests concerning Jews are never set in America and perpetuate the traditional stereotype of them as "the money-hunting tribe,"[90] so that surprise occurs when the Jew acts against the stereotype: "At Bath, some years ago, lived two physicians of considerable eminence in their professions, the one a Jew, but of liberal disposition, and moderate in his demand for his fees. Hence, the first was called the christian Jew, and the other the Jewish christian."[91] Even normal maternal feelings cannot transcend supposed Jewish concern over money:

> On one of the nights when Mrs. Siddons first performed at Drury-Lane, a Jew boy, in his eagerness to get to the first row in the shilling gallery, fell over into the pit, and was dangerously hurt. The managers of the theatre ordered the lad to be conveyed to a lodging, and he was attended by their own physician; but, notwithstanding all their attention, he died, and was decently buried at the expence of the theatre. The mother came to the playhouse to thank the managers, and they gave her his cloaths and five guineas, for which she returned a curtsey, but with some hesitation added, "They had forgot to return her the shilling which Abraham had paid for coming in."[92]

So deep is the prejudice that even when they show a Jew transcending the stereotype, appreciation is expressed in racist terms, in the manner of Huck praising Jim by saying, "I knowed he was white inside." So we are told how Judge Mansfield decides for a Jewish plaintiff unfairly accused by a Christian defendant, whom he admonishes by saying, "you are the greater Jew of the two."[93]

In *Humor and Laughter*, Mahadev Apte makes a convincing case for the importance of ethnic humor as a cultural text. "Ethnic humor," he writes, "like all other types of humor, is an integral part of expressive culture. It reflects a group's perception and evaluation of other groups' personality traits, customs, behavior patterns, and social institutions by the standards of ingroup culture, with its positive or negative attitudes towards others."[94] We have seen these jest books do all that. We have also seen how the stereotypes of out-groups in America are mirrors of what the in-group that created them hoped or feared itself to be. Although over the centuries the image of Native Americans has shifted according to different psychic and political needs, in the eighteenth century and through the early decades of the nineteenth century Native Americans formed a reference group that administered to the settlers' own desired self-image. At the same time, however, the Cooper who created Natty Bumppo did so from the bedroom of his Paris hotel, and the Franklin who earned his reputation as an architect of the American Revolution administered thereafter to American pride as the ambassador who could hold his own in any drawing room in Europe. We should therefore not be surprised that the French, while mocked at times for their struggles with English, are also admired for a sophistication, an ability to express the bon mot, that Americans wanted to be able to emulate. Humor aimed at black Americans, on the other hand, may give us a different mirror image of the American psyche, and we have seen how the degraded, dehumanizing Sambo stereotype may be rooted in ambivalent feelings that could not be entirely repressed. Stereotypes of the Irish, Scottish, Germans, Dutch, and Jews, different as they were, nonetheless all served to mark these groups as outside the boundaries of the dominant culture. Their negative characteristics, whether stupidity, laziness, drunkenness, pride, or money hunting, were those the dominant culture wanted to disassociate from its image when it looked in the mirror. Whether we value such humor for what it tells us about the ways differences among various ethnic groups are perceived, or for the way such humor, by control and conflict, protects social and political boundaries and helps the dominant culture to create its own image, these jest books present us with a cultural text of the eighteenth and early nineteenth centuries that we have overlooked for too long.

Notes

1. Keith Thomas, "The Place of Laughter in Tudor and Stuart England," *Times Literary Supplement* (January 21, 1977), 77.

2. Christie Davies, "Ethnic Jokes, Moral Values and Social Boundaries," *British Journal of Sociology* 33:3 (September 1982), 393.

3. James Sully, *An Essay on Laughter: Its Forms, Its Causes, Its Development, and Its Value* (London: Longmans Green, 1902), 257. The best review of theories of humor as they relate to ethnic humor is John Lowe, "Theories of Ethnic Humor: How to Enter, Laughing," *American Quarterly* 38:3 (1986), 439–60.

4. Charles E. Schutz, "The Sociability of Ethnic Jokes," *Humor* 2:2 (1989), 167–68.

5. *The New Entertaining Philadelphia Jest Book* (Philadelphia, 1790), 80–81.

6. Werner Sollors, *Beyond Ethnicity: Consent and Descent in American Culture* (New York: Oxford University Press, 1986), 132.

7. Mahadev Apte, *Humor and Laughter: An Anthropological Approach* (Ithaca, N.Y.: Cornell University Press, 1985), 119–20.

8. Daniel Bowen, *Collection of Funny, Moral, and Entertaining Stories and Bon Mots* (New Haven, 1787), 30.

9. *The Laughing Philosopher* (Boston, 1825), 3.

10. Lowe, 445.

11. William H. Martineau, "A Model of the Social Functions of Humor," in Jeffrey Goldstein and Paul McGhee, eds., *The Psychology of Humor* (New York: Academic Press, 1972), 118.

12. *The American Jest Book* (Philadelphia, 1789), 19–20.

13. Thomas Jefferson, *Notes on the State of Virginia* (1787; reprinted, New York: Literary Classics of the United States, 1984), 188–89. I am grateful to my colleague, Carla Mulford, for alerting me to Jefferson's comments and for sharing with me her sense of their significance, as they are discussed in the context of her introductory essay for the pre-1800 section of the *Heath Anthology of American Literature*.

14. Jefferson, 185.

15. Cited in Sollors, 104.

16. Cited in Sollors, 205.

19. *The Merry Fellow's Companion* (Philadelphia, 1789), 11; reprinted in *Philadelphia Jest Book,* 38–39. The anecdote also appeared in *The Columbian Almanac* for 1793. Robert Dodge puts the story under the heading "Indians as Cruel and Degraded Savages" (*Early American Almanac Humor* [Bowling Green, Ohio: Bowling Green State University Popular Press, 1987], 72–73). Certainly the noble savage is a savage, living in a world that includes persecution and torture, but the emphasis of the story is not on the savagery but

rather on the nobility of the escapee, who undergoes his severe torture with stoic courage, so that "his countenance and his behavior were as if he suffered not the least pain." We are meant to marvel at his cleverness and his athletic prowess as he makes his escape and returns to be a constant thorn in the side of his enemies.

18. *Merry Fellow's Companion,* 12.

19. *The American Magazine of Wit* (New York, 1808), 49–50.

20. Frederick Jackson Turner first articulated his thesis in "The Significance of the Frontier in American History," a paper read before the American Historical Society in 1893. His *Frontier in American History* was published in 1920.

21. R. W. B. Lewis, "The Hero in the New World: William Faulkner's *The Bear,*" *Kenyon Review* 13 (Autumn 1951); reprinted in Charles Fiedelson, Jr., and Paul Brodtkorb, Jr., eds., *Interpretations of American Literature* (New York: Oxford University Press, 1959), 342.

22. D. H. Lawrence, *Studies in Classic American Literature* (New York: Thomas Seltzer, 1923), 67–92.

23. Richard Slotkin, *Regeneration through Violence: The Mythology of the American Frontier, 1600–1860* (Middletown, Ct.: 1973), 191.

24. *American Jest Book* (1789), 18.

25. *The Galaxy of Wit* (Boston, 1830), I, 37.

26. *Merry Fellow's Companion,* 27; reprinted in *Philadelphia Jest Book,* 10–11.

27. *Merry Fellow's Companion,* 26. The Pope couplet was repeated in the 1833 edition of *The American Jest Book,* 167.

28. *American Jest Book* (1833), 13.

29. Sollors, 131.

30. Richard Dorson, "Comic Indian Anecdotes," *Southern Folklore Quarterly* 10 (June 1946), 115. Dawson sees this as a version of a soldier story circulating in the nineteenth century and told by John Whitcomb Riley as "The Old Soldier's Story."

31. Sollors, 132.

32. *Galaxy,* I, 66.

33. Joseph Boskin, "The Complicity of Humor: The Life and Death of Sambo," in John Morreall, ed., *The Philosophy of Laughter and Humor* (New York: State University of New York Press, 1987), 252.

34. Jefferson, 270.

35. *Merry Fellow's Companion,* 27.

36. *The Youthful Jester* (Baltimore, 1800), 58.

37. *American Jest Book* (1833), 20–21.

38. *American Jest Book* (1800), 96.

39. *Merry Fellow's Companion,* 22; reprinted in *Philadelphia Jest Book,* 77.

40. *The Chaplet of Comus* (Boston, 1811), 157.

41. *Philadelphis Jest Book,* 37–38.

42. *Merry Fellow's Companion,* 26; reprinted in *Philadelphia Jest Book,* 10.

43. *Philadelphia Jest Book,* 29.

44. *Youthful Jester,* 58.

45. *American Magazine of Wit,* 20.

46. *American Magazine of Wit,* 39–40.

47. *American Magazine of Wit,* 51–52.

48. *American Magazine of Wit*, 76–78.

49. Cited in Schutz, 175.

50. *American Jest Book* (1833), 26.

51. *American Jest Book* (1833), 17–18; variant in *The Laughing Philosopher*, 87.

52. *American Jest Book* (1833), 7–9.

53. *The Harvard Encyclopedia of Ethnic Groups*, ed. Stephen Thernstrom, Ann Orlov, and Oscar Handlin (Cambridge: Harvard University Press, 1980), 530.

54. *Laughing Philosopher*, 137.

55. *The Feast of Merriment* (Burlington, 1795), 39–40.

56. *American Jest Book* (Wilmington, 1800), 97.

57. Seth Kravitz, "London Jokes and Ethnic Stereotypes," *Western Folklore* 36:4 (October 1977), 276.

58. *Feast of Merriment*, 59–60.

59. *Youthful Jester*, 19; reprinted in *Chaplet*, 175–76, and *Joke upon Joke* (New Haven, 1818), 95.

60. *Feast of Merriment*, 87; reprinted in *Youthful Jester*, 24.

61. *Laughing Philosopher*, 91.

62. *Feast of Merriment*, 62; reprinted in *A Mess or Salmagundi* (Philadelphia, 1817), 62–63.

63. Mark Twain, "How to Tell a Story," *Youth's Companion* (October 3, 1895); reprinted in Waller Blair, ed., *Selected Writings of Mark Twain* (Boston, 1962), 239. For a discussion of the transformations the story underwent from its earlier appearances in English jest books, and what these transformations might tell us about differences between American and English storytelling, see Robert Secor, "The Significance of Pennsylvania's Eighteenth-Century Jest Books," *The Pennsylvania Magazine* 110:2 (April 1986), 282–85.

64. *Feast of Merriment*, 15.

65. *Feast of Merriment*, 83; reprinted in *Youthful Jester*, 44.

66. *Mess*, 68–69.

67. Davies, 387.

68. *Chaplet*, 165; reprinted in *Mess*, 5.

69. *Chaplet*, 41; reprinted in *Mess* (1817) and *Joke upon Joke*, 21.

70. *New Jest upon Jest* (Baltimore, 1809), 84.

71. *Feast of Wit* (Boston, 1821), 33–34.

72. *Feast of Merriment*, 31.

73. *American Jest Book* (1789), 96; and *American Magazine of Wit*, 255.

74. *Chaplet*, 133–34.

75. *American Magazine of Wit*, 15–18.

76. *American Jest Book* (1789), 83–84.

77. *Merry Fellow's Companion*, 61.

78. *Merry Fellow's Companion*, 5.

79. *Merry Fellow's Companion*, 76.

80. *Merry Fellow's Companion*, 6–7. The anecdote also appeared in the *Massachusetts Centinel* (November 1, 1788), the *Georgia State Gazette* (March 28, 1789), and in an earlier form (without the profanity), in the *Pennsylvania Chronicle* (March 23, 1767).

81. *American Magazine of Wit*, 26.

82. *Chaplet,* 30.

83. *Merry Fellow's Companion,* 8.

84. *The Post Chaise Companion* (Baltimore, 1828), 124; variant in *Laughing Philosopher,* 163.

85. See Twain's "The Awful German Language," in *A Tramp Abroad* (1876).

86. *Chaplet,* 42.

87. *American Magazine of Wit,* 72–73.

88. Davies, 384.

89. *Feast of Wit,* 38.

90. *The Aurora Borealis* (Boston, 1831), 9.

91. *Post Chaise Companion* (Philadelphia, 1821), 142.

92. *New Jest upon Jest,* 101.

93. *Merry Fellow's Companion,* 25.

94. Apte, 121.

10

The Gratification of That Corrupt and Lawless Passion: Character Types and Themes in Early New England Rape Narratives

Daniel Williams

The crime of rape was not always a crime. In early New England, the legal status of rape was left unsettled throughout the colonial period. When Nathaniel Ward drafted the Body of Liberties in 1641, the Bay Colony's first code of laws, he omitted rape from his list of twelve capital crimes, having found no biblical sanction for its inclusion.[1] Not until after the notorious Fairfield case of the same year was rape included among the colony's most serious crimes. Daniel Fairfield, a "half Dutchman" about 40 years old, was discovered to have been having frequent sexual relations with the three daughters of a neighbor, all of whom were under the age of 10. Popular opinion demanded his execution, but the magistrates hesitated for several months while they debated what to do with both the rapist and the issue of rape. Finally, "after much dispute," the General Court concluded that Fairfield, though he was not to be executed, was to be severely punished. He was sentenced to be

> severely whipped at Boston and at Salem, and confined to Boston neck, upon the pain of death, if he went out, etc., he should have one nostril slit and seared at Boston, and the other at Salem, and to wear an halter about his neck visibly all his life, or to be whipped every time he were seen abroad without it, and to die if he attempted the like upon any person.[2]

After the Fairfield case, the General Court soon passed laws stipulating the death penalty for the rape of a child under 10 years of age and for the rape of "any mayde or woman that [was] lawfully married or contracted." Yet these laws were not incorporated in later legal codes, possibly owing to the lingering question of biblical sanction and to the inability of the magistrates to define what constituted rape. A new law, more flexible in application but narrower in focus, was then passed. The rape of "any mayde or single woman" above the age of 10 would be punished either by death or by some "other greivous punishment."[3] Although the issues of children and of married women were left unresolved for several decades, the magistrates could now punish rape as they wished. As the legal system in New England evolved over the next century, the use of discretionary justice in cases of rape continued, and by the eighteenth century all cases of nonconsensual intercourse were punished at the discretion of the judges.

Yet rape was rarely punished. As Susan Brownmiller has argued, rape "is nothing more or less than a conscious process of intimidation by which *all men* keep *all women* in a state of fear." As a "control mechanism" used to keep women in a "thrall of anxiety and fear," rape has never been consistently or vigorously prosecuted in judicial systems traditionally dominated by men.[4] When it was prosecuted, rape convictions were limited to those of marginal status who attacked women classified as valuable property by the patriarchal order, particularly young highborn virgins. The inability of the Massachusetts Bay Colony to legally define rape was (and is) indicative of a broader cultural hesitancy to punish the crime. According to one recent legal history, rape, although a capital felony, "rarely appeared" in early colonial court records.[5] When it did appear, rapists rarely received the maximum sentence of death.[6] Only for the most egregious of crimes and criminals was the sentence of death invoked.

In the criminal literature of early New England, rape was similarly neglected. During the eighteenth century, well over two hundred criminal narratives were published in New England; of this number only a few specifically concerned the crime of rape, and even fewer focused on the character of the rapist.[7] In his survey of colonial crime, Richard Slotkin estimated that 70 percent of all criminal narratives focused on murder, while only 6 percent dealt with rape.[8] Clearly, the crime of rape was an infrequent subject in the popular literature of early America. Ironically, although the sentimental novels of the early republic dwelled on all forms of sexual transgression, including rape, the genre's closest antecedents scarcely touched upon either the issue or the subject.[9] As in the formal judicial system, rape was ignored until only the most egregious crimes and criminals aroused enough popular outrage to attract the notice of colonial printers, and this was precisely the reason why these texts were—and are—significant. Because there were so few, rape narratives were unique commodities in the eighteenth-century print culture.

As it was depicted, rape was a symbolic crime. The woman's body was property, and thus the act of rape was a theft, the transgression of taking without permission. Yet it was more than a theft. Sexuality and criminality were linked in the traditional cultural perception of New England, and rape revealed the rapist's capacity to commit all that was evil.[10] The inability to control sexual impulse indicated a more dangerous inability to control all vicious impulses of self. As both nonmarital and nonconsensual sex, rape represented a threat to the family unit, the structural foundation of New England's patriarchy. Not only was sex outside marriage forbidden, but when such sex involved a subversion of family roles, such as the assault of a virgin daughter, then the crime signified an attack on New England's most fundamental social structures. Moreover, rape further challenged the order of both family and society because of the rapist's status as an outsider. An inferior by class and culture, if not by race or ethnic difference, the rapist embodied a defiance of the boundaries that were constructed to maintain the social hierarchy. As he was perceived, he was the Other, an alien whose trespasses represented an alternative world of sinful self-indulgence. Consequently, when fashioned into a popular commodity, the rapist character was depicted as wildly—and stupidly—self-destructive. In order to reaffirm social order, the rapist's life was presented as a pathetic progression from rebellion to execution.[11]

Those few narratives focusing on a rapist character all appeared during the latter part of the eighteenth century. Only once was a rapist described in the early Puritan narratives. "One W.C.," one of Cotton Mather's anti-apostles in *Pillars of Salt* (1699), became the subject of narration owing to the *"Rape* committed by him on a Girl, that Lived with him; though he had then a Wife with Child by him, of a Nineteenth or Twentieth Child."[12] One of the shorter passages in Mather's anthology of the damned, it said nothing concerning the actual rape; instead, Mather narrated the process in which W.C. "was *Ripened* for the Gallows." Although "his *Parents,* were Godly Persons," he "began

Early, to Shake off his Obedience unto *Them;* and Early had *Fornication* laid unto his Charge.'' According to the minister, the profligate sinner "Lived very Dissolutely" until "the Instances of his Impiety, grew so Numerous and Prodigious, that the wrath of God could bear no longer with him." W.C., then, as he was presented, was not so much condemned for rape as he was for his dissolute life, particularly for disobeying his parents and ministers. Significantly and indicative of the use of discretionary justice, Mather mentioned that "a *Reprieve* would have been obtained for him, if his foolish and froward Refusing to hear a *Sermon* on the Day appointed for his Execution, had not hardened the Hearts of the Judges against him." Obviously, W.C. became a pillar of salt, not because of his crime, but because "he had horribly slighted all calls to repentance."[13]

As brief as this passage is, Mather's description of W.C. nevertheless adumbrates the later rape narratives. Although his age was not given, W.C. was described as still being youthful, and although her age was not given, his victim was described as a "Girl," in all probability a virgin. What made his crime so egregious, and what attracted the official indignation of the judicial system, was that W.C. had violated the sacred order of the family, having abused his moral responsibilities as head of his household, by attacking one of his dependents. Equally important, W.C. already had identified himself as an outsider, having early transgressed the boundaries of acceptable (conventional) behavior. His execution for rape was merely the culmination in a life of depravity. Consequently, the overall narrative focus was placed on the process from disobedience to death rather than on the act or issue of rape. In all of the later accounts, this same structural focus was repeated. For late eighteenth-century readers, the life of the rapist, and not the rape, was dramatized. Besides the use of the word "rape," the only indirect reference to the actual assault was made inchoately by the emphasis on W.C.'s hypersexuality, as indicated by the number of children he fathered and by the early age at which he became sexually active. W.C. could not control himself.

In all of the later narratives, a similar lack of self-control was evident. In the earliest narrative, for example, *The Life and Dying Speech of Arthur* (1768), the character of the rapist was developed through a progressive series of transgressions.[14] Arthur, a black slave executed at the age of 21, began to exhibit his corrupt tendencies when still young. Although no mention of his father was made—a symbolic omission—

his mother was a servant in a pious home, where Arthur was taught to read and write. At the age of 14, however, he was sent away to another household, and once separated from the benevolent influences of master and mother, he soon manifested his rebellious spirit. On the pretext of quarreling with his new mistress, he ran away, thus discarding his ordained role and responsibilities, according to his society's standards.

Not only did Arthur reject his prescribed station, he also ran away from what his society defined as "civilization." In describing his first full immersion into corruption, he stated, "I fell in Company with some Indians, with whom I lived for two Months, in a very dissolute Manner, frequently being guilty of Drunkenness and Fornication, for which crimes I have since been famous." According to the narrative, the degenerate Indians represented the antithesis of Arthur's proper place in the world. Discarding piety and industry, he took up licentious liberty. The racism here is implicit. Arthur (the character), a young black man of inferior status and talents, lacked the moral strength to resist temptation. Once removed from his master's discipline, he succumbed to sin, allowing himself to be carried along in a process of corruption. Because of his weak, inferior nature, because of the base propensities inherent in his blackness, he was more receptive to vice than he was to virtue.

The movement of running away from good to evil was repeated throughout Arthur's short life. During his first year of dissolute freedom, he completely gave himself over to corruption, adding burglary and theft to his crimes. Twice he was publicly whipped for stealing, but punishment and humiliation reinforced rather than reformed his sinful status. In describing himself, he declared that he had become "hardened in . . . Wickedness." Unable to control himself, he "whored and drank, to great Excess" when his master permitted him to sail to the West Indies. On returning from this second excursion into excess, he attempted good behavior, but this was beyond him: "I behaved well for six Weeks, at the Expiration of which Time, going to Town with some Negroes, I got intoxicated; on returning home [I] went into an House where were several Women only, to whom I offered Indecencies, but was prevented from executing my black Designs." As punishment for his "black Designs," Arthur again was whipped, but like his previous public humiliations, this experience merely reconfirmed his sinful status.

In response to his outrages, Arthur was sold and then resold several times, including by one master who sold him "with a Drove of Horses."

His response to such property transactions was to run away, usually back to his Indian friends, during which times he continued his descent into depravity. During one of his sprees, he became involved with an Indian woman, who gained considerable—yet evil—influence over him. Continually he would run away to her, stealing horses and money along the way, each time separating himself further from his place within the dominant community. During one incident, he drunkenly became involved with a white woman at a husking frolic, leading him to exclaim, "And as our Behavior was such, as we have with Reason to be ashamed of, I shall for her sake pass it over in Silence." Similar to his previous "black Designs," this passage teased readers with the possibilities of his hypersexuality, yet it also introduced the final series of events in Arthur's life, outrages that could not be passed "over in Silence." Pursued and prosecuted by the woman's husband, Arthur was once more told that he was to be sold, and once more he responded by running away to his Indian mistress. Captured, convicted, and sentenced to yet another whipping, he escaped this last punishment through the intervention of his master, who paid his fines and took him home. But he repaid this kindness with one last transgression: "I one Night, after having stolen some Rum from my Master, got pretty handsomely drunk, took one of his Horses, and made the best of my way to her [his Indian mistress's] usual Place of Abode; but she not being at home, the devil put it into my Head to pay a Visit to the Widow *Deborah Metcalfe,* whom I, in a most inhumane manner, ravished." As he confessed himself, Arthur was beyond all control.

The narrative, which continued for another column of the broadside, stated nothing else about the rape or the victim, other than saying that Metcalfe made complaint against Arthur the following day. Instead, focus was quickly shifted from the rape back to the rapist's inability to submit. He was captured and jailed but soon escaped jail. He was once again captured and again escaped. For the next year this process of jail and jail breaking continued, until he was finally tried and convicted. Although he "prayed for the Benefit of Clergy," his request for mercy was denied, and he was sentenced to death. According to the narrative, he repented before his execution, and conforming to the conventions of the genre, his account concluded with a final confession and warning. He repented and confessed, however, for the sum of his vicious life rather than for the rape. When acknowledging the justness of his sentence, the now pious Arthur declared, "I must confess [that the execution] is but too just a Reward for my many notorious Crimes.'' Like W.C., he was executed less for rape than he was for his continual disruptions of the social order. The narrative was written, not to announce the crime of rape, but to warn masters and servants to abide by their prescribed roles. Moreover, the narrative was written to reassert control over the runaway rapist. Just as his execution demonstrated the ultimate submission to authority, so too did his narrative dramatize a return to the dominant order. By imposing the textual conventions of the criminal genre on his life, those responsible for his narrative placed him once more—and for good—within the lines of social conventions. The penitent Arthur concluded,

> I earnestly desire that this Recital of my Crimes, and the ignominious Death to which my notorious Wickedness has bro't me, may prove a Warning to all Persons who shall become acquainted therewith, But in a particular Manner, I would solemnly warn those of my own Colour, as they regard their own Souls, to avoid desertion for their Masters, drunkenness, and Lewdness, which three Crimes was the Source from which have flowed many Evils and Miseries.

As the first black rapist in American literature, Arthur set the foundation for what would later become an unfortunate stereotype—the immoral, hypersexual black wildly pursuing women to satisfy his prodigal lusts. "Black Designs" became a convenient metaphorical link between racial character and vicious impulse.

Yet all of the rapists were out of control, regardless of their race. Although a character's blackness served as an obvious symbol of depraved self-indulgence, this was not necessarily a uniquely black tendency. Though expedient, skin color was only one means used to identify the Other. In the next two narratives, both published during the 1770s, both of the rapists were Irish, and both similarly indulged their carnal appetites whenever and wherever they could. In *An Account of the Life of Bryan Sheehan* (1772), for example, Sheehan also was characterized as being trapped in a dissolute progression.[15] But unlike the previous accounts, his narrative dwelled at length on his rape, emphasizing the outrage of his crime and its symbolic function. As it was presented, his rape represented even more of a social insurrection than Arthur's. While Arthur was wildly self-indulgent, Sheehan was practically defiant.

Born in Ireland in 1732, Sheehan came over to New England when he was 20 as a Newfoundland fisherman but soon settled in Boston as a servant. During the next two decades, he was never able to overcome his marginal status. His descent into sin, however, began while he was still in Ireland, when his family was broken apart over religious issues. His father, a Catholic, raised Sheehan and his brothers "in the principles of the church of Rome," while his mother, an Anglican, raised the daughters in "the church of England." In view of his later outrages, specifically directed against wives and mothers, his early experiences foreshadowed his inability to respect the family unit.

According to the narrative, however, once in enlightened New England he was given the chance to receive proper training in both religious practice and social custom. As a servant, Sheehan was taken into the household of Benjamin Hollowell, a Boston shipbuilder, who was depicted as being the ideal patriarch of his family. Hollowell required his servant "to be present at the Exercises of family religion" and "to attend public Worship at the old South meeting," but Sheehan abused these opportunities. Such "duties," the narrative stated, "were no ways agreeable to him, and he performed them with carelessness and reluctance." By slighting religious instruction, he failed to cultivate the necessary reverence for the dominant values of his culture, thus allowing more perverse priorities to develop.

The movement toward his inevitable ruin began after he left the benevolent influence of Hollowell. He was immediately "ill-treated" by another master who, having "got him drunk," made him sign papers of indenture. Then, to escape this servitude, he ran away to Casco Bay, where he attempted to start a new life, marrying a woman there and enlisting in a local regiment raised for the Seven Years' War. The narrative, however, said nothing about his six-and-a-half-year enlistment; instead, attention was given to an unexpected homecoming. When he returned, he "found his wife had married, during his absence, to a Frenchman." Enraged to find his own family structure violated by a former enemy, he resolved to kill the Frenchman but relented. According to the narrative, "it was agreed that the wife should have her choice of the two husbands, on which she chose *Sheehan*." But Sheehan was incapable of accepting his role either as husband or father. Despite being chosen, he was "so disgusted" at his wife for "having a child . . . by the Frenchman, that he could not live very peaceably with her." Previously his wife had given birth to four children of his own, and although three had died shortly, one remained, but Sheehan refused to accept responsibility for his wife and either of the two children. Instead, he ran away.

As the narrative presented his life, the abandonment of his own family led directly to the final abandonment of all social boundaries. He went to Marblehead, where he soon acquired "the character of a wicked, profligate person." To document this, the narrative mentioned his attempt to burglarize a store, for which "he was confined a considerable time [in Salem jail], and publickly whipped." Similar to Arthur's experiences, the pain and humiliation he experienced in public served to reinforce his outsider status, setting him further apart from society. This separation was increased when he learned that his wife had died, which left him— as he was described—"considerably affected." It was at this point, then, publicly humiliated and emotionally isolated, that Sheehan committed rape. Unlike other accounts, nearly a third of the narrative dealt with the rape and the events that led up to it. The actual description, however, began with his arrest on September 13 for the rape of Abiel Hollowell of Marblehead. Significantly, not only did the victim have the same family name as Sheehan's first American master, but also her husband had the same given name, Benjamin.

Although the narrative made no direct comment, the fact that Sheehan raped the wife of a man who bore the same name as his first master could not be overlooked by readers. His outrage was all the greater as it was a symbolic attack on the family structure he had failed to become a part of or to imitate. And indeed the rape was an outrage. Switching the focus to the victim's perspective, the narrative related Mrs. Hollowell's testimony, "as near as can be recollected." From the first moment he saw her, Sheehan had pursued his victim with maniacal fervor. After encountering her in a house of another woman, he had "sent for some drink, and offered it to her, but she refused to taste it." He then "made some proposals to her, and offered her Money, both of which she rejected." When the other woman in the house informed him that "she [Hollowell] was a married woman, and not one for him, he became enraged, threatening the woman and demanding to know where Hollowell was hiding. On this night, however, the victim eluded his search by concealing herself in a closet and later under a pile of "bed cloaths," but this only increased Sheehan's determined malevolence. The narrative stated that on the following night,

> she was in bed with her two children, and he came up with a lighted candle, when she was much affrighted, she asked him what he wanted, and bid him gone . . . That he offered her money, which she refused, and again bid

> him gone . . . That he then blow out the candle, and swore by GOD that if she made any noise he would kill her: That he then stopt her mouth with one of his hands and perpetrated the villainy; abusing her with his other hand in so shocking a manner that she had little hope or expectation of life.

Were the two children still in bed while the mother was raped? The narrative made no mention of them other than the original statement, leaving readers to conclude that they were either still in the bed or in the room when the attack occurred. Moreover, there was enough narrative possibility to suggest that he perversely enjoyed the outrage all the more because his victim was both his wife and mother. The narrative, of course, offered no interpretation as to whether or not Sheehan's rape represented the acting out of repressed rage, a symbolic revenge for a life of humiliation brought on by the parental feuds, patriarchal masters, a French rival, or an unfaithful wife.

Instead, the narrative immediately proceeded to Sheehan's arrest, trial, and conviction. Although the attorney general stated that he "never knew one [a case] so plain, and the evidence so full against the prisoner,'' Sheehan maintained his innocence, claiming that the sexual intercourse "was done according to a agreement.'' His denials, however, did not stop him from confessing and repenting. Following the conventions of criminal narrative closure, he penitently renounced his former life. Rejecting "the belief of the erroneous [Catholic] principles in which he was educated,'' he attended "public worship in one or the other of the congregational churches'' and "appeared very desirous of receiving instruction from the ministers of the gospel.'' Accepting in death what he had rejected in life, Sheehan, according to the narrative, allowed himself to become an example of the wages of sin. The narrative concluded that his "total disregard and neglect of public worship of *GOD* . . . ha[d] probably been a principle introduction to most of his vices.'' The narrative's racial and ideological implications were clear; like Arthur, once Sheehan had abandoned his roles and responsibilities, he could not resist the vicious propensities of his ethnic/outsider background.

In *The Last Words and Dying Speech of Robert Young* (1779) a similar disregard for boundaries was evident, but unlike Arthur and Sheehan, Young was presented as manifesting his depraved spirit in only one direction, lust.[16] Of all the rapists depicted in early criminal narratives. Young was the most dedicated to satisfying his hypersexual appetite, and as he was depicted, he was the most libertine of all rapist characters and most resembled the rakes in sentimental novels. Rape became merely another form in which he indulged himself for physical pleasure. As it was presented, the pursuit of sexual gratification began as soon as he escaped his father's influence. Born in Ireland in 1750, he was sent away as an apprentice to a Dublin merchant at the age of 15, and as soon as he was beyond his family circle, he committed himself to sexual conquest: "At that early age I was much inclined to the company of women. . . . I made large promises to one of my employer's servant maids, if she would yield to my unlawful embraces, to which, by constant importunity, she consented." Like the later libertines of sentimental novels, Young used promises to seduce and, once he had achieved his goal, exhibited not the slightest regard for the woman involved. In this case, "to prevent discovery," he "studied all means to have her discharged." As he described himself in the narrative, he was without feeling or emotion, existing purely on a physical level.

Young was myopic in his pursuit of pleasure, refusing to recognize anything but the objects of his desire. Consequently, he served his apprenticeship more with "several lewd women" than he did with the Dublin merchant. When his master finally reprimanded him, demanding that he cease his immoral transactions and apply himself to business, he promptly ran away. Sexual gratification had become his profession, and in order to pursue this business, he joined the British army, where, he stated, "I gave myself up to all manner of debauchery." By connecting debauchery and soldiery, the narrative supported the colonial view that the British army was a haven for the depraved. Published during the fateful year of 1779, it conveniently exploited Young for the purpose of unmistakable propaganda. The school of vice that completed his process of corruption turned out to be the enemy. For readers during the Revolutionary period, Young became the Other, ethnically, morally, and politically.

Young stayed in the British army for most of his remaining years. His various duty stations gave him new opportunities for seduction, despite bouts of venereal disease. On the Isle of Man, for example, he declared, "There I betrayed three girls, but after leaving them, have scarce thought of them." Once in Canada as part of Burgoyne's ill-fated force, he continued to seduce and discard without the slightest pangs of conscience. Complaining that he had little money in Quebec, he explained how he used one woman: "At length I cast my eyes on a widow, paid her several visits, and strove to deceive her; she was for some time deaf to my protestations, but so closely did I pursue my purpose of deceiving her, that at length she gave heed to my request, and believed my falsehood.'' Once the woman had surrendered herself, he squandered her money on "plenty of liquor" and "lewd companions.'' When the woman's "affections" became oppressive, he abandoned her, preferring to march to Saratoga and defeat rather than to remain with her in Quebec. After his capture, Young still pursued his pleasure. As a prisoner in Hadley, he became involved with "a girl,'' who advised him to desert. After making love to her, he escaped, but instead of returning to the young woman, he journeyed to Pelham, where he spent three months, then to Shelburne, where he remained five months. He declared, "At both these . . . places, I studied to deceive the fair sex, and betrayed a young woman in each of them.'' Continuing his own private conquest of America, he next followed his "rambling inclination" to Greenfield, where he developed a new strategy for seduction—he opened a school.

Like his previous counterparts, Young held little regard for the social institutions and conventions. In proclaiming his new profession, he exhibited no awareness of his iniquity. Self preceded society, and all actions and situations were judged according to how they promoted personal interests and pleasures. He stated, "After keeping school here about two months I began my old practice of seducing the young women. I gained the consent of one in particular, who I often went to see in private.'' Seduction for Young was power, a way of controlling women and magnifying himself. Like the Quebec widow who gave him everything for nothing, the Greenfield woman also fell under his spell, surrendering everything she held in value for her lover, including family, friends, and community. Boasting of his conquest, he stated, "She like me so well, that she promised to go with me,'' although "her parents tried all means to keep her from me.'' Equally without feeling, he declared that "the girl left her friends in order to see me[,] which she often did.'' But the more given, the more was taken, and nothing was offered in return. Despite the young woman's vows to follow him, he abandoned her.

Yet this abandonment, as atrocious as it was, was only the penultimate step in Young's corrupt progression. Mixing instructional discourse with sexual intercourse, he continued to enjoy the position of a schoolteacher in several more towns, in all of which he claimed to have found "good acceptance." And in Brookfield, he set himself up in a similar position in the house of Samuel Green, keeping school during the day and boarding at night. Despite the false front of propriety, within a short period of time he abused both professional trust and personal kindness in the Green household: "I was not long there before I got acquainted with *Ann Green,* and kept her company some time before her parents knew of it, which when they did they strongly opposed it, knowing me then to be doing the same with others, and that I was many nights from home." Young, however, claimed that he actually fell in love with the daughter and offered to reform his behavior: "I promised to quit all other company . . . and offered marriage to *Ann;* she agreed." His story, then, might have turned out to be a sentimental tale with a happy ending; owing to the love of a good woman, the reprobate reforms and rebuilds his life within the social community. For the first time in the narrative, he expressed affection for another. "Many arguments were used," he declared, "and means tried, to diswade her from my company, but nothing could shake her constancy: When I was sick, she shewed such cordial affection that I loved her without deceit, and against much opposition we were published, and intended to marry in a few days."

But there was no possibility for a happy ending. From the beginning, indeed from the very structure of the criminal narrative genre, readers knew what to expect. Condemned criminals did not live happily ever after. The closure was obvious. Young's narrative was presented as his "Last Words," and as it was published on the day of his execution, it clearly demonstrated his status as an outsider. Only through the ritual of execution could he reenter the social community. Moreover, the narrative's subtitle not only declared Young's sentence and crime in boldface, but it also included a provocative description of the victim, stating that the rape was "committed on the body of Jane Green, a Child, eleven years of age." By the time readers encountered the supposed love relationship, they already knew of the outrage. The promises and possibilities of love, then, were used to arouse indignation rather than sympathy. Despite his declarations, Young could not resist raping his fiancée's younger sister. Despite his outward propriety, he was as out of control as Arthur or Sheehan.

Young, as he was presented, had fooled himself. After deceiving others for so long, he finally had deceived himself into believing his empty promises. His attempt at genuine feeling only served to emphasize the foulness of his crimes. Basically, he destroyed a family. Having separated daughter from parents, he then ruined the daughter and raped the younger sister. Again, the rape symbolized a much wider process of transgression. Fulfilling the expectations of readers, Young, when confronted with death, repented his many trespasses and offered his last words as evidence of his sincerity. But he confessed the rape only in the larger context of a life spent in defiance of all social institutions and conventions. Rather than the specific crime, his narrative publicized his failure to control his lust, a failure that developed into a subversive amorality.

Unlike Young, Joseph Mountain never had the opportunity to hide his Otherness. As a black, he could not occupy anything but the most marginal of social spaces. Consequently, his execution for rape in 1790 neither illustrated nor confirmed his all too apparent status as an outsider. Yet Mountain, as he was characterized, never attempted to gain acceptance within the boundaries of the hegemonic social order. Rather than accept low status within the sanctioned hierarchy, he chose to elevate himself within the framework of a counter social structure. Rather than use the scaffold as a stage from which to beg for acceptance, he exploited his death scenes to dramatize his membership in an entirely antithetical society, the criminal underworld of thieves, robbers, and highwaymen. Defying the boundaries by which his readers lived, he embraced his exclusion from society.

In *Sketches of the Life of Joseph Mountain* (1790), Mountain was presented to readers as a figure of contradistinction.[17] The blackness of his skin served as a convenient (and obvious) symbol for his antithetical values. Yet like most other criminal characters, his iniquity was not developed until after he had abandoned the moral influences of his youth. The child of a free "Molatto" father and a slave mother, he was raised as a servant in one of the wealthiest families of Philadelphia, where he received religious instruction, but as soon as he left the household, such "sentiments of virtue" were forgotten. In March 1775 Mountain joined the crew of a merchant ship bound for England, and shortly after his arrival he "was strolling the streets of London in quest of amusements." In an aside to readers, he commented, "In this situation, the public will easily conceive, I could not long remain an idle spectator. It will not be surprizing to find me speedily initiated in practices disgraceful to human nature, and destructive of every moral virtue."[18]

Mountain's narrative descent into disgrace and destruction was partly the result of his own vicious inclinations and partly the result of his corrupt environment. Soon after arriving in London he met two men who juggled during the day and who robbed at night. Without the slightest hesitation, he stated, "They soon found me susceptible of almost any impressions, and neither incapable of, nor averse to, becoming a companion in their iniquity."[19] Indeed, because of the stereotypically perceived weaknesses inherent in his race, he was "susceptible"; once initiated into the English underworld of footpads and highwaymen, he fully adopted the life-styles of his corrupt companions, revealing a talent for wickedness. During the next year he and his two companions frequently robbed travelers along the roads of England, and as "gentlemen of pleasure," they soon spent their illicit wealth indulging "in every species of debauchery."[20]

According to the narrative, Mountain's cycle of robbery and debauchery led him to discover a countersystem of values. The English underworld offered an alternative social hierarchy where footpads aspired to be highwaymen and where esteem was awarded for vice rather than for virtue. Early American readers could not help but notice the parodic contrast between the highborn gentlemen victimized by the robberies and the robbers who cavorted in the taverns on their spoils. Nor could they fail to recognize Mountain's ambitions to rise within this countersociety. Referring to his desire to rise from footpads to highwaymen, he stated, "The business which now seemed most alluring to me was that of *highway-men*. Considering myself at the head of foot-pads, I aspired for a more *honorable* employment, and therefore determined to join myself to . . . [a] gang of highway men."[21] The obvious irony conveyed by the word "honorable," emphasized by the printer's italics, clearly illustrated the world of inversions Mountain inhabited. To stress the parodic structure of this countersociety, he referred to robbery as his "business," "profession," "employment," and "occupation." And similar to more conventional professions, his success was judged according to the wealth he acquired. After his first successful tour as a highwayman, he—and the narrative—remarked,

> Upon my arrival [at the gang's tavern retreat] . . . I gave a faithful narrative of my transactions, and produced the plunder as undeniable proof. I never shall forget with what joy I was received. The house rang with the praises of Mountain. An elegant supper was provided, and he placed at the

head of the table. Notwithstanding the darkness of his complexion, he was complimented as the first of his profession.[22]

Living in a world where racism was a social convention, eighteenth-century readers would not have so easily dismissed the "darkness of his complexion." Here and throughout the narrative this "darkness" was used to heighten the perverseness inherent in Mountain's underworld, where those commonly perceived as "base" rose to the top of their counterhierarchy. Matched against his skin color, his ambitions defied what most readers would have understood as the natural order.

Mountain simultaneously inhabited two antithetical worlds: in one he was celebrated; in the other he was condemned. Continually the narrative focused on the contrast between these two worlds, increasing the distance between them in order to enhance the effect of the inevitable closure. No matter how great a highwayman he was, readers perceived his accomplishments through the conventions of the criminal narrative genre that ultimately would lead to his ignominious end. From the outset of their reading experience they knew that their world would be affirmed, not his, and that Mountain, regardless of the distances he traveled away from their world, both literally and figuratively, eventually would return in death to his original base position. The irony of this progression (the farther he went, the closer he returned) was emphasized during the latter part of the narrative. As readers reached the final scenes of his textual life, Mountain reached the farthest point from his lowly beginnings. In the company of his original companions, he invaded the Continent, robbing in France, Spain, and Holland, and acquiring enough booty to invest in part ownership of a tavern near London. According to the narrative progression, the highwayman had passed from being property to becoming a property owner.

Yet all his accomplishments were merely the ironic backdrop for the narrative's anticlimax. Unable to remain in England because of his previous iniquities, Mountain returned to the sea, making several voyages on merchant ships between Europe, Africa, and America (including one voyage on a slave ship). He made his last voyage to Boston, where he arrived in the spring of 1790. While traveling to New York, he "stole five dollars from the cabin of a sloop lying in the Connecticut River" near East Hartford.[23] For this offense he was sentenced to a public whipping, and it was at the whipping post where Mountain's two worlds collided.

No event in my antecedent life produced such mortification as this; that a highway-man of the first eminence, who had robbed in most of the capital cities of Europe, who had attacked gentlemen of the first distinction with success; who had escaped Kings-bench prison and Old-Bailey, that he should be punished for such a petty offence, in such an obscure part of the country, was truly humiliating.[24]

According to the narrative, Mountain's exalted self-conception was merely another perversion of values belonging to the underworld he inhabited, but "the highway-man of the first eminence" disdained this view. Refusing to perceive himself as socially inferior, he set out to reaffirm his more elevated status by seizing whatever he wanted along the open road. Instead of plundering gold and watches, however, he assaulted a young woman.

At the distance of one mile [from New Haven], I met the unhappy girl whom I have so wantonly injured. She was in company with an elder sister. . . . I began a conversation with them, and attempted by persuasion, to effect my purpose. They were terrified at my conduct and endeavored to avoid me. Upon this I seized the eldest girl; she, however, struggled from me. I then caught the younger, and threw her to the ground.[25]

As it was presented to the readers, the crime of rape was merely another form of robbery. Sexual gratification had nothing to do with the attack; Mountain wanted revenge against the social structure that had humiliated him, and as a material object, indeed as property, the young woman represented this social structure. His actions during and after the attack confirmed that rape, as forced sexual intercourse, simply was the medium through which he attempted to reassert his control over property and to reaffirm his reputation as a "highway-man of the first eminence." Consequently, in order to reassert and to reaffirm, Mountain needed an audience. In describing the attack, he—as he was characterized—denied that rape specifically was his intention while alluding to his need for witnesses.

I have uniformly thought that the witnesses were mistaken in swearing to the commission of a *Rape:* That I abused her in a most brutal manner—that her tender years and pitiable shricks were unavailing—and that no exertion was wanting to ruin her, I frankly confess. . . . When her cries had brought to her assistance some neighboring people, I still continued my barbarity, by insulting her in her distress, boasting of the fact, and glorying in my iniquity. Upon reflection I am surprized that I did not attempt my escape; opportunity to effect it frequently presented before I was apprehended. Yet, by some unaccountable fatality, I loitered unconcerned.[26]

By "insulting . . . boasting . . . and glorying," Mountain demonstrated that he was no ordinary thief. His actions after the rape, as significant as the rape itself, dramatized his contempt for the laws that denied him the privileges of ownership.

But in whose view—and in whose words—was his loitering an "unaccountable fatality"? In conventional Christianity, such hesitation would have been understood as the inevitable end of the sinner's chain of wickedness, and indeed the highwayman appropriately commented that "the counsel of heaven determined that such a prodigy of vice [as himself] should no longer infest society."[27] Yet, with the exception of the final paragraph's all too expected cries for mercy, Mountain had never acknowledged any authority higher than the hangman. Why, then, did he suddenly recognize a "counsel of heaven" sitting in judgment upon him? The obvious answer has more to do with the genre's narrative requirements than with the man. Readers expected that, once having run the length of their wickedness, sinners would renounce their defiance and reaffirm both sacred and secular orders. The conventions of closure required a transformation of character from resistance to repentance, and the dying confession, as an act of humiliation, was intended to dramatize this crucial change.

Mountain's closure was contrived; his final transformation revealed more a manipulation of character than a conviction of faith. Certainly, all criminal characters were manipulated, but Mountain's conclusion demonstrated an obvious attempt to situate the robber-rapist within the boundaries of the social community, regardless of all previous instances of scorn for these boundaries.[28] Throughout the text, his character had been created through the collaboration of two authors, a balancing of the experiences provided by the historical figure and the words provided by his ghostwriter, but in drawing the narrative to a close, this collaboration broke down. According to the narrative and to the conventions it followed, Mountain began attending church and expressing remorse after the "Sentence of Death" was pronounced, but this short paragraph of piety was not enough to direct attention away from the previous twenty pages of impiety.[29] At this point the ghostwriter, the voice of the social community, overwhelmed the robber. Mountain's ghostwriter was David Dagget (1764–1851), a most appropriate representative of the community. He was the justice to whom Mountain was first brought for arraignment, and among his many accomplishments he was at one time or another a U.S. senator, the mayor of New Haven, chief justice of the Connecticut Supreme Court, and one of the founders of the Yale Law School. According to one of the title pages, Mountain's narrative was "taken from his own mouth in the presence of several respectable witnesses." Moreover, to stress the authenticity of Mountain's voice, the narrative included the following postscript:

> The writer [Dagget] of the foregoing narrative assures the public, that the facts related were taken from the mouth of the culprit. In no instance has any fact been substantially altered or in the least exaggerated. On the 28th of September the writer applied to Joseph, to learn if he persisted in affirming the truth of the foregoing story. By the direction of the criminal his name was then set to this history, and he declared . . . that it contained nothing but the truth.

In order to tell his story, Mountain was seemingly forced to accept in the end the conventions of Dagget's legal discourse, but for all that his story also remains.

Throughout a century of criminal-narrative production, American readers had never before encountered a character like Mountain. He was the first English highwayman specifically shaped for a colonial audience, and he was the first to so clearly affirm his outsider status. The interviews that took place in the New Haven jail and his ghostwriter only can be faintly imagined; the reality of the actual person's experiences were lost the moment his neck snapped. But as the historical Mountain disappeared, his character emerged, and readers were presented with a personality in stark contradistinction to their own world. Imprisoned with a hostile environment and confronted with death, Mountain, the man, might have told a different story, one more appropriate for a sinner struggling desperately for salvation, but he apparently embraced the narrative opportunity to affirm his world, not the reader's. When given the chance to give an account of his life, he boasted of his accomplishments within his own antithetical society. Those involved in fashioning the narrative into a marketable commodity also might have told a different story, one less scornful of their own social conventions, but they equally embraced the narrative opportunity to present the alterity of their character's life—at least until the final paragraph.

As he approached death, Thomas Powers similarly voiced a somewhat sudden remorse for his transgressions, including for the crime of rape that brought him to the gallows. According to his 1796 *Narrative and Confession,* Powers, a 20-year-old black man, remained "hardened beyond all description" until hearing his death sentence; then, when faced with the reality of execution, he fainted, and after regaining consciousness the rapist, now repentant, asked to see his victim. When she refused, he declared, "I then set down and wrote a full confession of my crime, and of the justness of my punishment. I begged pardon, most sincerely for the injury, I had done her."[30] Through the act of confession, Powers, although previously stubborn and scornful, humbled himself in order to demonstrate the sincerity of his repentance. Seeking forgiveness from his victim, and undoubtedly mercy from the court, he abased himself by publicly accepting the wickedness of his crime.

Yet immediately after this moment of contrition, the narrative depicted a less than contrite character. Although several ministers and his master struggled to save his soul, Powers admitted that while awaiting death, he was unable to sustain a sincere level of self-surrender: "the secret hope of making my escape, and, the jollity of countenance that appeared in most of my spectators, did in some measure banish the idea of death from my mind." Caught between two audiences, one expecting piety and the other impiety, Powers acted out a role of careless complacence. Ironically, his one profitable action during his imprisonment was to sell his body for dissection to a group of doctors for ten dollars. After refusing to be either useful in life or repentant in death, he hoped that his "BONES [would] be of service to mankind." A wryly comic closure, but one not likely to encourage readers to perceive Powers as a member of the elect. Although he had the impulse to repent, he failed to achieve the strength of conviction necessary to transform sinners into saints. Yet this was not a failure of the narrative. Those responsible for shaping his characterization did not attempt to convince readers that the rapist was capable of conviction; instead, they concluded the narrative by refocusing attention not on his strengths but on his weaknesses.

In writing to his victim, Powers assumed the role of a penitent, an imposture that reflected greater patterns of infidelity and iniquity. Unlike Mountain, he never openly challenged the boundaries of his social community, even when confronted and confused. More deceitful than defiant, he remained within the hierarchy that oppressed him, using the blackness of his skin to mask his wickedness. Published in order to satisfy and exploit public curiosity, the narrative exposed the sinister reality behind the character's poses, in effect confirming his Otherness. Although less exotic than the black highwayman, Powers was a more disturbing character. Other than acknowledging his crimes, his *Confession* confessed little, as the character revealed a capacity to commit evil unreconciled by either conscience or cognizance. Since he overtly remained within his community, and thus supposedly within the sphere of proper influence, his narrative raised the issues of how to identify such evil, issues that it answered by reinforcing—and popularizing—racist stereotypes.

On both the title page and headnote, Powers was identified as "A NEGRO," a label that not only immediately set him at the bottom of his social environment but also suggested the base proclivities of his racial character.[31] Within the first paragraph, the narrative promptly confirmed both his low status and fallen nature. Like previous criminals, he stated that he rejected the lessons of his youth, defying both parents and masters: "my father, who being a very pious man, endeavored to instruct me in my several duties, to God, to my parents, and to all mankind . . . But I as naturally too much inclined to vice, to profit by his precepts or example: for I was very apt to pilfer and tell lies."[32] The natural inclinations Powers alluded to were ascribed to his race as well as to his character. According to the narrative, he was naturally weak, more disposed to corruption than to correction. Lacking the strength of self-discipline, he tended toward dissipation, and without supervision he could not resist the temptations of such tendencies. The sequence that led Powers to the scaffold, in fact, symbolically was begun when the young boy surrendered to his evil inclinations. When he was 9 years old, he "was put out to live" with a new master, and it was at this point that he "began the practice of villainy and debauchery." Appropriately, his baptism in carnal sin occurred on a Sabbath when his master's family was at church: "Being one Sunday at home from meeting, with nobody but a young Negro woman . . . she, enticing me to her bed, where she was sitting, soon taught me the practice of that awful sin, which now costs me my life." While commenting on his initiation into iniquity, Powers declared, "It was here I began my career in the gratification of that corrupt and lawless passion."[33] Certainly, the choice of the word "career" is apt, since profligacy was the only activity to which Powers committed himself; the use of "corrupt" and "lawless" to describe his "passion" provided even greater insight into his characterization. Throughout the narrative incontinence and disobedience were linked; not only was the former a version of the latter, but sexual excess, as a lack of restraint, also represented an inability to restrain the self in all areas of social participation, particularly within the family. Physical pleasure dominated all motivations, reducing Powers to a brutish reflex of wanting and taking.

After being "put out" with a second master, the first having grown tired of his incontinence and disobedience, Powers continued to develop his vicious habits. Despite the attempts of his new master to instruct him, he applied himself to more immoral pursuits. According to the narrative, he could not help surrendering to his nature:

> being naturally vicious I improved my talents . . . to very bad purposes. I used to make a point of pilfering whenever I could; for when I saw an opportunity, the devil, or some other evil spirit, always gave me a strong inclination. I suppose it was because I was naturally inclined to be light-fingered; for I never hesitated to touch anything that came my way.[34]

By referring to his natural inclinations, Powers exposed the corruption inherent in his character, and readers, unable to distinguish between racial character and literary characterization, were encouraged to use their prejudices to comprehend the sources of evil. This narrative mixture of racial and literary character was reinforced by the connection between lewdness and lawlessness. Following the above passage, Powers added, "Here too I played my pranks, with young black girls about the streets; and indulged myself as freely as I could without discovery." Indeed, as the narrative emphasized, he "never hesitated to touch anything" that came his way. Any desire, whether sexual or material, was indulged.

When describing the actual rape, Powers presented his crime as a similar impulse of wanting and taking. Previous to the attack, he had neither forethought of what he was about to do nor malice toward his victim. As it was described, the rape was a random, spontaneous event, the result of a rash, vicious impulse. Although he admitted that he had once before "attempted to ravish a young girl," an attempt frustrated by "providence," Powers stated that on this particular night he was "without any evil intention." While riding along on his way "to wrestle" with someone, he explained that he simply encountered his victim on the road:

> I overtook a young woman, whom I knew to be ————. I passed on by her . . . till after a little querying with myself, and finding nothing to oppose, but rather the devil to assist me, I determined to make an attempt on her virgin chastity. —So I waylaid her, and as she came up, seized her

with one hand, and her horse's bridle with t'other, she asked me what I
wanted? —I told her to dismount and I would tell her. At the same time
taking her from the horse, I threw her on the ground, and in spite of her
cries and entreaties, succeeded in my hellish design.[35]

The description itself was brutal enough, but the lack of premeditation,
the sudden surrendering to an evil inclination, made Powers seem all the
more perfidious. Yet this lack of intention was equaled by a similar lack
of guilt. As he was described, after as well as before, Powers was
thoughtless, a creature of reflex rather than reflection. Describing his
actions following the rape, he stated, "Then [I] left her, and went to the
place proposed, where I found my antagonist; but the evening being far
spent, I returned to my master's house and sat down, as usual, to play
chequers with the children."[36]

Such a graphic account of a black man raping a white virgin indeed
would have shocked eighteenth-century readers, but, by describing the
rapist soon sitting down "as usual" to play checkers with his master's
children, the narrative revealed a more alarming level of evil. As he was
presented, Powers threatened readers not only because he was wicked
but also because he so easily masked his wickedness behind a deceptive
pose of docility. The narrative further dramatized the subtle and seduc-
tive quality of this deceit by describing the confusion that occurred
during the first attempt to arrest Powers: "It was not long before I heard
people round the house, and was afterwards informed they were after
me; but seeing me so lively at play, says the Esq. 'It can't be Tom'—so
they went away."[37] According to the narrative, Powers committed evil
without either deliberation or contrition and then attempted to conceal
his crime by appearing to be the exact opposite of what he was. In effect,
in order to hide his iniquity, he acted out a role of passive submission.
While reinforcing the racist stereotype of the oversexed black, his characterization, then, added an element of deviousness that promoted even
greater racial distrust.

Powers was arrested, despite his master's confused objections, but
even after officially receiving the label of "prisoner," he refused to
surrender his pose of ignorance and innocence. When being taken to jail,
he stated, "As we were passing by the place, where the crime was
committed, I was questioned concerning the fact; but, I, like a hardened
villain, as I was, denied every syllable of the truth." Throughout the
months he spent in jail awaiting his trial, he continued attempting to

evade "the truth," and even afterward he demonstrated that official conviction had little to do with spiritual conviction. Twice he broke out of jail, and the last half of the narrative followed his attempts to elude his pursuers and their unequivocal reading of his character. Finally, after his master and former friends assisted in his recapture, after he stood physically and symbolically exposed on the scaffold, Powers was unmasked, stripped of his feigned ignorance and innocence. His participation in the ritual drama of execution, whether voluntary or involuntary, was his fullest confession.

Yet for readers the truth came prepackaged. By the conventions of the criminal-narrative genre, the guilt and the deceit of the character were expected, announced on the title page that publicly connected his name, his crime, and his execution. In substituting literary experience for historical occurrence, *The Narrative and Confession of Thomas Powers* offered readers a similarly unequivocal (and univocal) reading of the rapist's nature. The Powers text not only sanctioned the judicial conviction but also popularized it, allowing readers no ambiguity concerning the verity of its presentation. Promoting racism as an interpretive strategy, the narrative exposed the "hellish" designs of its central character. As he was presented, Powers was naturally inclined to wickedness, unable to resist the temptations of "the devil, or some other evil spirit." The narrative, however, offered masters a lesson in how to overcome such corrupt tendencies. As it was related, when Powers was 14 he was caught stealing a small sum of money from his master, and in describing his punishment, he stated, "I was forced to return the money, and take a few stripes on my back; but if I had received my just deserts I might possibly have escaped the fate, that now awaits me."[38] Given his weak character and evil inclinations, Powers needed his master's discipline in order to overcome his nature. And though his example was extreme, his ability to deceive implicated all blacks; his plea for "just deserts" represented an ideological demand that all black servants be subjected to strict discipline.

Since rape was neither commonly reported nor prosecuted, its appearance in eighteenth-century criminal narratives was infrequent, but it certainly was not an insignificant topic. Several aspects present in all of the accounts were later developed into stereotypes of immense cultural proportions. Consequently, the narratives not only reflected reader expectations but also influenced such expectations. How early Americans perceived rapists in society was shaped by how rapists were characterized in narrative form. And these characterizations were remarkably similar. Invariably the rape was presented as the final outrage of a life of sinful corruption. With a macabre focus the narratives described how the rapists were *"Ripened* for the Gallows,"* a process of dissolution that began early with the defiance of authority, first parental, then civil. Without the discipline of parents and masters, they quickly developed a pattern of disregard, if not disdain, for all social boundaries. Of marginal and minority status—each of the five rapists covered by a narrative was an ethnic Other in New England, either black or Irish—the rapist characters challenged the conventions of their readers by refusing to accept the responsibilities of their prescribed roles. At one time or another, all of the characters ran away, an action that not only symbolized a rejection of their proper place but also a severing of social and emotional connections. Therefore, they were depicted in more than one way as outsiders, and their narratives publicized their alien status in order to justify their executions.

As they were depicted, the most sensational tendency of the rapists was their hypersexuality, but this was indicative of all vicious impulses of self. Embracing self-gratification while abandoning self-sacrifice, they situated themselves in an antisocial wilderness, a morally unsettled territory from which they raided their communities. With one exception (Young), all of the rapists were thieves, and the narratives presented rape, not as a crime against women, but as a crime against property. Yet the theft of sex was symbolic. Characterized as ungrateful and ungovernable, the rapists disrupted the social order in their various pursuits of self, and thus their crimes represented a rebellion. Readers were not presented with narratives of white masters raping servants or slaves. The pattern of social relationships was always reversed, thus threatening the established patriarchy. The victims's body was only a boundary marker, outlining the privileges of property ownership. The victim herself did not matter.

Notes

1. Edwin Powers, *Crime and Punishment in Early Massachusetts, 1620–1692* (Boston: Beacon Press, 1966), 264.

2. Powers, 266.

3. Powers, 266, 267.

4. Susan Brownmiller, *Against Our Will* (New York: Simon and Schuster, 1975), 5.

In the critical discussion of rape, Brownmiller's study is still essential reading. For a helpful anthology of essays on rape, including a review of Brownmiller's work, see Duncan Chappell, Robley Geis, and Gilbert Geis, *Forcible Rape: The Crime, the Victim and the Offender* (New York: Columbia University Press, 1977). An equally valuable study in the discussion of rape is Susan Griffin, *Rape: The Politics of Consciousness* (San Francisco: Harper and Row, 1979). For a Marxist interpretation of rape issues, see Julia R. and Harman Schwendinger, *Rape and Inequality* (Beverly Hills: Sage Publications, 1983). For a recent and perceptive contribution to the study of rape, see Linda Brookover Bourque, *Defining Rape* (Durham, N.C.: Duke University Press, 1989).

5. Bradley Chapin, *Criminal Justice in Colonial America, 1606–1660* (Athens: University of Georgia Press, 1983), 126.

6. Powers, 281.

7. For the most recent listing of early American criminal narratives, see Wilfred J. Ritz, *American Judicial Proceedings First Printed before 1801: An Analytical Bibliography* (Westport, Ct.: Greenwood Press, 1984). For a still helpful bibliography, see Ronald A. Bosco, "Early American Gallows Literature," *Resources for American Literary Study* 8 (1978), 81–107. The present study focuses on the narratives of five rapists. A sixth narrative, *The Life and Confession of Daniel Wilson* (Providence, 1774), offered Wilson's final remarks before his execution for rape, yet nothing of either his victim or his rape was mentioned; however, after listing his experiences as a thief, Wilson merely acknowledged that he was "apprehended for committing a rape." Although no narrative was published, the execution of Anthony for rape in 1798 prompted Timothy Langdon to publish the sermon he preached to the condemned rapist (*A Sermon, Preached at Danbury, November 8th, 1798, being the Day of the Execution of Anthony, a Free Negro . . . for the crime of Rape*). During the eighteenth century there were also three trial accounts of rapists published: *Bedlow's Trial for Rape* (New York, 1793); *Price's Trial for Rape* (New York, 1797); and *Croucher's Trial for Rape* (New York, 1800). In addition, *The Last Words and Dying Speech of Edmund Fortis, A Negro Man* (Exeter, Mass., 1795) combined the crimes of rape and murder. Only one criminal account of seduction was published, the trial account of John Baker: *The Hypocrite Unmask'd. Trial and Conviction of John Baker, A Methodist Teacher . . . for Seducing Miss Ann Burns* (New York, 1798).

8. Richard Slotkin, "Narratives of Negro Crime in New England, 1675–1800," *American Quarterly* 25 (1973), 17.

9. For a valuable discussion of the seduction motif in early American fiction, see Cathy N. Davidson, *Revolution and the Word* (New York: Oxford University Press, 1986).

10. For a recent discussion of American sexuality, see John D'Emilio and Estelle B. Freedman, *Intimate Matters: A History of Sexuality in America* (New York: Harper and Row, 1988). The link between sexuality and criminality was, of course, traditional in Western society, and early New Englanders were by no means unique in viewing one as an indication of the other. Yet according to D'Emilio and Freedman, attitudes toward sexuality underwent great change during the latter part of the eighteenth century. For the first time sexual pleasure was no longer seen simply as a secondary by-product of the procreative act but as an end in itself. Such a change in attitude, by no means universally shared, would have increased the social anxiety concerning sexual relations, since it tended to deemphasize the family unit.

11. Certainly most eighteenth-century criminal characterizations followed the same basic conventions. Generally, criminal narratives were published to offer warnings, give justifications, and provide explanations for crime while exploiting a popular audience. Inevitably, in order to warn, justify, and explain, the narratives, situated the criminal characters in a process of defiance that began early in childhood, more often than not with filial disobedience. In that his crime or rape was described as the final outrage in a series of outrages, the rapist resembled other criminal characters. As an insurrectionary, however, the rapist was unique. Since the woman's body was sacred property, the rapist was depicted as defying both social and sexual codes.

12. Cotton Mather, *Pillars of Salt* (Boston, 1699), 69.

13. Mather, 69–70, 71.

14. *The Life and Dying Speech of Arthur* (Boston, 1768) was published as a broadside. Kneeland and Adams, its printers, also published Arthur's execution sermon, delivered by Thaddeus Maccarty, *The Power and Grace of Christ display'd to a dying Malefactor* (Boston, 1768).

15. Sheehan's *Account* was published in Salem as a broadside and, again, was probably sold on his execution day, January 16, 1772. A second undated and imperfect edition of the broadside was also published. Along with the broadside, his execution sermon also was published: James Dimon, *A Sermon, Preached at Salem, January 16, 1772* (Salem, 1772).

16. Young's *Last Words* was published in Worcester as a broadside and, again, probably was sold on his execution day, November 11, 1779. At the same time a ballad, supposedly written by Young, was also published as a broadside; Robert Young, *The Dying Criminal: Poem* (Worcester, 1779). Both broadsides were republished shortly afterward in New London.

17. Mountain's *Sketches* was one of the more popular criminal narratives published in the eighteenth century. The original narrative was published in New Haven at some time around his execution, October 20, 1790. Three more editions were also published in 1790 at Norwich, Hartford, and Boston. Under two different titles, *The singular adventures,* n.p., and *The Life and Adventures,* Bennington, the narrative was again published in 1791. Also, two German translations were published: *Die Wunderbare Lebens-Beschreibung von Joseph Mountain* (Lancaster, n.d.), *Das Leben und die Begebenheiten von Joseph Mountain* (Philadelphia, 1791). In addition to the different editions, Mountain's execution sermon was also published: James Dana, *The Intent of Capital Punishment* (New Haven, 1790).

18. Mountain, 2. Although unstated, readers could assume Mountain jumped ship once he arrived in England, running away from slavery as well as his specific responsibilities. His status as a runaway slave, then, emphasized the narrative's general lesson that inferiors, both social and racial, needed strict discipline and supervision. Moreover, since he ran away just when the first shots of the Revolution were being fired, he could be perceived as abandoning his country as well as his master.

19. Mountain, 3.

20. Mountain, 5.

21. Mountain, 8.

22. Mountain, 10–11.

23. Mountain, 16.

24. Mountain, 17.

25. Mountain, 17.

26. Mountain, 17–18.

27. Mountain, 18.

28. Mountain's *Sketches* exhibits conflicting narrative impulses. The criminal narrative began as authoritarian discourse. While exploiting the popular hunger for the lurid and the sensational, early narratives generally suppressed the criminal voice, replacing it with the dominant voice of the community. Words were literally "taken from his [the criminal's] mouth." But as printers became more competitive, forces of the market place began to influence the production of criminal narratives. Readers came to desire the criminal's story more than his warning, and printers responded by including more sensational material and a more authentic criminal voice. As a result, the original narrative intentions to warn, to justify, and to explain became conventions used to make the sensational material more socially acceptable. As one of the later narratives, Mountain's reveals an obvious attempt to surround the criminal's voice with that of the community, thus using literary conventions to return the robber-rapist to an acceptance of social conventions.

29. According to contemporary accounts, including Dana's execution sermon, Mountain did not conform to the model of penitence the narrative imposed upon him. Referring to Mountain's "levity" during his imprisonment, Dana stated: "Since your confinement you have by no means given the best evidence of true contrition" (22).

30. Thomas Powers, *The Narrative and Confession of Thomas Powers, A Negro* (Norwich, 1796), 12. Powers's *Narrative* was published roughly three weeks after the day of execution, July 28, 1796. The title page noted that Powers was "formerly of Norwich in Connecticut." Evans also lists three other editions, one of which was published in Haverhill where Powers was executed. This edition was probably the original, but it and the other two have not been located. The execution sermon, however, was published and is available: Noah Worcester, *A Sermon delivered . . . at the Execution of Thomas Powers* (Haverhill, N.H., 1796).

31. The identification of Powers as "A Negro" was not unusual in early American narratives. As a rhetorical strategy intended to provide white readers with an ideological context to view the characters, racial epithets were commonly used on title pages. Both Mountain and Arthur similarly had been identified.

32. Powers, 3–4.

33. Powers, 4.

34. Powers, 5.

35. Powers, 6.

36. Powers, 6–7.

37. Powers, 7.

38. Powers, 5.

III

Individual Confrontations

11

Phillis Wheatley and the Black American Revolution

Betsy Erkkila

In the years leading up to the American Revolution, those who advocated a break with England did so in the language of the two primary social tropes: the family and slavery. The position of America was figuratively represented as the natural right of the son or daughter to revolt against a tyrannical parent and the natural right of a slave to revolt against a master. Through a masterful deployment of these parent/child and master/slave tropes in *Common Sense,* which was published in 1776, Tom Paine galvanized popular support for the formal break with England that would occur six months later. In his attempt to "divest" the king and monarchy of their traditional authority, Paine represented the king as a slave master seeking to deprive Americans of their natural liberties: "When the republican virtue fails, slavery ensues. Why is the constitution of England sickly, but because monarchy has poisoned the republic, the crown has engrossed the Commons?" Pleading the cause of "final separation" from Britain in the language of the "violated unmeaning names of parent and child," Paine says,

> No man was a warmer wisher for a reconciliation than myself, before the fatal nineteenth of April, 1775, but the moment the event of that day was made well known, I rejected the hardened, sullen tempered Pharoah of England for ever; and disdain the wretch that with the pretended title of FATHER OF HIS PEOPLE can unfeelingly hear of their slaughter, and composedly sleep with their blood upon his soul.[1]

In a political economy in which the rights of women were absorbed and legally "covered" by the constituted authority of the male and blacks were held as property under the institution of slavery, the widespread rhetorical representation of America as child of liberty or enchained slave oppressed by the tyranny of father/master had a particularly potent social appeal. This appeal was heightened by the violent and bloody visual iconography that accompanied the written representation of the American cause.

In the newspaper cartoon "Britannia Mutilated" (1774), for example, Britain appears as a naked female figure, enchained, amputated, and deprived of her former power by the aggressive colonial policies of king and Parliament. In "The able Doctor, or America Swallowing the Bitter Draught" (1774), America is figured as a half-clad Indian woman who is violated by a number of male figures who force her to submit to the "bitter draught" of the Boston Port Bill and other British policies while Britannia turns away in distress. In the etching "Liberty Conquers Tyranny" (1775), Liberty leans on a pillar with her foot on the neck of a man whose crown and chain represent the oppression of Britain as monarch and enslaver. The old world order of the patriarch is represented as a barren landscape of war and violence in which a female appears to be at the mercy of an aggressive male figure. The new world order of female liberty is represented as a pastoral landscape of abundance, fertility, and peace where male and female dance in apparent harmony. In "Columbia Trading with all the World" Columbia as a figure of the United States takes her sovereign place among the four female continents: America, Africa, Asia, and Europe. Liberated from the oppressions of patriarch and slave master, she freely engages in commerce and exchange with the entire world.

The radicalizing effect that Revolutionary rhetoric and iconography could have on women's self-conceptions and the traditional relations between male and female is particularly evident in the correspondence between Abigail and John Adams during the Revolutionary years. Abigail Adams was one of the first to note and draw out the Revolutionary implications of the analogy between the political position of America and the position of the female within a masculine economy. "I long to hear that you have declared an independancy," she wrote John on March 31, 1776,

> and by the way in the new Code of Laws which I suppose it will be necessary for you to make I desire you would Remember the Ladies, and be more generous and favourable to them than your ancestors. Do not put such

unlimited power into the hands of the Husbands. Remember all Men would be tyrants if they could. If perticular care and attention is not paid to the Laidies we are determined to foment a Rebelion, and will not hold ourselves bound by any Laws in which we have no voice, or Representation.[2]

In this justifiably famous passage Adams not only challenges traditional orders of masculine authority in family or in state; her masterful deployment of the rhetoric of representation and consent, desire and power, self-sovereignty and natural law, also illustrates the importance of the American Revolution in giving women the language and metaphors to "foment" further rebellion in their struggle for citizenship, suffrage, and full human rights.

Whereas John Adams and the Founding Fathers wanted a change of regime, Abigail Adams was asking for a change of world. Like such male satirists as Alexander Pope in England and John Trumbull in America, John Adams seeks to diffuse the logic and power of Abigail Adams's Revolutionary appeal through humor.

As to your extraordinary Code of Laws, I cannot but laugh. We have been told that our Struggle has loosened the bands of Government every where. That Children and Apprentices were disobedient—that schools and Colleges were grown turbulent—that Indians slighted their Guardians and Negroes grew insolent to their Masters. But your Letter was the first Intimation that another Tribe more numerous and powerfull than all the rest were grown discontented.

Recognizing the dangerous loosening of traditional bonds of rank and subordination brought by the Revolutionary situation, John insists on reconstituting the absolute authority of patriarchy: "Depend upon it, We know better than to repeal our Masculine systems."[3] His bantering tone does not disguise the fact of his self-contradiction. While he was advocating the right of rebellion in the political sphere, asserting that "the people have a right to revoke the authority that they themselves had deputed and to constitute abler and better agents, attorneys, and trustees," he was attempting to suppress the rebellion in his own household by reasserting the absolute authority of a "Masculine" system that was hereditary, divinely sanctioned, and beyond repeal.[4]

Abigail Adams refused to be silenced. She pointed out the contradiction between the antiauthoritarian rhetoric of the Revolution and her husband's insistence on maintaining the divine right of the father as king. "I can not say that I think you very generous to the Ladies," she wrote, "for whilst you are proclaiming peace and good will to Men, Emancipating all Nations, you insist upon retaining an absolute power over Wives. But you must remember that Arbitrary power is like most other things which are very hard, very liable to be broken."[5] Like other Revolutionary women, Abigail Adams took advantage of the Revolutionary situation to press for widespread political reform both within and outside marriage. Alarmed by a "conspiracy of the Negroes" in Boston, who had agreed to fight on the side of the royalist governor in return for arms and liberation, she expressed her essential sympathy with the slave's demand for liberation: "I wish most sincerely there was not a Slave in the province," she wrote John in 1774, pointing the contradiction between the rhetoric of liberty and the fact of slavery in America. "It allways appeard a most iniquitous Scheme to me—fight ourselfs for what we are daily robbing and plundering from those who have as good a right to freedom as we have. You know my mind on this Subject."[6]

During the American Revolution, the challenge to constituted authority came not only from privileged and highborn women like Abigail Adams, but, also as John Adams had grudgingly noted, from apprentices, Indians, and Negroes who "grew insolent to their Masters." The potential danger of this challenge is evident in the life and work of the black poet Phillis Wheatley, who was abducted from Africa and sold as a slave in Boston in 1761. Whereas Abigail Adams compared the condition of women in America to "Egyptian bondage," for Wheatley, drawing upon the same Old Testament image to describe the captivity of her people to "our Modern Egyptians," the language of bondage and freedom was no longer metaphoric but real. Knowing the truth of slavery as part of her daily experience as the slave of a prosperous Boston merchant, she, too, pointed out the contradiction between rhetoric and reality in America. In a letter to the Native American preacher Samson Occom, Wheatley expressed hope for "Deliverance" from the "Avarice" that impelled Americans to "countenance and help forward" the enslavement of "their fellow Creatures." In this letter, which was printed in the *Boston Post-Boy* and the *Boston News-Letter* in 1774, she noted ironically "the strange Absurdity of their Conduct whose Words and Actions are so diametrically opposite. How well the Cry for Liberty, and the reverse Disposition for the Exercise of oppressive power over others agree,—I humbly think it does not require the Penetration of a Philosopher to determine."[7] Positioning herself in the breach between trope and truth, between the rhetoric of republican liberty and her actual experience of black African enslavement, Wheatley transformed the discourse of liberty, natural rights, and human nature into a subtle critique of the color code and the oppressive racial structures of Revolutionary America.

It is no coincidence that Wheatley's *Poems on Various Subjects Religious and Moral* (1773), which was the first full-length book published by an African American, appeared during the Revolutionary period. According to her "Master" John Wheatley, "Phillis was brought from *Africa* to *America,* in the Year 1761, between Seven and Eight Years of Age. Without any Assistance from School Education, and by only what she was taught in the Family, she, in sixteen Months Time from her Arrival, attained the English Language."[8] By age 12 she was reading and translating Ovid, at age 15 she published her first poem, and she was 20 when *Poems* was published. Wheatley and her book were, in effect, a Revolutionary phenomenon.

In *Home* Leroi Jones criticizes what he calls Wheatley's "ludicrous departures from the huge black voices that splintered southern nights."[9] But his criticism misses the point. Within the discourse of racial inequality in the eighteenth century, the fact of a black woman reading, writing, and publishing poems was in itself enough to splinter the categories of white and black and explode a social order grounded in notions of racial difference. The potential danger of her enterprise is underscored by the doubleness of the authenticating picture that represents her in the Revolutionary figure of a black woman reading, thinking, and writing at the same time that it enchains her in the inscription "Phillis Wheatley, Negro Servant to Mr. John Wheatley of Boston."

Her volume of poems was accompanied by the authenticating documents, a picture and a "Notice to the Public" signed by several local authorities, which would frame and mark later African-American writing. Wheatley's complex position as black woman slave in Revolutionary America is suggested by the fact that the signatures of the royalist governor Thomas Hutchinson and the leader of Boston resistance John Hancock were joined for a brief moment over the body of her *Poems*. But while Wheatley was the "property" of John Wheatley and the authenticating male figures who "notice" her text, she was possessed by the insurrectionary "Goddess of Liberty" who stalks her poems as she was at that very moment stalking the landscape of Revolutionary America.

Even before Wheatley's book was published, the Philadelphia physician and antislavery advocate Benjamin Rush cited her poetry as a sign at once of black humanity and the sameness of human nature. In his antislavery tract, *An Address to the Inhabitants of the British Settlements in America upon Slave Keeping* (1773), he wrote, "There is now in the town of Boston a Free Negro Girl, about 18 years of age, who has been but 9 years in the country, whose singular genius and accomplishments are such as not only do honor to her sex, but to human nature. Several of her poems have been printed, and read with pleasure by the public."[10]

Within the context of Revolutionary America, loyalist and patriot alike laid claim to Wheatley's voice: for the loyalists she might serve as a means of garnering slave support for the cause of Britain in America, and for the patriots she represented a sign of human progress rather than degeneration within America. But while Wheatley appears to utter the ideals of her time in the ordered and allusive heroic couplets of Pope and the neoclassical writers, she also knew how to manipulate language, image, and phrase in a manner that destabilizes while it appears to reinforce the categories of the dominant culture. As the poet Naomi Long Madgett says in a recent tribute to "Phillis," she "learned to sing / a dual song":

> *Show to the world the face the world would see;*
> *Be slave, be pet, conceal your Self—but be.*
>
> Lurking behind the docile Christian Lamb,
> Unconquered lioness asserts: "I am!"[11]

Within the Revolutionary matrix of eighteenth-century America, Phillis Wheatley learned the power of speaking doubly as African and American.

From the dedication to the countess of Huntington that opens her *Poems* to her tribute "To the Right Honorable William, Earl of Dartmouth" enclosed within, Wheatley's book is enmeshed in a web of Revolutionary associations. Margaret Burroughs exaggerates only slightly when she says, "If the Continental Congress had possessed an intelligent counter-intelligence service, Phillis Wheatley might have been interned for the duration as a security risk, on the principle of guilt by association."[12] The countess of Huntingdon was a well-known supporter of both the evangelical and the antislavery movement in England. Her friend and associate, the earl of Dartmouth, supported the British policy of inciting slaves to revolt against rebel masters when he served as secretary of state for North America between 1772 and 1775.

As a book of poems by a woman slave celebrating the cause of American liberty, Wheatley's *Poems* is loaded with the irony of a cause and a country at odds with itself. While Wheatley was in London in 1773, where she met several supporters including the earl of Dartmouth and Benjamin Franklin, no less than five petitions for freedom were presented to the Massachusetts General Council by Boston slaves: "We have no Property. We have no Wives! No Children! We have no City! No Country!," one exclaimed. In February 1774 an article in the *Massachusetts Spy,* signed by an "African" patriot, invoked the rhetoric of natural right and consent to point out the analogy between America's defiance of Britain and the slaves' defiance of their masters in America: "Are not your hearts also hard, when you hold them in slavery who are intitled to liberty, by the law of nature, equal as yourselves? If it be so, pray, Sir, pull the beam out of thine eye."[13] At the time Wheatley's *Poems* was published, there was widespread fear of slave revolt; Abigail Adams's September 1774 letter to John on the conspiracy of Boston Negroes is only one of a number of signs that fear of slave insurrection was spreading from the South to New England. Perhaps because of this growing fear of blacks, whether free or enslaved, Wheatley's book, having failed to receive an adequate subscription in America, was sponsored and published in England.

Like others who have lived and written in a dangerous social environment, Phillis Wheatley knew the art and necessity of speaking with a double tongue. In her poetry, she makes subtle use of ambiguity and irony, double meaning and symbolic nuance, to speak what was otherwise unspeakable from her position as an African woman slave in Revolutionary America. Wheatley's *Poems* opens with an address "To Maecenas," the patron of Horace and Virgil, who appears to represent her image of an ideal patron and audience for her poems. Wheatley enters the literary community by invoking the classical tradition of Homer and Virgil, but she ends with an invocation to Terence, the Roman slave of African descent who was able to use his literary talent to attain freedom:

> The happier *Terence* all the choir inspir'd,
> His soul replenish'd, and his bosom fir'd;
> But say, ye *Muses,* why this partial grace,
> To one alone of *Afric's* sable race;
> From age to age transmitting thus his name
> With the first glory in the rolls of fame?

Self-consciously placing herself and her poems within a specifically African tradition, Wheatley registers her own ambitious desire to share—or perhaps transcend—the "first glory" of her African forbear in a poetics of ascent "That fain would mount, and ride upon the wind."

In "To the University of Cambridge, in New England," which was one of the earliest poems she wrote, Wheatley begins by representing her passage into American slavery as a paradoxical Christian deliverance out of the bondage of African paganism:

> 'Twas not long since I left my native shore
> The land of errors, and *Egyptian* gloom:
> Father of mercy, 'twas thy gracious hand
> Brought me in safety from those dark abodes.

In the remainder of the poem, the "intrinsic ardour" of God's grace becomes the source of her moral authority, enabling her not only to speak as a poet but also to become a kind of female preacher who delivers a jeremiad to the unredeemed Harvard students:

> Let sin, that baneful evil to the soul,
> By you be shunn'd, nor once remit your guard;
> Suppress the deadly serpent in its egg.
> Ye blooming plants of human race devine,
> An *Ethiop* tells you 'tis your greatest foe;
> Its transient sweetness turns to endless pain,
> And in immense perdition sinks the soul.

The racial underscoring—"an *Ethiop* tells you"—appears to be a rhetorical maneuver that increases the persuasiveness of the poet's lesson by drawing upon the negative social equation of black and African with sin and evil. But Wheatley's emphatic *Ethiop* also suggests a figure of racial pride who speaks to the privileged white race from a position of moral superiority.

The ambiguity of the passage is particularly evident in a 1767 manuscript version of the poem, in which the concluding lines read:

> Let hateful vice so baneful to the Soul,
> Be still avoided with becoming care;
> *Suppress the sable monster in its growth,*
> Ye blooming plants of human race, divine
> An Ethiop tells you, tis your greatest foe,
> Its transient sweetness turns to endless pain,
> And brings eternal ruin on the Soul. [emphasis added]

The line "Suppress the sable monster in its growth" is syntactically double, functioning as both command against evil and statement against the "sable monster" of black enslavement. Read this way, the "transient sweetness" of sin becomes linked with the economics of slavery, the production of molasses and sugar, and the "eternal ruin" that will be visited upon the white race by a divine order of retribution. Although Wheatley herself ultimately suppressed the figure of the "sable monster," the fact of her suppression suggests her underlying awareness of the potentially dangerous doubleness of language—a doubleness that still marks the final version of the poem.

In her most anthologized poem, "On Being Brought from Africa to America," Wheatley speaks with a similarly double voice. The poem is, like the title, formally split between Africa and America, embodying the poet's own split consciousness as African American. In the opening quatrain, the poet speaks as an American, representing slavery as a paradoxical Christian deliverance, a necessary stage in the black person's advance toward redemption and civilization; in the second quatrain the poet speaks as an African, turning the terms of Christian orthodoxy into a critique of white hypocrisy and oppressive racial codes.

> 'Twas mercy brought me from my *Pagan* land,
> Taught my benighted soul to understand
> That there's a god, that there's a *Saviour* too:
> Once I redemption neither sought nor knew.
> Some view our sable race with scornful eye,
> "Their color is a diabolic die."
> Remember, *Christians, Negroes,* black as *Cain,*
> May be refin'd and join th' angelic train.

As in "To the University of Cambridge," Wheatley's "redemption" becomes the source of her moral authority, signaling her transformation from being passively "brought" and "taught" by God's Providence to being the active black subject who speaks and instructs in the second quatrain of the poem.

The poem operates on what Maya Angelou has called the "Principle of Reverse": "Anything that works for you can also work against you."[14] Speaking as a black woman slave, Wheatley turns the racial codes of the dominant culture back upon themselves, giving them an ironic inflection. What appears to be repetition is in fact a form of *mimesis* that mimics and mocks in the act of repeating. This process is particularly evident in the final lines of the poem, in which Wheatley challenges and destabilizes the white discourse of racial difference by placing that discourse in quotation marks—"Their color is a diabolic die." As the racially conscious voice of her people, Wheatley literally "mimics" the white view of "our sable race" in a manner that recasts the discourse of racial difference in an ironic mode.

Within the context of the poem, the use of italicization has a similarly destabilizing effect: the italicized terms *Pagan, Christian, Negroes,* and *Cain* are simultaneously underscored and marked for interrogation. The slipperiness of these terms is evidenced in the final lines of the poem, in which through punctuation and italicization the phrase "Remember, *Christians, Negroes,* black as *Cain*" might be read doubly as an address to Christians about black humanity and an address to Christians *and* Negroes that links them both in the figurative image "black as *Cain.*" Both readings undermine the color code by emphasizing the equality of spiritual condition shared by whites and blacks alike as sinful descendants of Adam and potentially "redeemed" heirs of Christ's saving grace.

Wheatley's most overt criticism of the institution of slavery occurs in "To the Right Honorable William, Earl of Dartmouth, His Majesty's Principal Secretary of State for North America, &c." Here again the poet speaks doubly as American patriot and African slave, celebrating "Fair Freedom" as the cause of New England patriots and "the *Goddess* long desir'd" by enslaved blacks. She associates the 1772 appointment of Dartmouth as secretary of state for North America with the return of Freedom, "Long lost to realms beneath the northern skies":

> Elate with hope her race no longer mourns,
> Each soul expands, each grateful bosom burns,
> While in thine hand with pleasure we behold
> The silken reins, and *Freedom's* charms unfold.

When one remembers that as secretary of state for the colonies and president of the Board of Trade and Foreign Plantations between 1772 and 1775 the earl of Dartmouth became engaged in the British policy of inciting American slaves to revolt against their patriot masters, the poet's "hope" of freedom for "her race" takes on a particularly insurrectionary cast.

Wheatley draws upon the Revolutionary rhetoric of tyranny and enslavement to promote the cause of America, but as the language of an

American slave her words bear specific reference to the cause of black liberation:

> No more, *America,* in mournful strain
> Of wrongs, and grievance unredress'd complain,
> No longer shalt thou dread the iron chain,
> Which wanton *Tyranny* with lawless hand
> Had made, and with it meant t'enslave the land.

Wheatley further literalizes the slave metaphor by calling attention to her own condition as an American slave:

> Should you, my lord, while you peruse my song,
> Wonder from whence my love of *Freedom* sprung,
> Whence flow these wishes for the common good,
> By feeling hearts alone best understood,
> I, young in life, by seeming cruel fate
> Was snatch'd from *Afric's* fancy's happy seat:
> What pangs excruciating must molest,
> What sorrows labour in my parent's breast?
> Steel'd was that soul and by no misery mov'd
> That from a father seiz'd his babe belov'd:
> Such, such my case. And can I then but pray
> Others may never feel tyrannic sway?

Transforming the Revolutionary trope of enslavement into the thing itself, the poet becomes self-authenticating, authorizing her voice as the poet of freedom in her historical experience as an American slave. Wheatley's most direct personal statement about her African past becomes as well her most direct protest against the reality of slavery as the true tyranny in America.

Wheatley's reference to her "seeming cruel fate" might be read as a sign of the mutilating influence of slavery, the mark of the black poet's capitulation to the codes of the dominant culture.[15] But her words are self-protectively ambiguous. Read within the context of Wheatley's ardent Christian faith, her words also suggest a moving attempt to make sense of the fate of herself and her people as slaves within a "seeming cruel" providential order. The poet is not "brought" but "seiz'd" and "snatch'd from *Afric's* fancy'd happy seat," a phrasing that represents her enslavement as a kidnapping and Africa as a site not of illusory but of *still* imagined happiness. Bearing witness to slavery and the slave trade as a cold-blooded violation of the fundamental social unit, the familial bond between father and child, Wheatley turns her personal history into an emotionally charged "case" against the institution of slavery. Her prayer that "Others may never feel tryannic sway" is a prayer that encompasses not only American colonists but the "Others" of her own African race.

According to her nineteenth-century biographer Margaretta Matilda Odell, Wheatley's only memory of her African homeland was the daily sunrise ritual of her mother, who "poured out water before the sun at his rising."[16] In Wheatley's writings, the memory of African sun worship merges with the language of evangelical Christianity and the language of Revolutionary freedom to produce a poetics of ascent and liberation. In this poetics the sun/son is the central figure of a constellation of images that moves from dark to light, white to black, sin to redemption, bondage to deliverance.

The intersection of these languages is particularly evident in "On Imagination," in which Wheatley imagines herself mounting on the "silken pinions" of *"Fancy"* toward the sun, toward God, and toward liberation:

> Soaring through air to find the bright abode
> Th'empyreal palace of the thund'ring God,
> We on thy pinions can surpass the wind,
> And leave the rolling universe behind:
> From star to star the mental optics rove,
> Measure the skies, and range the realms above.
> There in one view we grasp the mighty whole,
> Or with new worlds amaze th'unbounded soul.

Like Memory (*"Mneme"*) in "On Recollection" and Liberty ("the goddess") in "To Washington" and "Liberty and Peace, a Poem," Wheatley's *"Imagination"* is a potent female figure, an "imperial queen" whose wings carry the poet into "new worlds" of the "unbounded soul." These "new worlds" are at once the heavenly other world of biblical revelation and the poet's own "raptur'd" vision of an alternative earthly economy. In the last stanza of the poem the "rising fire" of Wheatley's poetic aspiration fuses with the language of revelation and revolution and her memory of the African sunrise, leading her on to an insurrectionary vision of deliverance out of the "iron bands" of an oppressive white order—figured in the poem as the "frozen deeps" of *"Winter"*—into the "radiant gold" of a new dawn on earth. The poet's voice and vision "cease" in the final lines of the poem: *"Winter austere forbids me to aspire, / And northern tempests damp the rising fire; / They chill the tides of Fancy's flowing sea."* But the poet's closing images of herself as a "rising fire" and "flowing sea" suggest that she will continue to sing against and beyond the damp and chill of white northern oppression.

The visionary language of evangelical Protestantism gave Wheatley the means of engaging in the Revolutionary struggle for black freedom without losing her devout Christian faith. Commenting on the "natural Rights" of Negroes in her 1774 letter to the Native American activist Samuel Occom, Wheatley envisions the black struggle against American slavery as a type of the Old Testament struggle of Israel "for their Freedom from Egyptian Slavery." "In every human Breast," she says,

> God has implanted a Principle, which we call Love of Freedom; it is impatient of Oppression, and pants for Deliverance; and by the Leave of our modern Egyptians I will assert, that the same Principle lives in us. God grant Deliverance in his own Way and Time, and get him honour upon all those whose Avarice impels them to countenance and help forward the Calamities of their fellow Creatures.[17]

Wheatley was the first in a long line of African-American writers to merge the Revolutionary language of liberty and natural rights with the biblical language of bondage and deliverance in a visionary poetics that imagines the deliverance of her people not as a religious translation only but as a revolutionary change of world.

A few months after the publication of her *Poems* and at the urging of her English supporters and her mistress, Susannah Wheatley, Phillis Wheatley was freed by John Wheatley. In a letter to Colonel David Wooster on the sale of her book in Connecticut she wrote, "I am now upon my own footing and whatever I get by this is entirely mine, & It is the Chief I have to depend upon."[18] Both literally and figuratively, Wheatley's poems—like those of her forbear, Terence—became a means of writing herself into freedom, and through them she continued to act, both directly and indirectly, toward the deliverance of her race.

On October 26, 1775, Phillis Wheatley sent a poem "To His Excellency George Washington." Inspired by "the goddess" Freedom and impelled by the "wild uproar" of Freedom's warriors, the poem is a subtle attempt to enlist Washington as a freedom fighter for real as well as for metaphoric slaves. "We demand," the poet says,

> The grace and glory of thy martial band.
> Fam'd for thy valour, for thy virtues more,
> Hear every tongue thy guardian aid implore!

Like the addresses to Washington written by other Revolutionary poets, including Joel Barlow and Philip Freneau, the poem suggests the potential power of writing at a time when poets as well as politicians were engaged in the process of creating a nation. As in Wheatley's addresses to other figures of cultural power, including the earl of Dartmouth, the preacher George Whitefield, and the lieutenant-governor of Massachusetts, Andrew Oliver, the poem also suggests a certain openness and indeterminacy in black-white relations during the Revolutionary years—an openness that would begin to close and rigidify once the war was over and slaves were written into the Constitution as three-fifths human.

In 1784, only a year after the close of the war, Phillis Wheatley died and was buried in an unmarked grave. Within the same year Thomas Jefferson set very distinct limits on the revolutionary discourse of freedom, equality, and "self-evident" truth when in *Notes on the State of Virginia* (1785) he advanced it "as a suspicion only, that blacks, whether originally a distinct race, or made distinct by time and circumstances, are inferior to the whites in the endowments of both mind and body." The potential danger of Wheatley's *Poems* as proof against Jefferson's "suspicion" of racial inequality is suggested by the fact that in advancing his argument, he singles out her work for criticism. In one of the earliest instances of the politics of canon formation in post-Revolutionary America, he not only dismisses her work from serious literary consideration; he also, and perhaps intentionally, transmutes her name from "wheat" to "what": "Religion indeed has produced a Phyllis Whately [*sic*]; but it could not produce a poet. The compositions published under her name are below the dignity of criticism. The heroes of the Dunciad are to her, as Hercules to the author of that poem."[19] At a time when the "loose and dangerous" notions of equality and consent were threatening to subvert traditional orders of masculine authority, subordination, and subjection, Jefferson's comment on the issue of race represents one of the first attempts of the white fathers to counter the Revolutionary discourse of equality with the post-Revolutionary discourse of racial and sexual difference.

"What do We Mean by the Revolution?" John Adams asked in 1815 in a letter to Thomas Jefferson. "The War? That was no part of the

Revolution. It was only an Effect and Consequence of it. The Revolution was in the Minds of the People, and this was effected, from 1760 to 1775, in the course of fifteen Years before a drop of blood was drawn at Lexington.''[20] While Adams recognized that the real American Revolution took place in the ''Minds of the People,'' he saw the Revolution as something that ended with the break from England. This reading of the American Revolution appeared to be confirmed by the 1787 Constitution, which reined in the egalitarian possibilities of the Revolution by representing slaves as three-fifths human and women as nonexistent under the supreme law of the land.

What the American Revolution gave to privileged white women like Abigail Adams and formerly enslaved black women like Phillis Wheatley was not real legal or political rights, but the knowledge, the moral ground, and perhaps most of all the language and the metaphors with which to ''foment'' further rebellion against the constituted orders of white masculine authority in the United States. Thus, it is no coincidence that the poetic and essentially political work of Phillis Wheatley would (re)emerge at the very center of the abolition movement in the 1830s and the Black Power movement in the 1960s. Nor is it any coincidence that as the first act of the women's suffrage movement, the Declaration of Principles at Seneca Falls in 1848 was a self-consciously female rewriting of the Declaration of Independence, and the still unratified Equal Rights Amendment of 1972 is phrased in the language of equal rights that had been proclaimed by the Declaration of Independence but denied to women in the Constitution of the United States. Abigail Adams was right; John Adams was wrong. The revolution was not over.

Notes

1. Thomas Paine, *The Complete Writings of Thomas Paine,* ed. Philip S. Foner (New York: Citadel Press, 1945), 16, 23, 25.

2. L. H. Butterfield, ed., *Adams Family Correspondence* (Cambridge: Harvard University Press, 1963), I, 370.

3. Butterfield, I, 382.

4. John Adams, *The Political Writings of John Adams,* ed. George A. Peek (New York: Liberal Arts Press, 1954), 13.

5. Butterfield, I, 402.

6. Butterfield, I, 162.

7. Phillis Wheatley, "To Samson Occom," in *The Poems of Phillis Wheatley: Revised and Enlarged Edition,* ed. Julian D. Mason, Jr. (Chapel Hill: University of North Carolina Press, 1989), 203–4. This letter was printed in several other New England newspapers about this time.

8. Wheatley, 47.

9. Leroi Jones, *Home* (New York: William B. Morrow, 1966), 106.

10. Quoted in William H. Robinson, Jr., "On Being Young, Gifted, and Black," in Robinson, ed., *Critical Essays on Phillis Wheatley* (Boston: G. K. Hall, 1982), 24. For a review of the debate on the nature of the Negro that surrounded the publication of Wheatley's *Poems,* see Henry Louis Gates, Jr.'s excellent essay "Phillis Wheatley and the Nature of the Negro," in his *Figures in Black: Words, Signs, and the "Racial" Self* (New York: Oxford University Press, 1987), 61–79.

11. Naomi Long Madgett, "Phillis," in Robinson, 207.

12. Margaret Burroughs, "Do Birds of a Feather Flock Together?" in Robinson, 145.

13. Quoted by Charles Akers, "'Our Modern Egyptians': Phillis Wheatley and the Whig Campaign against Slavery in Revolutionary Boston," *Journal of Negro History* 60 (1975), 404.

14. Maya Angelou, *I Know Why the Caged Bird Sings* (New York: Random House, 1969), 215.

15. Merle A. Richmond comments on the "warping influence" of slavery. "It mutilated her," he says in *Bid the Vassal Soar: Interpretive Essays on Life and Poetry of Phillis Wheatley . . . And George Moses Horton* (Washington, D.C.: Howard University Press, 1974), 66. For others who have commented on Wheatley's internalization of racist attitudes, see Vernon Loggins, *The Negro Author* (New York: Columbia University Press, 1931), and Terence Collins, "Phillis Wheatley: The Dark Side of the Poetry," *Phylon* 36 (1975), 78–88.

16. Margaretta Matilda Odell, *Memoir and Poems of Phillis Wheatley* (Boston: George W. Light, 1834), 10–11.

17. Wheatley, 204.

18. Wheatley, 197.

19. Thomas Jefferson, *Notes on the State of Virginia,* ed. William Peden (Chapel Hill: University of North Carolina Press, 1954), 143, 140.

20. Lester J. Cappon, ed. *The Adams-Jefferson Letters* (Chapel Hill: University of North Carolina Press, 1959), II, 455.

12

The Heritage of American Ethnicity in Crèvecoeur's Letters from an American Farmer

Doreen Alvarez Saar

Spurred on by the controversy over the nature of the canon, American scholars, particularly after the publication of Werner Sollors's *Beyond Ethnicity*,[1] have turned their attention to a reevaluation of the place and function of ethnic literature. Sollors's work was an important corrective to the tendency to see ethnic literature as a nineteenth- and twentieth-century phenomenon; in fact, as this essay attempts to show, the mechanism of ethnic culture was set in place during the colonial period.

J. Hector St. John de Crèvecoeur's *Letters from an American Farmer*,[2] published in 1782, is a key text in the development of American cultural codes of ethnicity because it is the first text to define the nature of the emerging American. However, insufficient attention has been paid to *Letters* as a text about ethnicity. A primary reason for this neglect is that readers have not understood the eighteenth-century context of the work and therefore have not seen how the historical context—the uneasy melding of the new theories of the individual with other cultural theories—influenced many of our contradictory attitudes about ethnicity.

Letters cannot be read in the same way as a modern text because the narrator of the letters has no self-consciousness about the ethnic experience or even an ethnic identity. Rather, *Letters* is an eighteenth-century text about the nature of life in America from which the narrator's occasional, albeit important, comments on ethnic experience have been culled. *Letters* is a fictional account of life in America: the work consists of twelve letters purported to be sent by a colonial innocent, James, the American farmer, to a friend in London. In the letters, James recounts his life on his farm, several trips he takes through the colonies, and his feelings about the Revolution. Although the boundaries between genres in the eighteenth century could be remarkably fluid, *Letters* is in many ways like Samuel Johnson's *Rasselas* and Voltaire's *Candide* in its consideration of political, social, and philosophical issues and thus might be considered a philosophical pseudo-novel.[3] Consequently, it would be impossible to do justice to *Letters* without some sense of the overt philosophical and some might even say political intention of its author.

In his dedication to the Abbe Raynal, Crèvecoeur suggests that it was Raynal's *Political and Philosophical History* that caused Crèvecoeur to think and to write about the state of nations and by implication to write *Letters:*

> For the first time in my life I reflected on the relative state of nations; I traced the extended ramifications of a commerce which ought to unite but now convulses the world; I admired that universal benevolence, that diffusive good will, which is not confined to the narrow limits of your own country, but, on the contrary, extends to the whole human race. (37)

The Letters from Crèvecoeur's fictional narrator, James the American farmer, may be seen as representative of the eighteenth-century quest for "the knowledge of permanent, common human nature."[4] While the text begins "in the centre of the individual personality," that is, in James's descriptions of his own family and his own farm, its purpose is public and moves outward from the private considerations of character "through systems of objectively meaningful rhetorical symbolism to the destination of the journey,"[5] that is, to James's discussions of slavery, the nature of personal allegiance, and war. When we read *Letters,* although we see the personal journey of the narrator from content colonial to a nonaggressive, even Quakerish, nationalist as the narrative core of the text, we must recognize that James's journey moves forward not in physical space as much as in intellectual and emotional reevaluations of the public, social, political, and philosophical questions of his time. When his respondent poses the theme "What is an American" for the third letter, James addresses questions of enduring importance for the history of ethnicity.

Conscious of the demands and biases of his audience, Crèvecoeur's purpose in the opening letters is to convince the English that the colonies represent "the most perfect society now existing in the world" (67). Letter three, "What is an American," begins with the assertion that the English will find that the colonies have surpassed their expectations:

> I wish I could be acquainted with the feelings and thoughts which must agitate the heart and present themselves to the mind of an enlightened Englishman when he first lands on this continent. He must greatly rejoice that he lived at a time to see this fair country discovered and settled; he must necessarily feel a share of national pride when he views the chain of settlements which embellish these extended shores. (66)

The need for such appeasement and persuasion of Crèvecoeur's eighteenth-century reader probably expresses actual historical conditions. England was beginning to manifest real concern about the exodus of its population to the American colonies. Bernard Bailyn describes the fears of the English about the disruption caused by emigration:

> By 1773 it was commonly believed that emigration was leading to virtual depopulation in certain regions of the British Isles. . . . It was the manifest, demographic and economic, losses involved that created the general public concern, a concern that grew wildly as the crisis in Anglo-American political relations swelled to the point of explosion.[6]

The stories of the immigrants are meant to calm the fears of Crèvecoeur's English readers and prove that America transforms anyone who enters its shores into a worthy colonial.

The tales of immigrants are a subtext and support Crèvecoeur's contentions about the happiness of James's own situation, the situation of any immigrant to the colonies and, by extension, the colonies as a whole. The many asides relating the success of a new arrival are intended not only to praise James and America but also to indirectly criticize Europe: "I knew a man who came to this country, in the literal sense of the expression, stark naked; I think he was a Frenchman and a sailor on board an English man-of-war. Being discontented, he had stripped himself and swam on-shore, where . . . he settled . . . in Maraneck" (89). The happy transformations of immigrants into Americans are used to exemplify the wonders possible in America:

> I had rather attend on the shore to welcome the poor European when he arrives; I observe him in his first moments of embarrassment, trace him throughout his primary difficulties, follow him step by step until he pitches

his tent on some piece of land and realizes that the energetic wish which has made him quit his native land, his kindred, and induced him to traverse a boisterous ocean. It is there I want to observe his first thoughts and feelings, the first essays of an industry, which had been hitherto suppressed. I wish to see men cut down the first trees, erect their new buildings . . . and say for the first time in their lives, "This is our own grain, raised from American soil; on it we shall grow fat and convert the rest into gold and silver." I want to see how the happy effects of their sobriety, honesty, and industry are first displayed; and who would not take a pleasure in seeing these strangers settling as new countrymen, struggling with arduous difficulties, overcoming them, and becoming happy? (91)

As in this paragraph, Crèvecoeur's method is to generalize the immigrant experience, often subsuming the many into one.

Despite the fact that Crèvecoeur often converts immigrants' stories into the unit of experience, there are actually four distinct and different "ethnic" experiences in *Letters*. The primary one is that of the loyal English colonist. It is told through the medium of James and was once considered the only matter of importance in the work; modern readers in search of true ethnicity tend to reject this transformation as not ethnic. However, it is in this story that the potential for ethnicity is created. While in England and Europe, there was no practical method by which the nonroyal foreigner could become a recognized member of that nation; in America, a theory of individual rights, citizenship, and allegiance would allow *almost* anyone to become an American. The principles that James espouses as universals and on which he eventually bases his rejection of England are crucial to the development of a theory that assimilates the Other and allows modern ethnicity to exist. The second is that of the non-English and European immigrant (in this period this group includes Scots and Irish). These immigrants get the full benefit of the political and social modifications that the English colonists make in received English culture. They are treated, and think of themselves, as English. They appear in a patchwork of stories and observations scattered throughout the letters. Often, these stories convey varying attitudes toward their behavior. Particularly on a first reading, some of Crèvecoeur's comments seem outdated and hence embarrassing to the modern reader; for example, Crèvecoeur says of the Irish: "Their potatoes, which are easily raised, are perhaps an inducement to laziness: their wages are too low and their whiskey too cheap" (85). The treatment of the third and fourth groups is radically different from that accorded the English and European immigrants. These two groups, Africans brought to be slaves and Native Americans, are considered outsiders by the colonists. A careful reading of *Letters* reveals that these groups have been covertly excluded from the process of Americanization: they remain outside the melting pot process open to the English and the Europeans. Without an understanding of the fact that Crèvecoeur, although he abhors slavery and praises the Native American way of life, acknowledges that the African and the Native American are treated differently, we would be guilty of obscuring the realities of life and ethnicity in eighteenth- and twentieth-century America. Further, we would be promoting "the erroneous view of immigration and assimilation as the primary modes by which groups of people enter and then rise in American society,"[7] a statement that, as we will see, is true even in colonial America.

It is likely that Crèvecoeur's own observation of the four major historical and cultural patterns of ethnic life in the eighteenth century shaped his portrayal of the four patterns of ethnic experience. Like Crèvecoeur's narrator, English settlers hammered out a political identity in the new nation while never entirely rejecting their English culture. According to Michael Zuckerman's study of colonial society in "Identity in British America: Unease in Eden," the colonists of British America "always strove to be Britons."[8] The Anglo-centrism of English colonial culture was such that European nationals in colonial America assimilated first on the basis of English political principle, that is, as English, and then confronted their practical cultural differences from the English colonists. As Willi Paul Adams details in "The Colonial German-language Press and the American Revolution," immigrant Germans fought the Revolution on the basis of English political principles. The determinants of their political consciousness toward events in colonial America were English in origin. For example, Henry Miller, the publisher of a prominent German-language newspaper, "did not publish an emigrè gazette full of news about home. . . . He addressed his readers primarily as inhabitants of a British colony . . . as subjects of the British crown whose daily lives, curiosity, and interests were determined by the fact that they lived in a colony in America."[9] At the same time, the existence of a German-language press was an indication of the distinction between these "Americans" and other Americans. It is likely that, to some degree, Crèvecoeur's text also mirrors the racism of the English colonists. Rejecting the Indian mode of life was an important element of British colonial identity: "Englishmen everywhere kept indigenes at a distance, to one degree or another, Spaniards, Portuguese, and French incorporated the American Indian into their colonial cultures."[10] Further, among the British colonies, "there emerged 'a growing racialist conviction that negroes were a nonhuman form of life.'"[11]

Implicit in the four ethnic strands of *Letters* is a hierarchy of culture. Crèvecoeur's test is Anglocentric, not only in its handling of the character of the narrator, but because the sociopolitical context that allows for the creation of the American grows out of an English political environment. In some sense, then, we are looking at the roots of what Werner Sollors calls the "consent" and "descent" traditions of American identity,[12] as well as identifying the limits that reject people of color. To become an American, the non-English immigrant must fit the definition provided by English political tradition as modified by Crèvecoeur's notions of individual rights. Crèvecoeur's extensions of individual rights, extended to include mankind (however severely restricted that definition may be) paved the way for assimilation and thus, American ethnicity. In letter III, as we shall see, James naively presents the radical political theories, the theories of volitional allegiance and individual rights, that allow for a combination of many ethnic groups into a new national identity. However, this mélange of eighteenth-century ideas also carries with it some peculiar attitudes toward emerging Americans and their ethnicity.

The most significant concept for the development of the American ethnicity is the idea of volitional allegiance, that is, the right of the individual to chose a country. In *Letters,* James makes the startling observation that individuals may determine their allegiance on economic grounds and that individuals have the ability to determine what might be best for them:

> In this great American asylum, the poor of Europe have by some means met together, and in consequence of various causes; to what purpose should they ask one another what countrymen they are? Alas, two thirds of them had no country. Can a wretch who wanders about, who works and starves, whose life is a continual scene of sore affliction of pinching penury—can that man call England or any other kingdom his country? A country that had no bread for him, whose fields procured him no harvest, who met with nothing but the frowns of the rich, the severity of the laws, with jails and punishments, who owned not a single foot of the extensive surface of this planet? No! (68)

Despite James's blithe presentation of this idea, the notion of consensual allegiance was one that was not generally accepted in England in this period. In *The Development of American Citizenship, 1608–1870,* James Kettner explains the history of national identity:

> Although Englishmen might move away from the notion that their obligations as subjects stemmed from natural principles of hierarchical order and toward the concept that those obligations in theory originated in consent, the practical conclusion remained the same: no subject could of his own independent volition give up his membership in a community of allegiance.[13]

In other words, in the English tradition, the individual was ruled by a concept of perpetual allegiance. In the eyes of the English law, place of birth locked an individual into a fixed and subject position. It was almost unthinkable that a person not born on English soil could become English: Kettner describes a few instances of a foreigner being allowed to be naturalized largely to demonstrate to the reader the complex and arduous legal process the foreigner had to endure. Therefore, had the colonists not modified English tradition, modern American ethnicity would not have been possible.

This mention of volitional allegiance is not a random event in James's letter but is part of the logic supporting his development of a definition of American. In the same paragraph, James dismisses traditional reasons for national allegiance. He describes allegiance as a matter of individual choice driven by significant economic determinants over which he assumes the individual to have control:

> What attachment can a poor European emigrant have for a country where he had nothing? The knowledge of the language, the love of a few kindred as poor as himself, were the only cords that tied him; his country is now that which gives him land, bread, protection and consequence, *Ubi panis ibi patria* is the motto of all emigrants. (69)

This apparently simple description of the right of the individual to choose actually encompasses a variety of radical historical changes in the eighteenth century. Modern concepts of nationalism do not take recognizable form until the eighteenth century and even then were limited to certain classes. One of the best summaries of this process is Otto Dann's introduction to *Nationalism in the Age of the French Revolution:*

> From the time of the decline of the Carolingian Empire, nations began to emerge as a new force in the process of state-building in Europe. The

leading social groups which shared a common language and other characteristics intensified their mutual links in order to pursue their common
interests. A new sense of identity, national consciousness, came into being
and formed the basis of a common state.[14]

However, as Dann points out, this phenomenon was linked to the rise of
the aristocracy and intelligentsia because "the 'nation' in these periods
never included—nor did it ever claim to include—the whole population,
but only those classes which had developed a sense of national identity
and begun to act upon it."[15] In the eighteenth century, a new concept of
patriotism was promulgated by the educated middle class, based on an
altered model of the state. Patriotism became nationalism, as the state
recognized the sovereignty of the people and each individual's inalien-
able human rights.[16] In *Letters,* James extends these rights to the lowest
class of Europeans. He posits a new class for whom loyalty and patriotism must be a matter of economic well-being, not a mere acceptance of
tradition.

James's claims for individual choice arose not merely from political
ideology but from the historically documented practical needs of the
new colonies. The demand for population caused changes in the traditional practices of naturalization. In England, the intricate legal procedures for naturalization and citizenship worked to prevent all but a
small number of aliens from gaining rights as Englishmen, but in the
American colonies, the pressing need for population altered British policy: "the American colonists had not waited for Parliament's formal
delegation of authority, but had adopted aliens as fellow subjects almost
from the beginnings of the settlement."[17] Easy amalgamation of immigrants was possible because the demand was driven by the needs of the
companies seeking to develop America and its markets: "England alone
could not supply the numbers needed to settle the colonies, and both
public and private promoters saw the value of inviting foreigners to
people the king's new dominions."[18] The colonies ignored precedent
and legal authority and established local procedures for incorporating
aliens, procedures that gave the aliens "extensive rights and benefits."[19] Thus, James's theory of the new American race ("they are a
mixture of English, Scotch, Irish, French, Dutch, Germans and Swedes.
From this promiscuous breed, that race now called American have
arisen") also grew from Crèvecoeur's practical observation of European
immigration to the colonies.

While most ethnic interpretations of *Letters* rely heavily on the paragraph cited below, it is important to remember that Crèvecoeur's discussion of the new man, the American, relies upon the development by his narrator of the new principles of the society and the rejection of traditional ideas about allegiance:

> What, then, is the American, this new man? he is neither an European nor the descendant of a European; hence that strange mixture of blood, which you will find in no other country. I could point out to you a family whose grandfather was an Englishman, whose wife was Dutch, whose son married a French woman, and whose present four sons have now four wives of different nations. He is an American who, leaving behind him all his ancient prejudices and manners, receives new ones from the new mode of life he has embraced, the new government he obeys, and the new rank he holds. He becomes an American by being received in the broad lap of our great Alma Mater. Here individuals of all nations are melted into a new race of men. (69–70)

While this paragraph is often quoted in the literature of ethnicity, Crèvecoeur's emphasis on the new social and political environment in America is overlooked: ''He is an American who, leaving behind him all his ancient prejudices and manners, receives new ones from the new mode of life he has embraced, the new government he obeys, and the new rank he holds.'' The ''new race'' is not merely the product of intermarriage but can only result from broader political changes and practical changes wrought by a new environment.

According to *Letters,* the political and social environment shapes a new ethnic reality. In the following paragraph, the immigrant becomes an American by a change in political and social status and the mechanism of naturalization:

> He is become a freeholder, from perhaps a German boor. He is now an American, a Pennsylvanian, an English subject. He is naturalized; his name is enrolled with those of the other citizens of the province. Instead of being a vagrant, he has a place of residence; he is called the inhabitant of such a county, or of such a district, and for the first time in his life counts for something, for hitherto he had been a cypher . . . From nothing to start into being; from a servant to the rank of master; from being the slave of some despotic prince, to become a free man, invested with lands to which every municipal blessing is annexed! What a change indeed! (83)

The political transformation of the individual has an important economic component. As he becomes an American, the immigrant gains power over his economic existence and "the rewards of his industry follow with equal steps the progress of his labour." Because personal industry is rewarded, the American becomes "a new man, who acts upon new principles" who "must therefore entertain new ideas and form new opinions." James attributes the immigrant's transfiguration to the immigrant's possession of his own labour: "By what invisible power hath this surprising metamorphosis been performed? By that . . . of their industry" (83). In *Letters,* the critical difference between the social systems of Europe and America lies in the individual's right to his own labor: "Here the rewards of his industry follow with equal steps the progress of his labour: his labour is founded on the basis of nature, self-interest; can it want a stronger allurement?" (70). However, as we shall see, this new power is not merely a gift but carries with it a demand for certain minimal standards of performance. When Crèvecoeur has America, "our great parent," speak to the newly arrived foreigner, America says, "If thou wilt work, I have bread for thee; if thou wilt be honest, sober, and industrious, I have greater rewards to confer on thee—ease and independence" (89). It is this moral obligation to be industrious that colors Crèvecoeur's notions of ethnicity and our own.

With individual rights comes individual obligations and, in the case of Crèvecoeur's *Letters,* a balancing of the implications of this theory with other deeply cherished eighteenth-century theories. Even as he is proposing equality, Crèvecoeur feels compelled to explain the distinctions within American society. For example, James remarks that the transformation from European to American is not always complete for all colonials. He uses the settlers in the frontier regions to illustrate this point: "In all societies there are cast-offs; this impure part serves as our precursors or pioneers" (73). These backwoods people exemplify a particularly American problem, people who refuse to act in accordance with the demands for industry, honesty, and sobriety:

> These new manners grafted on the old stock produces a strange sort of lawless profligacy. . . . The manners of the Indian natives are respectable compared with this European medley. Their wives and children live in sloth and inactivity; and having no proper pursuits, you may judge what education the latter receive. Their tender minds have nothing else to contemplate but the example of their parents; like them, they grow up a mongrel breed, half civilized, half savage. (77)

It is Crèvecoeur's accuracy about the real conditions in America that makes *Letters* a valuable record of American life and enduring features of its cultural landscape; thus, James's portrayal of the backwoods culture anticipates a stock character in Fenimore Cooper and in early westerns, the half-breed: "as old ploughmen and new men of the woods as Europeans and new made Indians, they contract the vices of both; they adopt the moroseness and ferocity of a native, without his mildness or even his industry at home" (78).

While the modern reader, educated in these cultural codes, may be aware of the racism implied by James's description, James's comments express a commonplace of English colonial thought, the idea that the intermixture of an original English stock and the native population would lead to a mongrel breed of unpleasant and immoral character. In an analysis of the emergence of an Anglo-Irish identity, Nicholas Canny shows that Edmund Spenser's *View of the Present State of Ireland* (1596) had already promulgated the notion that " 'the chiefest abuses which are now in that realm are grown from the English, and the English-that-were are now much more lawless and licentious than the very wild Irish.' ' '[20] Part of a culture accustomed to hierarchical ordering, Crèvecoeur had no problem recognizing a lesser form of American. The backwoods settlers can fit easily into his constellation of ideas about America and ethnicity because they have failed to meet their obligations; they are not industrious and proper and thus do not qualify as Americans. In Crèvecoeur's theory, the European had the ability to work but was not industrious because he was a serf. When his native industry is released by conditions in the New World, he as a new American can achieve suitable wealth if he is willing to work hard.

When "the voice of our great parent," the American continent, invites the European to become an American, she also requires that the immigrant accept the requirement of work: "If thou wilt work, I have bread for thee; if thou wilt be honest, sober, and industrious, I have greater rewards to confer on thee—ease and independence. . . . Go thou and work and till; thou shalt prosper, provided thou be just, grateful and industrious" (90). This obligation of industry may account for a rarely discussed section in *Letters* (84–86) in which James calibrates the success of ethnic groups by their ability to work. He rebukes the Scots for their lack of technical knowledge and because "their wives can not work so hard as German women." The Irish are described in what to the modern reader is a nineteenth-century stereotype: the Irish "love to drink and quarrel" and "their potatoes, which are easily raised, are perhaps an inducement to laziness; their wages are too low and their whiskey too cheap.'' Only the Germans seem to escape the harshest criticism: by ''dint of sobriety, rigid parsimony, and the most persevering industry,'' the Germans succeed, spurred on by the ''recollection of their former poverty and slavery.'' To balance these descriptions and to underline the necessity of labor, James ends this letter with the parable of a successful emigrant. He describes with loving care the history of a Scottish emigrant, Andrew the Hebridean. By tracing ''the progressive steps of a poor man, advancing from indigence to ease, from oppression to freedom, from obscurity and contumely to some degree of consequence—not by virtue of any freaks of fortune, but by the gradual operation of sobriety, honesty, and emigration'' in Andrew's history (90), James demonstrates to his reader, who may well be a potential emigrant, the wonders of America and the success that can only be achieved by a proper moral stance.

As we have seen, the success of the metamorphosis depends upon a notion of individual responsibility called industry by Crèvecoeur, and certain immigrants do not meet this standard. However, certain groups are excluded from even being considered for Americanization. Because of the Anglocentricity of the principles, both Native Americans and Africans brought to America as slaves remain outside the assimilation process. The ethnic experience of Africans is dominated by the relationship between slavery and the dominant capitalistic culture of the new society. Because Africans are held in a situation that parallels that of the European in Europe, that is, they can not exercise their industry for themselves, they are implicitly denied the ability to enter the transformation process: ''Day after day they drudge on without any prospect of ever reaping for themselves'' (169). The very situation that introduces them to America precludes their participation.[21]

Letters shows the ambiguity of the slave situation as an ethnic experience. Although most readers remember James's attack on slavery, when Africans are first introduced in the early pages of *Letters,* they are introduced as slaves. The very early references in *Letters* mention Africans only as they attach to the household. For example, in a catalog of James's blessings, James counts slaves with his cattle: ''Every year I kill from 1,500 to 2,000 weight of pork, 1,200 of beef, half a dozen of good wethers in harvest; of fowls my life has always a good stock; what can I wish more? My Negroes are tolerable faithful and healthy.'' However, *Letters* contains a continuing undertone of opposition to the institution of slavery: for example, while James generally finds the situation of slaves in the North good, he does note that the Quakers, who are his model of perfection, "lamenting that shocking insult offered to humanity, have given the world a singular example of moderation, disinterestedness, and Christian charity in emancipating their Negroes" (153).

In letter IX, a strong plea against slavery, the reader learns of the deep scars that America, even in the eighteenth century, inflicts on the newly arrived Africans. The greatest injury is to the family as a system, the very institution that James claims is supported and nourished by the American experience:

> If Negroes are permitted to become fathers, this fatal indulgence only tends to increase their misery; the poor companions of their scanty pleasures are likewise the companions of their labors; and when at some critical seasons they could wish to see them relieved, with tears in their eyes that behold them perhaps doubly oppressed, obliged to bear the burden of Nature—a fatal present—as well as that of unabated tasks. How many have I seen cursing the irresistible propensity and regretting that by having tasted of those harmless joys they had become the authors of double misery to their wives . . . they are not permitted to partake of those ineffable sensations with which Nature inspires the hearts of fathers and mothers; they must repel them all and become callous and passive. This unnatural state often occasions the most acute, the most pungent of their afflictions: they have no time, like us, to tenderly rear their helpless offspring, to nurse them on their knees, to enjoy the delight of being parents. Their paternal fondness is embittered by considering that if their children live, they must live to be slaves like themselves. (169)

The psychological and culture ramifications of this treatment will affect the African family for centuries. All of the elements that make America a haven for the immigrant—the ability to own one's own labor, the ability to establish a freehold, the ability to raise a family, the ability to establish certain rights against the government and the church—are denied the slave.

The ethnic experience of the Native Americans, as revealed in Crèvecoeur's text, manifests a paradox in that, while their culture is often praised, it is also seen as the bar to their acceptance by white society. While Africans, against their will, were implicated in the system of society that enables the white immigrant to become an American and so, as slaves, they occupy a peculiar place within the system, the Native American stands outside the system entirely. It is ironic that in

Letters the Native Americans are generally described or mentioned in positive ways. We need only look at the first lengthy mention of the Native American in the history of Andrew the Hebridean to see that Crèvecoeur did not denigrate Native American culture. In the story, the newly arrived Andrew, staying alone at an acquaintance's home, tries to keep several Native Americans who are friends of Mr. P. R., the acquaintance, from entering Mr. P. R.'s house. The Native Americans, accustomed to making themselves at home there, enter and effectively brush Andrew aside. The tale ends with the Native Americans being largely amused at Andrew's behavior, and Crèvecoeur's comment at this point is remarkable for the moral superiority it gives the Native American speaker: "I have heard one of the Indians say that he never laughed so heartily in his life" (99). Further, Mr. P. R. asserts the honesty and good sense of the Indians to Andrew while attempting to explain simply that the ways of the Native Americans are different. More often than not, the text praises Native Americans for their virtues, even if the manner is somewhat condescending: on Martha's Vineyard, for example, the Native Americans "appeared, by the decency of their manners, their industry and their neatness, to be wholly Europeans and no way inferior to many of the inhabitants" (133). In fact, the text concludes, if we are to take James's words at face value, that Native American culture is superior to that of whites, both English and American: "Without temples, without priests, and without laws, they are in many instances superior to us. . . . What system of philosophy can give us so many necessary qualifications for happiness?" (215). Crèvecoeur invests Native American society with many of the values he had his narrator praise in the colonial society of British North America, and he finds their freedom from work and carefree nature one of the charms of the Native American culture.

Despite genuine enthusiasm for the Native American way of life, Crèvecoeur and his narrator are still uncertain about the relationship of Native American life to European ideals of culture. James's stories of the white children who join Native American tribes and then refuse to return to white society and his inexplicable insistence on the "bewitching" character of Native American society are indications of James's deeper disease. Further, James's odd plans during his sojourn in the Native American village are premised on his desire to introduce those elements of agricultural economy to Native American society that James considers a prerequisite of society: "I will persuade them, if I can to till a little more land than they do and not to trust so much to the produce of the chase.'' These are attempts to remake Native American culture into a culture based on European norms. Unlike the Africans, Native Americans are so removed from Crèvecoeur's notions of individual industry and propriety that they can not be comprehended by the logic of ethnic transformation and thus must be changed so that they can become Americans.

Letters is an important text because, as this paper has attempted to show, it reveals the essential models of the cultural codes of American ethnicity. It is disquieting to acknowledge that the patterns of ethnic relationships that dominate modern American culture were so strongly shaped by our colonial experience and so little altered. We learn from *Letters* that our instinctive feel for acceptable ethnic behavior is based upon a model prescribed by the eighteenth century's notions of industry and propriety so that, even today, a variation in cultural forms and models is sufficient to exclude a group from entering ''real'' life in America.

Notes

1. Werner Sollors, *Beyond Ethnicity: Consent and Descent in American Culture* (New York: Oxford University Press, 1986).

2. J. Hector St. John de Crèvecoeur, *Letters from an American Farmer* and *Sketches of Eighteenth Century America,* ed. Albert E. Stone (New York: Penguin, 1981). All references will be to this edition and indicated parenthetically in the text.

3. Clive T. Probyn, *English Fiction of the Eighteenth Century, 1700–1789* (London: Longmans, 1987), 4.

4. Paul Fussell, *The Rhetorical World of Augustan Humanism Ethics and Imagery from Swift to Burke* (Oxford: Clarendon Press, 1965), 264.

5. Fussell, 265.

6. Bernard Bailyn, *Voyagers to the West: A Passage in the People of America on the Eve of the Revolution* (New York: Knopf, 1986), 36, 41.

7. Alan Wald, ''Theorizing Cultural Difference: A Critique of the Ethnicity School,'' *MELUS* 14:2 (1987), 23.

8. Michael Zuckerman, ''Identity in British America: Unease in Eden,'' in Nicholas Canny and Anthony Pagden, eds., *Colonial Identity in the Atlantic World, 1500–1800* (Princeton, N.J.: Princeton University Press, 1987), 115.

9. Willi Paul Adams, ''The Colonial German-language Press and the American Revolution,'' in Bernard Bailyn and John B. Hench, eds., *The Press and the American Revolution* (Worcester: American Antiquarian Society, 1980), 174.

10. Zuckerman, 145.

11. Zuckerman, 150.

12. Sollors, 5–6.

13. James Kettner, *The Development of American Citizenship, 1608–1870* (Chapel Hill: University of North Carolina Press, 1978), 60.

14. Otto Dann, "Introduction," in Otto Dann and John Dinwiddy, eds., *Nationalism in the Age of the French Revolution* (London: Hambledon Press, 1988), 5.

15. Dann, 5.

16. Dann, 5–8.

17. Kettner, 78.

18. Kettner, 78.

19. Kettner, 78.

20. Nicholas Canny, "Identity Formation in Ireland: The Emergence of the Anglo-Irish," in Nicholas Canny and Anthony Pagden, eds., *Colonial Identity in the Atlantic World, 1500–1800* (Princeton, N.J.: Princeton University Press, 1987), 169.

21. Although there was white indentured servitude in the colonies, white slaves were held only for a set period of time and, in the case of the English, presumably never lost their rights as citizens. See Abbot Emerson Smith, *Colonists in Bondage, White Servitude and Convict Labor in America, 1607–1776* (New York: Norton, 1947), 26–35.

13

Thomas Jefferson:
Race, Culture, and the Failure
of Anthropological Method

Frank Shuffelton

Thomas Jefferson's original reluctance to give wide circulation to his *Notes on the State of Virginia* for fear that his critique of slavery would provoke a backlash against attempts to end it seems more than somewhat ironic, since many readers have been greatly disturbed by the apparent racism that comes into play in his discussion of African Americans. Many readers who admire Jefferson for declaring that all men are created equal are dismayed that he could also proclaim of black men,

> Comparing them by their faculties of memory, reason and imagination, it appears to me that in memory they are equal to the whites; in reason much inferior, as I think one could scarcely be found capable of tracing and comprehending the investigations of Euclid; and that in imagination they are dull, tasteless, and anomalous.

It seems needlessly harsh to say, "Religion indeed has produced a Phyllis Whately; but it could not produce a poet. The compositions published under her name are below the dignity of criticism."[1] It is a severe judgment indeed for a man who thought a gentleman's library should certainly include the works of minor bards like Shenstone, Ogilvie, and those lesser talents in the poetic collections of Dodsley and Pearch.[2]

Jefferson's attitude seems even more problematic, coming as it does after he has vigorously defended the Native Americans' humanity and natural capacities. His denial of the poet's laurels to Phillis Wheatley follows what is perhaps an exaggeration in the other direction when he challenges "the whole orations of Demosthenes and Cicero, and of any more eminent orator, if Europe has furnished more eminent, to produce a single passage superior to the speech of Logan, a Mingo chief, to Lord Dunmore."[3] Obviously, something more complex is at work here than a mere prejudice against people of color, and Jefferson's original readers responded to these passages in contradictory ways that underlined the instability of his text. The editor of *The Columbian Magazine* in March 1788 extracted a long section that began with the statement "In general, their existence appears to participate more of sensation than reflection" and ended with the proposal that "when freed, he is to be removed beyond the reach of admixture." This presented the full criticism of the black's inherent abilities and was even more damning in the context of *The Columbian,* which in the previous month had printed two extracts from Edward Long's *History of Jamaica* arguing that blacks were void of genius, destitute of moral sense, and incapable of making progress in civilization or science.[4] *The Massachusetts Magazine* chose to print in September 1789 a much briefer passage in which Jefferson had qualified his earlier remarks by defending the blacks' moral sense—"we find among them numerous instances of the most rigid integrity, and as many as among their better instructed masters, of benevolence, gratitude, and unshaken fidelity,"—and by expressing reservations about his earlier criticism—"The opinion, that they are inferior in the faculties of reason and imagination, must be hazarded with great diffidence."[5] If *The Columbian* presents Jefferson as a racist theorist supporting the deportation of blacks, *The Massachusetts Magazine* offers an abolitionist man of feeling. Jefferson's friend David Ramsay of South Carolina took yet another approach and confronted him directly, arguing, "You have depressed the negroes too low," and a fellow member of the American Philosophical Society observed, "These remarks upon the genius of the African negro appear to me to have so little foundation in true philosophy that few observations will be necessary to refute them."[6] The ideological contradictions of Jefferson's text thus point to a corresponding uncertainty, a repressed anxiety even, in the culture at large when it confronted an ethnic and cultural Other and at the same time tried to be mindful of the Enlightenment ideals of "true philosophy."

To arrive at some clearer view of Jefferson's contradictory attitudes in *Notes,* we need to shift the terms of discussion from race, the usual frame of reference, to ethnicity, a broader and more subtle strain of discourse. The term "race," among the numerous and contradictory meanings it has gathered to itself, includes notions of biological inheritance and even determinism; ethnicity, a newer and less cluttered term, focuses more directly on differences in cultural behavior. The eighteenth century applied the term "race" variously from the context of family (e.g., "the Bourbon race") to that of nation (e.g., the "British race") to that of a larger physical type (e.g., "the Tartar race"), to say nothing of groups united only by spiritual affinity (e.g., "a generous race," "a race of heroes").[7] To speak of race is to embrace a word near the center of Jefferson's confusion; at one point he can affirm "that there are varieties in the race of man," and at another he can speak of separate red, black, and white races.[8] The language of race both in the eighteenth century and even in our own time inevitably entangles issues of biology and culture, of the underlying likeness of all human beings with the cultural diversity that differentiates us. It introduces notions of biological determinism that thrive upon the class or national ambitions of one group of people at the expense of another. For Jefferson and his contemporaries, however, it was an almost inescapable entanglement, since the major traditions of eighteenth-century discourse about the differences among groups of human beings had from Montesquieu on focused upon the connection between nature and culture, climate and law.

The precedence of nature or culture was a crucial question that could determine the limits of discourse about human difference, for nature was seen as fixed, whereas culture was fluid, susceptible to melioration or degeneration.[9] One branch of this tradition of discourse about human variety focused on anatomical differences among human population groups, culminating in the important work of Johann Friedrich Blumenbach, *On the Natural Variety of Mankind* (1776), which divided humanity into the Caucasian, Mongol, American, African, and Malayan races. Although some writers like Lord Kames seized upon such work to argue for a physical basis for the differences among races (and the inferiority of all to the Caucasian), the anatomists were intent upon taxonomy, upon establishing a fixed order of relationships among the varieties of human beings as Linnaeus had done for the plant and animal kingdoms. However doubtful the claims of the anatomists to scientific objectivity, they were enormously impressive in a rationalist age infatuated with the possible discovery of scientific laws that might put everything, and everyone, into its place. In fact it was the anatomists' rationalism rather than their objectivity that appealed so strongly, for they offered not merely tables of observed differences but ordered hierarchies of the races of humankind in which the standard of measurement was, consciously or not, the observer's own European culture, usually denominated as "civil society" or "civilization."[10] The hierarchical tendencies of the anatomists were reinforced by the theoretical principles of Buffon, the greatest natural historian of his age, who in his *Des epoques de la nature* (1778) supplied a foundation from which to argue for a natural hierarchy of races as the result of impersonal forces of nature.[11]

To use the terminology of "race" thus positioned eighteenth-century thinkers on a slippery slope beginning with science and ending in racism, and the difficulties remain alive for us in this century. One response to this difficulty in our own time has been the construction of a new term, "ethnicity," which is not without problems of its own but which hopes to be more free from the hierarchical assumptions attached to the word "race." Because it has been defined self-consciously against notions of an essentialist racism, it emphasizes culture as invented or constructed rather than as unvarying and objectively given. To speak of ethnicity allows us to step aside from a discourse of fixed verities and biological constraints such as that of the anatomists and the "scientific" racists of earlier ages in order to consider what the eighteenth century liked to call "national character" as a flexible cultural construct.[12]

Although Montesquieu was famous for noting the impact of climate on national character (but hardly the first to do so) and thus unintentionally giving aid and comfort to rationalist theorizers who hoped to show the laws of nature behind culture, he in fact had suggested that differences among national types needed more complex explanation: "Mankind are influenced by various causes: by the climate, by the religion, by the laws, by the maxims of government, by precedents, morals, and customs; whence is formed a general spirit of nations." Furthermore, this "general spirit of nations" was not grounded in a rationalist's absolute truth but in human reason—"Law in general is human reason," says Montesquieu—and therefore needed to be discussed with skepticism, the only means for human reason to critique itself. Since we can only know law in general in its particular cases, the political and civil laws of each nation, we should expect to find cultural variation as the human norm rather than as a mark of some people's ability to attain the norm; political and civil laws, Montesquieu claims, "should be adapted in such a manner to the people for whom they are framed that it should be a great chance if those of one nation suit another."[13] For Montesquieu truth is at the level of the observed local fact, the appropriateness of a nation's general spirit to its particular situation, and not in a fixed and static rationalization.

However, if truth was at the level of the local fact, it was not situated in any particular or privileged fact but in the relation all of the facts have with each other; laws should be considered

> in relation to the climate of each country, to the quality of its soil, to its situation and extent, to the principal occupations of the natives, whether husbandmen, or shepherds: they should have relation to the degree of liberty which the constitution will bear; to the religion of the inhabitants, to their inclinations, riches, numbers, commerce, manners and customs. In fine, they have relations to each other, as also to their origin, to the intent of the legislator, and to the order of things on which they are established; in all of which different lights they ought to be considered.[14]

Because Montesquieu's truth is situated not merely in the local fact itself but in the space between the facts where human reason plays, it balances a pragmatic acceptance of the fact with an attitude at once skeptical and welcoming toward reason as an agent of explanation. This skepticism, rational but tolerant of irony and difference, is a fundamental component of Enlightenment anthropological discourse, and it becomes a fundamental condition for a nonracist discussion of ethnicity.

Montesquieu's skeptical inquiring spirit should not be confused with moral indifference or genuine cultural relativism; he did not equally value despotisms and republics. What matters is that he projected a possible method of anthropological observation in which the observer's own culture is equally under question with that of the culture observed.[15] If there is no scheme for comparing cultures that is itself open to rational criticism, then cultural relativism or, as bad, cultural imperialism can vitiate consideration of the ethnic Other. Such a scheme appeared in the mid-eighteenth century when Anne Robert Jacques Turgot conceived his *Plan for Two Discourses on Universal History,* which applied a notion of historical change—"Universal history embraces the consideration of the successive progress of humanity, and the detailed causes which have contributed to it"—to a notion of culture as the production of signs—"Possessed of a treasure of signs which he has the faculty of multiplying to infinity, [man] is able to assure the retention of his acquired ideas, to communicate them to other men, and to transmit them to his successors as a constantly expanding heritage."[16] Turgot's theory of progressive history became a way to compare against a scale of measurable change human cultural groups themselves open to change, and as such it provided an alternative to the anatomists' categorization of races on the static grid of the Linnaean plan.

Philosophical history that saw individual cultures each with its own diachronic position on a synchronic historical frame received an enthusiastic reception. Adam Ferguson's *Essay on the History of Civil Society* (1767) explored the stages of savagism, barbarism, and civil society, analogous to Turgot's stages of historical development, but showed that progress was not inevitable; societies could degenerate as well as progress. Like Montesquieu, Ferguson set up no absolute theory of value or absolute scale of social complexity, but he measured complexity and differentiation in terms of the number and arrangement of social categories that the observed group itself recognized.[17] Jefferson's friend Condorcet gave the last twist to the theory in his *Sketch for a Historical Picture of the Progress of the Human Mind* (1795), which extended the idea of stages of development into recorded history and even, in discussion of the tenth and final stage, into a utopian future. The philosophical historians gave ethnologists a framework in which different cultures could be compared without having to make invidious distinctions; savagism described not congenital inability but only an ethnic group's mastery, comparatively speaking, of fewer and simpler cultural signs and of access to a more limited range of knowledge.

This being so, philosophical students of humanity ought to make a cultural catalog for each people they encounter and compare the facts of one society with those of another in order to determine their significance. The practice was at least as old as Roger Williams's *Key into the Language of America* (1643), but the notion of a cultural catalog was first methodically treated in the eighteenth century following the lead of Montesquieu. There are a variety of examples of lists of questions or guides for the philosophical traveler, including the culminating Enlightenment example of the genre, Joseph-Marie Degerando's *Considerations on the Various Methods to Follow in the Observation of Savage Peoples* (1800), prepared under the auspices of the Société des Observateurs de l'Homme as a guide for Nicolas Baudin's expedition to Australia. If Degerando operates from the assumption that "the idioms of the Savages are probably very scanty," he is also sure that they are like himself: "we shall in a way be taken back to the first periods of our own history." If Degerando's guide is ultimately an instrument of imperial domination, it also contains an egalitarian vision of semiotic exchange: "The first means to the proper knowledge of the Savages, is to become after a fashion like one of them; and it is by learning their language that we shall become their fellow citizens."[18] The notion that cultural progress could be measured by the complexity of signs was always a threat to the assumptions of "savage" intellectual and moral simplicity, since careful observers, such as Degerando hoped to send out, tended to discover the genuine richness and complexity of all human cultures. To discover the language and the cultural production of a people persuaded observers with a skeptical ethnographic sensibility to recognize their full humanity.

More to our immediate point, however, Thomas Jefferson, a few years after he had given an enthusiastic reading to Montesquieu's *Esprit des Lois,* received an earlier example of the cultural questionnaire from François Marbois, secretary of the French legation to the United States in 1780.[19] When Jefferson undertook the *Notes on the State of Virginia* in response to Marbois's queries, he was thus committing himself to, among other things, an act of anthropological exploration or, as he would later describe an inquiry into the American West, a "philosophical vedette at [a] distance." Jefferson took the list of queries seriously, reordering and expanding them as he felt was appropriate to fulfill "the mysterious obligation for making me much better acquainted with my own country than I ever was before."[20] His careful work on the *Notes* led him to see the usefulness of the anthropological method's cultural catalog for other projects as a philosophical traveler, but his own catalogs for philosophical travelers tended not to be disinterested programs for the acquisition of knowledge. His concerns for accurate scientific observation were frequently crossed by questions of national interest and policy or by other intellectual commitments.

In June 1788, for example, he sent to John Rutledge, Jr., and Thomas Lee Shippen pages of hints for Americans traveling in Europe based in part upon his own travels of the previous year. Much of the text contains specific instructions on the best inns, curious sights, best wines, and so on, but some paragraphs of "General Observations" and a list of "Objects of Attention for an American" reveal the influence of anthropological method. He recommends to the travelers, "Buy beforehand a map of the country you are going into." "On arriving at a town, the first thing is to buy the plan of the town, and the book noting its curiosities. Walk round the ramparts when there are any. Go to the top of a steeple to have a view of the town and its environs."[21] The first step toward understanding the character of a nation or town is thus to understand its physical situation; to make geography fundamental is to ground subsequent knowledge on a nature organized in time and space, rather than upon a system of rationalized categories. Similarly, the first five queries addressed in the *Notes* were "Boundaries of Virginia," "Rivers," "Sea-Ports," "Mountains," and "Cascades." Next he cautions the young travelers against the dangers of unreliable informants: "Take care particularly not to let the porters of churches, cabinets, &c. lead you thro' all the little details in their possession, which will load the memory with trifles, fatigue the attention and waste that and your time. . . . The people that you will naturally see most of will be tavern keepers, Valets de place, and postillions. These are the hackneyed rascals of every country. Of course they must never be considered when we calculate the national characters." Instead, the travelers should turn to those sites where a people acts out its public life, to "theatres, public walks and public markets . . . [for] At these you see the inhabitants high and low." Finally, he offers a list of eight objects of attention for an American, but here the skeptical spirit of the general observations is undercut by a utilitarian relativism. Thus, the first object is agriculture, where one ought to observe "everything belonging to this art, and whatever has a near relation to it," but this observation should be directed by considerations of "useful or agreeable animals which might be transported to America. New species of plants for the farm or garden, according to the climate of the different states." The rest of the objects of attention are similarly qualified by questions of utility to America, thus moving from a program of disinterested inquiry to a variety of low-level commercial espionage. Further betraying the anthropological spirit, Jefferson uses the last object as the occasion for a short political sermon; "Courts. [are] To be seen as you would see the tower of London or Menagerie of Versailles with their Lions, tygers, hyaenas and other beasts of prey, standing in the same relation to their fellows."[22]

A more fully worked out program for a cultural catalog came fifteen years later in the instructions to Meriwether Lewis regarding the conduct and objectives of his exploring mission. Since Lewis and Clark were entering unknown territory, the primary duty of their mission was to generate maps, to make possible a knowledge of the geography of the American interior. Jefferson followed the initial directions for mapmaking with a guide to acquiring a knowledge of the people they would meet. Like the program for Rutledge and Shippen, the instructions to

Lewis and Clark are flawed by the intrusion of national interest; after a model list of items of ethnographic information to be recorded comes the insidious call to learn what "articles of commerce they may need or furnish & to what extent." An additional ominous note sounded in the comment that such ethnographic information "may better enable those who endeavor to civilize & instruct them, to adapt their measures to the existing notions & practices of those on whom they are to operate."[23] The persistent intrusion of a language of exploitation in discussing the relations between the American and the Indian nations is more distasteful than the language of commerce as cultural exchange that occurs in the advice to Rutledge and Shippen. The point to be made, however, is that one learned the character of the Oto, Sioux, or Mandans as one learned the national character of the Germans, French, or Italians, by asking the same kind of questions and by assuming that their culture constituted one possible human ordering of things.

Despite the instability in Jefferson's mature scientific program, he entertained a sustained interest in the Native Americans that led him to respect their culture as an object of serious study. In one of the remarkable letters to John Adams he describes an early encounter with the Cherokees:

> Before the revolution they were in the habit of coming often, and in great numbers to the seat of our government, where I was very much with them. I knew much the great Outassete, the warrior and orator of the Cherokees. He was always the guest of my father, on his journeys to and from Williamsburg. I was in his camp when he made his great farewell oration to his people, the evening before his departure for England. The moon was in full splendor, and to her he seemed to address himself in his prayers for his own safety on the voyage, and that of his people during his absence. His sounding voice, distinct articulation, animated actions, and the solemn silence of his people at their several fires, filled me with awe and veneration, altho' I did not understand a word he uttered.[24]

Jefferson's account is first of all remarkable for an essentially romantic spirit that crosses ethnographic reporting with barely restrained feeling; in the famous head and heart letter to Maria Cosway, he gave the head empire over the field of science but put the heart in care of morals. The description of Outassete's speech is that of an observer fully engaged with both head and heart who will make a lifelong study of the Indian languages, of which on this occasion he did not understand a word. Second, it is suggestive that when he describes the early impressions that awakened his interest in the Indians, he focuses on the Indian as a producer of cultural objects and signs, in this case an oration as well as a kind of national meeting. It is hardly accidental that Jefferson offers Logan's speech as the clinching bit of evidence in his argument with Buffon about Native American inferiority, for if he wished to prove the full humanity of the Indians, he had to demonstrate the richness of their cultural signs.[25]

Anthropological method allowed Jefferson to record and order as scientific knowledge the information his youthful "awe and veneration" urged him to seek as the stuff of feeling. His account in the *Notes* of opening an Indian mound has been credited as a pioneering example of the archaeological technique of stratigraphy, opening a cut through a site that preserves the layers of accumulation and enables one to observe changing patterns of use.[26] His most significant line of inquiry, however, was his collection of Indian vocabularies, unfortunately lost in the move of his personal goods from the White House back to Monticello. He prepared printed vocabularies of English words with blank spaces that explorers such as Lewis could fill in with the appropriate Indian terms. Material such as this had been grist for the philosophical mills of earlier ethnographers such as James Adair who wished to identify the Cherokees with the Jews, but Jefferson maintained a skeptical distance from such rationalist presumptions. As he told the Abbe Correa,

> I had myself made a collection of about 40 vocabularies of the Indians on this side of the Mississippi, and Capt. Lewis was instructed to take those of every tribe beyond, which he possibly could. The intention was to publish the whole, and leave the world to search for affinities between these and the languages of Europe and Asia.

Writing in 1801 to William Dunbar of Natchez, he recognized a different form of bias inherent in the nature of language itself:

> I have at present about 30 [vocabularies] tolerably full, among which the number radically different, is truly wonderful. It is curious to consider how such handfuls of men came by different languages, & how they have preserved them so distinct. I at first thought of reducing them all to one orthography, but I soon became sensible that this would occasion two sources of error instead of one. I therefore think it best to keep them in the form of orthography in which they were taken, only noting whether that were English, French, German, or what.[27]

Jefferson's interest in the language of the Indians as their most reveal-ing cultural production is curiously appropriate, given his own logo-centrism, but it is also, as we have seen, a central concern of eighteenth-century anthropology. From Turgot's notion of culture as semiotic production to Degerando's insistence that his philosophical travelers learn the native systems of signs, linguistic and otherwise, eighteenth-century discussions of culture focused on the question of language as a sign of cultural production or individual moral development. It is pre-cisely this question of cultural production that lies at the heart of Jeffer-son's differing treatments of Indians and blacks.

He valued the Indians as masters of a native semiosis whose culture was in the process of change; their vocabularies revealed for him a history of cultural transformation as the linguistic groups had diverged from one another. As a result they were not fated to be trapped in the apparent savagery, the cultural simplicity, in which Europeans first found them; he was pleased to inform John Adams that the Cherokees and Creeks

> are far advanced in civilization; They have good Cabins, inclosed fields, large herds of cattle and hogs, spin and weave their own clothes of cotton, have smiths and other of the most necessary tradesmen, write and read, are on the increase in numbers, and a branch of the Cherokees is now institut-ing a regular representative government.[28]

The Creeks and Cherokees prove that the Indians have a vital culture that can advance up the ladder from savage simplicity, measured by a pov-erty of cultural objects, to civilization, measured by a relative richness of cultural objects. Jefferson's praise of the Native Americans turns out, however, to be a minefield of ironies. If he rescues them from a static, physically determined inferiority such as that to which the Abbe Raynal would have consigned them, he relegates most of the Indian nations to the level of cultural children, well down on the evolutionary ladder of the philosophical historians. The changing voice of his Indian addresses reflects the subversion of the Revolutionary egalitarian by the progres-sive historian and scientist. Early addresses such as those to Jean Bap-tiste de Coigne (1781), Handsome Lake (1802), or the representatives of the Choctaw Nation (1803) speak to Native Americans as "Brother," but later statements such as those to the Cherokee chiefs (1806) and to The Wolf and the people of the Mandans (1806) address Indians as "My children."[29] Above all, not the least of the ironies surrounding his praise of the Cherokees in the letter to Adams hangs on the observation that the cultural objects prized as evidence of native capacity and civility are ultimately his own cultural objects replicated in an ethnic frame.

The fact remains, however, that Jefferson could respect the Native Americans because they were culture producers, even when the objects of their culture resisted his understanding. If he values them because of their potential to become like the whites, producers of the same sort of cultural objects, he just as strongly fixes his attention upon them because of their difference, their ability to hold the imagination in the anthropological gaze. Their languages attract his interest precisely because they lie at the edge of his comprehension, and similarly the other major native cultural production he discusses in the *Notes,* the curious mounds left by earlier inhabitants, remain objects of skeptical speculation, even of romance. After his account of his exemplary and pioneering excavation of one of these mounds, he moves from explanation to mystery:

> But on whatever occasion they may have been made, they are of considerable notoriety among the Indians: for a party passing, about thirty years ago, through the part of the country where this barrow is, went through the woods directly to it, without any instructions or enquiry, and having staid about it some time, with expressions which were construed to be those of sorrow, they returned to the high road, which they had left about half a dozen miles to pay this visit, and pursued their journey.[30]

The cultural object here is clearly a sign for a range of mental phenomena, ideas about genealogy, about history, feelings of grief, of nostalgia perhaps, that can only be imagined, construed rather than defined, by the anthropological observer. If Jefferson ultimately wants the Indians to become "incorporated" with the whites, to become one body with them at least in a cultural sense, he also can recognize, at least in moments like this, the integrity of their own culture and its evidence that they are fully human agents in history.

When he turns to the blacks, however, he is unable to see any signs that they have a culture of their own or are capable of producing one. Continuing the argument for their inferiority in reason and imagination, he contends that even association with a more highly developed culture has failed to stimulate blacks removed from their supposedly savage African context:

> [M]any have been brought up to the handicraft arts, and from that circumstance have always been associated with the whites. Some have been liter-

ally educated, and all have lived in countries where the arts and sciences are cultivated to a considerable degree, and have had before their eyes samples of the best works from abroad. The Indians, with no advantages of this kind, will often carve figures on their pipes not destitute of design and merit. They will crayon out an animal, a plant, or a country, so as to prove the existence of a germ in their minds which only wants cultivation. They astonish you with strokes of the most sublime oratory; such as prove their reason and sentiment strong, their imagination glowing and elevated. But never yet could I find that a black had uttered a thought above the level of plain narration; never see even an elementary trait of painting or sculpture.[31]

What in fact astonishes here is Jefferson's blindness to the creativity of the black artisans in his own household who were accomplished cooks, cabinetmakers, storytellers, and so on.

It is clear that Jefferson puts the blacks in a double bind from the outset when he considers their ability to produce cultural objects. To denote a genuine cultural producer, he expects more than mere imitativeness, the chief characteristic of a childish mind as the eighteenth century saw it. Therefore, he discounts artisans who seemingly do no more than reproduce the objects of another culture, such as his own skilled cabinetmakers, carpenters, and nailmakers (and Phillis Wheatley). Yet at the same time he holds up the high culture objects of European society (e.g., painting and sculpture) as norms for the blacks' own production; even when he grants them some ability, their accomplishments, the products of a popular culture, are measured against the inappropriate standard of Europe's most sophisticated products. "In music they are more generally gifted than the whites with accurate ears for tune and time, and they have been found capable of imagining a small catch." W. C. Handy would be faulted for not being W. C. Handel, but if he wrote an oratorio like *The Messiah* he would be dismissed as a mere imitator. Unreasonable as it seems to demand originality of people caught up in a system of slave labor, forced to work to the masters' norms, it is yet more subtly mistaken to see as the only authentic cultural production that which is unaffected, or apparently unaffected, by some other culture. Carved figures on Indian pipes seem genuinely "native," whereas an elegant lady's writing desk made by John Hemings did not prove the existence of a "germ" in his mind but only his ability to follow Jefferson's plans.[32]

The reasons for Jefferson's blindness are complex, but at the outset, no matter how much we admire him as an opponent of slavery, we must recognize his racism, an abiding attitude that kept him from admitting more than grudgingly the intellectual or imaginative potential of black men and women. After his widely read comments in the *Notes* he received several examples of black intellectual accomplishment in refutation of his strictures, and he customarily returned a polite note of thanks expressing his sincere interest in seeing black ability vindicated but at the same time including some telltale phrase suggesting that he was not yet convinced. Benjamin Banneker is thus assured, "No body wishes more than I do to see such proofs as you exhibit, that nature has given to our black brethren, talents equal to those of the other colors of men," but Jefferson then goes on to say that he wishes to see a system to raise the condition both physical and mental of the blacks "as fast as the imbecility of their present existence, and other circumstances which cannot be neglected, will admit."[33] The mystification of "other circumstances" clouds the sincerity of philanthropic hopes that are nonetheless real for all the contradictory currents in this note. Jefferson's racism should not be confounded, however, with the virulent racist expressions of the nineteenth century that would deny humanity itself to blacks, for as we shall see, the skeptical ground of his anthropological attitude saved him from the racial determinism of a Gobineau or some American defenders of the "peculiar institution."

Allowing for Jefferson's inability to be a purely objective witness, something he never claimed to be, the situation of black culture in Virginia presented in itself unique problems for his comprehension of it. The deracination of blacks in their forced passage across the Atlantic is a truism, although there has been insufficient recognition of the survival of African cultural patterns, particularly in the mainland North American colonies. More important is the confounding of African ethnic distinctions in the New World; the slaves came from a stretch of coast ranging from Senegal to Angola and from a wide variety of ethnic groups, Igbo, Tiv, Kongo, Fante, Asante, Ibibio, Fon, and others, but these differences were lost to white masters. Jefferson's study of the Indians led him to make at least linguistic distinctions among the Creeks, Osages, and Oneidas, but to him and to all other white observers the Africans in America were simply "blacks," unlike European immigrants and their descendants who could continue to point to their origins as Scots, Welsh, Germans, or Dutch. Ironically in his farm book Jefferson listed slaves residing in settlements called Guinea and Angola, but these references to different African places of origin did not lead him away from his essentialization of blacks as an undifferentiated ethnic group.[34]

If the essentialization of African Americans as "blacks" contributed to an inability to perceive signs of their cultural distinctiveness, they were further masked from white observers, first, by their often unrecognized cultural similarity to Europeans and, second, by cultural consequences of the slave system. In a recent and quite remarkable book Mechal Sobel has examined the impact of African culture upon European culture in Virginia, neatly reversing the usual assumptions about the direction of cultural influence; in the first part of her study she points out that European and African immigrants to the New World through at least the mid-eighteenth century shared basic attitudes, despite culturally specific differences, toward nature, work, and time typical of "rural, prebourgeois and especially preindustrial" societies.[35] Shared expectations about housing appropriate for farming communities, for example, allowed Africans to teach Europeans perhaps as much as they learned, and "by mid-century," Sobel claims, "blacks and whites were in one family, by blood and adoption, all over Virginia. They were interacting in ordinary times and at times of celebration."[36] This degree of cultural assimilation meant that whites were frequently blind to the contributions of blacks to that culture; all culture, whether European or African in origin, had become "American," even as the slaves themselves were denied a fundamental human interest in that Americanness. A suggestive illustration in Sobel's study shows one of Jefferson's chess sets with clearly African features on both kings and on all of the black pieces. Possibly carved in Africa and brought west by Portuguese traders, these figures "not destitute of design and merit" never seemed to cause Jefferson to qualify his assessment of black creative abilities.

Second, because the demands of the system of enforced labor filled the daylight hours with few exceptions, uniquely black cultural activities took place at night and in relative isolation. The slaves met frequently after working hours, in what one observer called "nigger day-time," for hunting, dancing, or religious meetings. John F. D. Smyth noted in his account of travels in America,

> instead of returning to rest, as might naturally be concluded he would be glad to do, [a slave] generally sets out from home, and walks six or seven miles in the night, be the weather ever so sultry, to a negroe dance, in which

he performs with astonishing agility, and the most vigorous exertions, keeping time and cadence, most exactly, with the music of a banjor (a large, hollow instrument with three strings), and a quaqua (somewhat resembling a drum), until he exhausts himself.[37]

Whites were certainly aware of this activity and like Smyth might note the presence of non-European musical instruments and incomprehensible motions, but such a meeting was seldom regarded as a laudable cultural production. The exhaustion at its conclusion led to sleeping on the job during the next day, although this was often ascribed to "natural" black laziness. Jefferson thought it might be because "they seem to require less sleep. A black, after hard labour through the day, will be induced by the slightest amusement to sit up till midnight, or later, though knowing he must be out with the first dawn of the morning." He linked the black propensity for nighttime "amusements" to "a want of fore-thought," variously a sign of the childish or the savage.[38] More important, the night meeting's strangeness and dark setting aligned it with the irrational and the savage that threatened all cultural order and, especially after Gabriel's conspiracy of 1800, with the possibility of slave rebellions. Patrols were regularly constituted to keep black nighttime activity in check. For slave owners "authentic" black culture production was frightening, and they often associated it with savagism, the cultural nullity that marked the bottom of the hierarchical order of cultural progress.

The dominant white culture, then, either occulted the signs of ethnic black culture when its productions were congruent with the demands and expectations of European culture, or it marginalized and tried to obliterate those signs of black culture that emphasized ethnic difference. When Jefferson considered the examples of Phillis Wheatley or Ignatius Sancho as culture producers, he discounted them either as themselves products—"Religion indeed has produced a Phyllis Whately"—or as exemplars of the irrational and uncultivated—"his imagination is wild and extravagant, escapes incessantly from every restraint of reason and taste, and, in the course of its vagaries, leaves a tract of thought as incoherent and eccentric, as is the course of a meteor through the sky."[39] Thus, when he discusses American people of color in *Notes on the State of Virginia,* it is noteworthy that he takes up the Native Americans in query VI, "Productions, Mineral, Vegetable, and Animal," where his desire to refute Buffon's theory of New World degeneracy leads him to emphasize cultural production, a category in which he can include Logan as well as Franklin and David Rittenhouse; he considers the blacks in Query XIV, "Laws," where advocacy of slave emancipation is directly linked to a scheme for black colonization, a complete physical and cultural separation of black and white.

Because he can find no discrete system of black cultural production, he is unable to implement the discourse of eighteenth-century anthropology that tended to respect ethnic difference, in part because of its fundamental skepticism. He is instead forced back into the discourse of the anatomists, the language of race and of scientism that he inherits primarily from Linnaeus and Buffon. Christopher Looby has identified this strain of discourse as "a view of knowledge that [*Notes*] as a whole tries to promote: to know is to overrule the sensibly intuited bodies in nature by means of a universally-available, all-encompassing conceptual system that, not incidentally, makes time stand still."[40] Unable to see black cultural production, Jefferson is caught up in this taxonomic discourse that focuses not upon what human beings can *do* in a specific situation but upon what they inherently *are* as part of a fixed class. Thus when he speaks of the Native Americans, he talks of "varieties in the race of man" or "this part of the human race," but when he discusses blacks under the topic of "Law," he considers "the one or the other race" and "the two races."[41] The discourse of anthropological observation fails Jefferson when he is unable to turn it back upon his own culture, ironically just at the point when he criticizes the blacks' inability to lead lives of reflection. Unable to discuss ethnic differences as a function of culture, he is betrayed into the language of anatomy and the differentiation between species.

One consequence of this contradiction between the discourses of anthropology and of anatomy was the later direction of his policies toward native Americans and blacks. "More than once," as Bernard Sheehan has pointed out, "he told the Indians, 'Your blood will mix with ours; and will spread, with ours, over this great island.'" The plan as he sketched it out for Benjamin Hawkins, his agent among the Creeks, was "to let our settlements and theirs meet and blend together, to intermix, and become one people. Incorporating themselves with us as citizens of the U.S., this is what the natural progress of things will of course bring on."[42] "The natural progress of things" sketched out by Turgot and other philosophical historians can overcome cultural and ethnic differences to create a single body in blood and community. To the end of his life he insisted on the immorality of slavery and the necessity of ending it, but at the same time he insisted on the necessity of then separating the races. Writing in 1824 to Jared Sparks, editor of *The North American Review,* he approved the colonization of freed blacks in Africa and restated his plan for emancipation from Query XIV of *Notes:* "This was the result of my reflections on the subject five and forty years ago, and I have never yet been able to conceive any other practicable plan." By sending abroad American blacks, this colony would have the additional advantage, oddly enough, of introducing "among the aborigines the arts of cultivated life, and the blessings of civilization and science."[43] The natural progress of things could perhaps make blacks of one culture with other Americans, but it could apparently never make them of one body.

Ethnic assimilation on the one hand and ethnic denial on the other turn out to be two faces of the same coin, well-meaning disguises for a hegemonic assertion over the ethnic Other that has long been a central fact of American political life. But if eighteenth-century discussions of cultural and ethnic difference betrayed Jefferson (himself betrayed by his own racism), the framing skepticism of the anthropological vision he shared preserves him for us as a figure we can admire. To see others as equal to oneself does not require seeing them as the same as oneself, and Jefferson falls into this error when he takes the universalizing view of the philosophical historian. Conversely, to see others as different from oneself does not mean they are unequal, and Jefferson does not make this mistake. While his critique of blacks is couched in terms of rational intelligence, he never denies them the possession of the moral sense that is the fundamental qualification for all human rights; if "nature has been less bountiful to them in the endowments of the head, I believe that in those of the heart she will be found to have done them justice." By basing his opposition to slavery on the moral endowments of blacks, he ultimately is critical of reason itself and of its power to make binding categories for human behavior and judgment. His opinions about black intellectual ability are, after all, advanced as "conjecture," "a suspicion only," to "be hazarded with great diffidence."[44]

If he is never finally convinced of black Americans' abilities as culture producers, he always remains open to the possibility that he is wrong. After thanking Benjamin Banneker for the copy of his almanac, he sends it along on the same day to Condorcet as the work of "a very respectable Mathematician. . . . I shall be delighted to see these instances of moral eminence so multiplied as to prove that the want of talents observed in them is merely the effect of their degraded condition, and not proceeding from any difference in the structure of the parts on which intellect depends."[45] Here is none of the mystification about "other circumstances" that mars the letter to Banneker, and Jefferson's genuinely skeptical intelligence raises him above any impulse to diminish Banneker's achievement. In passing on the almanac to Condorcet, one of the culminating figures in the Enlightenment discourse about cultural difference, he enrolls Banneker in the record of the human sciences as an instance of "moral eminence" rather than as merely one of "them." Scientific observation of human possibility passes to a fully human regard, for this moment at least.

One continuing problem with the notion of race in the old South was the difficulty of determining exactly how to classify some individuals under the law, of seeing the individual within the species. In 1806 in Virginia, for example, a judge required to determine if a person were legally black or white delivered as his opinion, "It is said that the distinguishing characteristics of the different species of the human race are so visibly marked, that those species may be readily discriminated from each other by inspection; and that, in the case of a person visibly appearing to be of a slave race, it is incumbent upon him to make out his freedom."[46] This remark appalls because of the judge's confidence in a privileged observer's ready discrimination and in his imposition of accidents of appearance on fundamental moral questions. In contrast, Jefferson's anthropologically based skepticism distances him from the brutal self-assurance of racism even as it is finally unable to free him from the tyranny of a racist discourse of anatomy and appearance. Succeeding eras of American history have shown the extraordinary dangers that this confusion of motives holds for all of us; the example of Thomas Jefferson presents a ground for the reexamination we must continually make of the relationships among ourselves and the enormously varied cultural possibilities lived out by our fellow Americans.

Notes

1. Thomas Jefferson, *Notes on the State of Virginia,* ed. William Peden (Chapel Hill: University of North Carolina Press, 1954), 139–40 (hereafter *Notes*).

2. See *The Papers of Thomas Jefferson,* ed. Julian Boyd et al. (Princeton, N.J.: Princeton University Press, 1950), I, 79 (hereafter *Papers*).

3. *Notes,* 62.

4. John C. Greene, "The American Debate on the Negro's Place in Nature, 1780–1815," *Journal of the History of Ideas* 15 (1954), 384–96.

5. *Notes,* 143.

6. *Papers,* IX, 441; Samuel Stanhope Smith, *An Essay on the Causes of the Variety of Complexion and Figure in the Human Species,* ed. Winthrop D. Jordan (Cambridge: Harvard University Press, 1965), 162.

7. See, for example, the entries under "race" in the Oxford English Dictionary; Ashley Montagu claims "race" enters scientific literature with Buffon in 1749 and the publication of his *Histoire naturelle, generale et particuliere.* Montagu, *Man's Most Dangerous Myth: The Fallacy of Race* (Cleveland: World Publishing, 1964), 46.

8. *Notes,* 63, 142–43.

9. Note, for example, Linnaeus's contention about the stability of species, that there are precisely as many species now as at the moment of creation. Cf. Winthrop Jordan, "Introduction" to Smith, xxvii–xxviii.

10. On Blumenbach and Kames, see Jordan, "Introduction." On the tradition of rationalist anthropology, see Murray J. Leaf, *Man, Mind, and Science: A History of Anthropology* (New York: Columbia University Press, 1979).

11. Phillip R. Sloan, "The Idea of Racial Degeneracy in Buffon's *Histoire Naturelle,"* *Studies in Eighteenth-Century Culture* 3 (1973), 307. Buffon's follower, the Abbe Raynal, argued more strenuously for environmental determinism and was more directly the target of Jefferson's rebuttal in *Notes,* cf. p. 64. For the role of environmental determinism in late eighteenth- and early nineteenth-century America, see Bernard W. Sheehan, *Seeds of Extinction: Jeffersonian Philanthropy and the American Indian* (Chapel Hill: University of North Carolina Press, 1973).

12. Thus, responding to a special issue of *Critical Inquiry* entitled " 'Race,' Writing and Difference," Tzvetan Todorov comments, "It is with good cause that the word 'race' was placed in quotation marks in the title of this issue: 'races' do not exist." " 'Race,' Writing and Culture," *Critical Inquiry* 13 (1986), 172. Werner Sollors points to the difficulties of separating race and ethnicity as categories but then chooses "to keep looking at race as one aspect of ethnicity." *Beyond Ethnicity: Consent and Descent in American Culture* (New York: Oxford University Press, 1986), 38–39.

13. Charles Secondat, baron de Montesquieu, *The Spirit of the Laws,* trans. Thomas Nugent (New York: Hafner, 1949), 293, 6.

14. Montesquieu, 6–7.

15. The method is perhaps demonstrated more clearly in his *Persian Letters* than in *The Spirit of the Laws:* see Dena Goodman's discussion in *Criticism in Action: Enlightenment Experiments in Political Writing* (Ithaca, N.Y.: Cornell University Press, 1989), 19–106.

16. Quoted in Marvin Harris, *The Rise of Anthropological Theory* (New York: Harper, 1968), 14.

17. Leaf, 38.

18. Joseph-Marie Degerando, *The Observation of Savage Peoples,* trans. F. C. T. Moore (Berkeley: University of California Press, 1969), 63, 70.

19. Douglas S. Wilson suggests he was reading Montesquieu as recently as the period when he was revising the laws of Virginia in the late 1770s. He received Marbois's queries in the summer of 1780; Gilbert Chinard has suggested that these may have been framed by Buffon. See *Notes,* xii. The queries may have been sent to persons in all the states;

certainly it went to New Hampshire and New Jersey where John Sullivan and John Witherspoon made attempts to answer it.

20. Thomas Jefferson, *Writings* (New York: Library of America, 1984), 1084; *Papers,* iv, 168.

21. *Papers,* xiii, 268; cf. Leaf, 42, on Kant's movement from geography to anthropology.

22. *Papers,* xiii, 268–69.

23. *Writings,* 1128.

24. *Writings,* 1262.

25. Logan's speech was immensely popular in the nineteenth century as a schoolboy declamation, but it was also vigorously debated, both by defenders of Cresap, the supposed killer of Logan's family, and by disbelievers in Logan's oratory and his civility. Thus, the speech remained a focus of argument about the "savageness" of the Indian.

26. See C. W. Ceram, "The President and the Mounds," in *The First Americans: A Story of North American Archaeology* (New York: Harcourt, Brace, 1971), 3–10.

27. *Writings,* 1389, 1083–84.

28. *Writings,* 1263.

29. Bernard Sheehan comments on the Indian speeches in *Seeds of Extinction.*

30. *Notes,* 100.

31. *Notes,* 139–40.

32. *Notes,* 140; see Silvio A. Bedini, *Declaration of Independence Desk: Relic of Revolution* (Washington: Smithsonian Institution Press, 1981), 33, for details of the desk made by John Hemings as a wedding gift for Ellen Randolph Coolidge.

33. *Writings,* 982.

34. *Thomas Jeffersons' Farm Book,* ed. Edwin M. Betts (Princeton: Princeton University Press, 1953), 9.

36. Sobel, 119–20, 166.

37. John F. D. Smyth, *A Tour in the United States of America* (London, 1784), I, 46, quoted by Sobel, 34, who notes African analogues to this sort of celebration.

38. *Notes,* 139.

39. *Notes,* 140.

40. Christopher Looby, "The Constitution of Nature: Taxonomy as Politics in Jefferson, Peale, and Bartram," *Early American Literature* 22 (1987), 267. I disagree, however, with Looby's identification of this taxonomic strain as the essential voice of *Notes.* Equally important is a discursive line marked by skepticism, recognition of change, and a belief in the right of future generations to change the present.

41. *Notes,* 63, 100, 138, 139.

42. Sheehan, 174; *Writings,* 1115.

43. *Writings,* 1484–85.

44. *Notes,* 142, 142–43.

45. *Papers,* xxii, 98–99.

46. Quoted by James Hugo Johnston, *Race Relations in Virginia and Miscegenation in the South, 1776–1860* (Amherst: University of Massachusetts Press, 1970), 194.

Index